500
RECIPES FOR QUICK MEALS

500

RECIPES FOR QUICK MEALS

EDITED BY
NORMA MACMILLAN

CHANCELLOR
PRESS

Notes

All measurements in this book are given in Metric, Imperial and American. Follow one set only because they are not interchangeable.

Standard spoon measurements are used in all recipes
1 tablespoon = one 15 ml spoon
1 teaspoon = one 5 ml spoon
All spoon measurements are level.

Ovens and grills (broilers) should be preheated to the specified temperature or heat setting.

First published in Great Britain in 1982 by
Reed Consumer Books Limited
as *501 Recipes for Quick Meals*

This edition published in 1993 by
Chancellor Press, an imprint of
Reed Consumer Books Limited
Michelin House, 81 Fulham Road, London SW3 6RB
and Auckland, Melbourne, Singapore and Toronto

ISBN 1 85152 412 6

Printed in the Slovak Republic

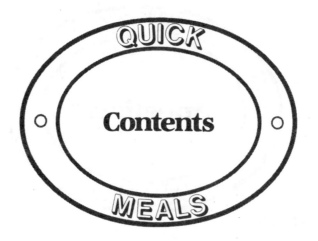

Contents

QUICK

Appetizers

MEALS

Guacamole

Metric/Imperial
4 large ripe avocados, peeled
   and stoned
juice of 1 lemon
4 tomatoes, skinned and
   chopped
1 small onion, grated
1 garlic clove, crushed
¼ teaspoon Tabasco sauce
salt and pepper

American
4 large ripe avocados, peeled
   and seeded
juice of 1 lemon
4 tomatoes, peeled and
   chopped
1 small onion, grated
1 garlic clove, crushed
¼ teaspoon hot pepper sauce
salt and pepper

Mash the avocados with the lemon juice, then beat in the remaining
ingredients, with salt and pepper to taste, until smooth. Serve with crisps
(potato chips or taco chips) for dipping.
Serves 4 to 6

Tuna Pâté

Metric/Imperial
1 × 200 g/7 oz can tuna fish,
   drained and flaked
2 hard-boiled eggs, chopped
1 × 225 g/8 oz packet cream
   cheese
2 tablespoons chopped chives
2 tablespoons chopped parsley
2 tablespoons brandy (optional)
salt and pepper

American
1 × 7 oz can tuna fish,
   drained and flaked
2 hard-cooked eggs, chopped
1 × 8 oz package cream cheese
2 tablespoons chopped chives
2 tablespoons chopped parsley
2 tablespoons brandy (optional)
salt and pepper

Put all the ingredients, with salt and pepper to taste, in a bowl and beat
until well combined. For a very smooth pâté, use a blender or food
processor. Spoon into a small serving dish and chill before serving with
hot toast and butter.
Serves 4 to 6

Savoury Cheese Log

Metric/Imperial
225 g/8 oz Cheddar cheese,
    grated
4 hard-boiled eggs, chopped
½ teaspoon made mustard
2 tablespoons mayonnaise
2 tablespoons single cream
2 teaspoons chopped parsley
salt and pepper
To serve:
lettuce leaves
tomato slices
parsley sprigs

American
2 cups grated Cheddar cheese
4 hard-cooked eggs, chopped
½ teaspoon prepared mustard
2 tablespoons mayonnaise
2 tablespoons light cream
2 teaspoons chopped parsley
salt and pepper
To serve:
lettuce leaves
tomato slices
parsley sprigs

Mix together the cheese, eggs, mustard, mayonnaise, cream, parsley and salt and pepper to taste. Shape into a roll and wrap in foil. Chill for at least 1 hour.

Line a serving plate with lettuce leaves. Place the cheese roll on top and garnish with tomato slices and parsley sprigs.
Serves 4 to 6

Melon Antipasto

Metric/Imperial
½ honeydew melon, seeded
    and chopped
50 g/2 oz walnuts, chopped
3 tablespoons raisins
lettuce leaves
8 salami slices
canned sardines, drained
Dressing:
3 tablespoons bottled French
    dressing
2 tablespoons double cream
½ teaspoon French mustard
2 tablespoons chopped parsley

American
½ honeydew melon, seeded
    and chopped
½ cup chopped walnuts
3 tablespoons raisins
lettuce leaves
8 salami slices
canned sardines, drained
Dressing:
3 tablespoons bottled Italian
    dressing
2 tablespoons heavy cream
½ teaspoon Dijon-style mustard
2 tablespoons chopped parsley

Mix together the dressing ingredients in a bowl. Add the melon, walnuts and raisins and fold together.

Arrange a bed of lettuce leaves on a serving platter. Pile the melon mixture in the centre. Roll the salami slices into cornets and arrange around the edge with the sardines.
Serves 4

Avocado Dip

Metric/Imperial	American
2 ripe avocados, peeled, stoned and chopped	2 ripe avocados, peeled, seeded and chopped
2 tomatoes, skinned and chopped	2 tomatoes, peeled and chopped
3 hard-boiled eggs, chopped	3 hard-cooked eggs, chopped
3 tablespoons lemon juice	3 tablespoons lemon juice
2 tablespoons mayonnaise	2 tablespoons mayonnaise
salt and pepper	salt and pepper
paprika	paprika

Put the avocados, tomatoes, eggs, lemon juice and mayonnaise in a blender or food processor and purée until smooth. Spoon into a bowl and season to taste with salt and pepper. (If liked, the dip may be served in the avocado shells.) Sprinkle the top with paprika and serve with raw vegetable sticks or savoury biscuits (crackers) for dipping.
Serves 8 to 10

Devilled Crab Dip

Metric/Imperial	American
1½ × 225 g/8 oz packets cream cheese	1½ × 8 oz packages cream cheese
4 tablespoons soured cream	¼ cup sour cream
2 teaspoons mild chilli sauce	2 teaspoons mild chili sauce
2 teaspoons Worcestershire sauce	2 teaspoons Worcestershire sauce
¼ teaspoon cayenne pepper	¼ teaspoon cayenne
salt and pepper	salt and pepper
1 cucumber, peeled and grated	1 cucumber, peeled and grated
1 × 225 g/8 oz can crabmeat, drained and flaked	1 × 8 oz can crabmeat, drained and flaked

Cream the cream cheese with the sour cream until softened. Beat in the chilli and Worcestershire sauces, cayenne and salt and pepper to taste. Fold in the cucumber and crabmeat.

Chill before serving with savoury biscuits (crackers).
Serves 8 to 10

Melon and Prawn (Shrimp) Cocktail

Metric/Imperial
½ honeydew melon, seeded
225 g/8 oz cooked peeled
   prawns
2 tomatoes, chopped
½ cucumber, diced
Dressing:
3 tablespoons mayonnaise
1 tablespoon tomato ketchup
3 tablespoons soured cream
salt and pepper

American
½ honeydew melon, seeded
½ lb cooked shelled shrimp
2 tomatoes, chopped
½ cucumber, diced
Dressing:
3 tablespoons mayonnaise
1 tablespoon tomato ketchup
3 tablespoons sour cream
salt and pepper

Scoop the melon flesh out of the shell with a melon baller, or cut it into cubes. Place the melon, prawns (shrimp), tomatoes and cucumber in a bowl. Combine the dressing ingredients with salt and pepper to taste. Add to the salad ingredients and fold together gently. Serve lightly chilled.
Serves 4 to 6

Ham and Avocado Rolls

Metric/Imperial
1 red pepper, cored, seeded
   and cut into strips
4 tomatoes, skinned, seeded
   and cut into strips
1 celery stick, chopped
3 tablespoons mayonnaise
1 ripe avocado, peeled, stoned
   and sliced
lemon juice
salt and pepper
8 slices of cooked ham

American
1 red pepper, seeded and cut
   into strips
4 tomatoes, peeled, seeded
   and cut into strips
1 celery stalk, chopped
3 tablespoons mayonnaise
1 ripe avocado, peeled, seeded
   and sliced
lemon juice
salt and pepper
8 slices of cooked ham

Blanch the red pepper strips in boiling water for 5 minutes. Drain well and dry on kitchen paper towels.

Mix the red pepper strips with the tomatoes, celery and mayonnaise. Toss the avocado slices in lemon juice to prevent discoloration, then fold into the mayonnaise mixture. Season to taste with salt and pepper.

Divide the avocado mixture between the ham slices and roll them up.
Serves 4

Horseradish Dip

Metric/Imperial	American
2 × 75 g/3 oz packets cream cheese	2 × 3 oz packages cream cheese
4 tablespoons double cream	¼ cup heavy cream
1 teaspoon grated dried horseradish	1 teaspoon grated dried horseradish
1 teaspoon grated lemon rind	1 teaspoon grated lemon rind
stuffed olive halves to garnish	pimiento-stuffed olive halves for garnish

Beat the cream cheese with the cream until smooth, then beat in the horseradish and lemon rind. Spoon into a serving dish and chill.
Garnish with olive halves and serve with raw vegetable sticks for dipping.
Serves 6 to 8

Bagna Cauda

Metric/Imperial	American
15 g/½ oz butter or margarine	1 tablespoon butter or margarine
1 small onion, finely chopped	1 small onion, finely chopped
1 large tomato, skinned and finely chopped	1 large tomato, peeled and finely chopped
1 teaspoon plain flour	1 teaspoon all-purpose flour
1 tablespoon anchovy essence	1 teaspoon anchovy paste
few drops of Tabasco sauce	few drops of hot pepper sauce
salt and pepper	salt and pepper
100 g/4 oz Cheddar cheese, grated	1 cup grated Cheddar cheese
raw vegetables to serve	raw vegetables to serve

Melt the butter or margarine in a flameproof serving dish or chafing dish. Add the onion and tomato and fry until the onion is softened. Stir in the flour and cook for 1 minute, then stir in the anchovy essence (paste), Tabasco sauce and salt and pepper to taste. Stir in the cheese and cook gently for 5 minutes.
Serve hot with raw vegetables for dipping. Select from radishes, quartered canned artichoke hearts, spring onions (scallions), small tomatoes, cauliflower florets, green and red pepper strips, carrot and celery sticks, cucumber and courgette (zucchini) chunks.
Serves 4 to 6

Stuffed Peaches

Metric/Imperial
225 g/8 oz cottage cheese
2 celery sticks, diced
2 tablespoons chopped walnuts
juice of ½ lemon
2 tablespoons grated cucumber
2 tablespoons mayonnaise
garlic salt
salt and pepper
8 canned peach halves
lettuce leaves

American
1 cup cottage cheese
2 celery stalks, diced
2 tablespoons chopped walnuts
juice of ½ lemon
2 tablespoons grated cucumber
2 tablespoons mayonnaise
garlic salt
salt and pepper
8 canned peach halves
lettuce leaves

Mix together the cottage cheese, celery, walnuts, lemon juice, cucumber, mayonnaise, and garlic salt, salt and pepper to taste. Pile the mixture on the peach halves.

Arrange a few lettuce leaves on each of four serving plates and place the stuffed peach halves on top. Serve lightly chilled.
Serves 4

Kipper Pâté

Metric/Imperial
500 g/1 lb frozen
   boil-in-the-bag kipper fillets
1 × 225 g/8 oz packet
   cream cheese
juice of ½ lemon
pepper

American
1 lb frozen boil-in-the-bag
   kipper fillets
1 × 8 oz package cream cheese
juice of ½ lemon
pepper

Cook the kipper fillets according to the instructions on the packet. Cool slightly, then scrape off the grey/black skins. Mash the kippers with the cream cheese until smooth, or purée in a blender or food processor. Add the lemon juice and pepper to taste. Chill before serving.
Serves 6 to 8

Variations:
Smoked Trout Pâté: Make as above, substituting smoked trout for kippers. Smoked trout does not require cooking, but remove all the skin and bones. Use 1 tablespoon creamed horseradish (or more to taste) instead of lemon juice.
Smoked Mackerel Pâté: Make as above, substituting smoked mackerel for kippers. Smoked mackerel does not require cooking, but remove all the skin and bones. Add 1 crushed garlic clove and cayenne pepper to taste. If you like, pack the pâté into small pots and cover with melted butter. Chill before serving.

Stuffed Cucumber

Metric/Imperial
2 cucumbers, halved lengthways
1 red dessert apple, cored and
  diced
100 g/4 oz mushrooms, diced
1 onion, finely chopped
75 g/3 oz cheese, grated
4 tablespoons mayonnaise
1 teaspoon French mustard
salt and pepper
stuffed olive slices to garnish

American
2 cucumbers, halved lengthwise
1 red-skinned apple, cored and
  diced
1 cup diced mushrooms
1 onion, finely chopped
¾ cup grated cheese
¼ cup mayonnaise
1 teaspoon Dijon-style mustard
salt and pepper
pimiento-stuffed olive slices
  for garnish

Scoop the seeds out of the cucumber halves, then blanch in boiling water for 1 minute. Drain and cool. Cut each half crossways into four pieces.

Mix together the apple, mushrooms, onion, cheese, mayonnaise, mustard and salt and pepper to taste. Pile the mixture into the cucumber pieces and garnish with olive slices.
Serves 4 to 6

Green and Yellow Noodles

Metric/Imperial
225 g/8 oz egg noodles
225 g/8 oz green noodles
  (fettuccine verde)
salt and pepper
2 tablespoons olive oil
2 garlic cloves, crushed
300 ml/½ pint double cream
2 tablespoons chopped parsley
1 teaspoon dried oregano
25 g/1 oz butter or margarine
50 g/2 oz Parmesan cheese,
  grated

American
½ lb egg noodles
½ lb green noodles
  (fettuccine verde)
salt and pepper
2 tablespoons olive oil
2 garlic cloves, crushed
1¼ cups heavy cream
2 tablespoons chopped parsley
1 teaspoon dried oregano
2 tablespoons butter or
  margarine
½ cup grated Parmesan cheese

Cook the noodles in boiling salted water until just tender.

Meanwhile heat the oil in a large frying pan (skillet). Add the garlic and fry for 1 minute, then stir in the cream and herbs and simmer gently for 2 to 3 minutes. Stir in the butter or margarine until melted.

Drain the noodles thoroughly and add to the sauce in the pan with the cheese. Toss to coat the noodles and serve hot.
Serves 6

Roe Pâté

Metric/Imperial	American
225 g/8 oz smoked cod's roe	½ lb tarama (salted fish roe)
25 g/1 oz fresh breadcrumbs	½ cup soft bread crumbs
15 g/½ oz butter or margarine	1 tablespoon butter or margarine
1 garlic clove, crushed	1 garlic clove, crushed
1 tablespoon lemon juice	1 tablespoon lemon juice
1 teaspoon chopped parsley	1 teaspoon chopped parsley
salt and pepper	salt and pepper
lemon twists to garnish	lemon twists for garnish

Mix all the ingredients together with salt and pepper to taste. A blender or food processor will speed things up considerably.

Pack into four small pots and chill. Serve garnished with lemon twists.
Serves 4

Grapefruit Tuna Pâté

Metric/Imperial	American
1 × 200 g/7 oz can tuna fish	1 × 7 oz can tuna fish
grated rind and juice of	grated rind and juice of
1 grapefruit	1 grapefruit
75 g/3 oz fresh breadcrumbs	1½ cups soft bread crumbs
2 teaspoons grated onion	2 teaspoons grated onion
1 egg, beaten	1 egg, beaten
salt and pepper	salt and pepper

Put the tuna in a bowl with its oil. Mash until smooth, then mix in the remaining ingredients with salt and pepper to taste. Spoon into a greased 500 g/1 lb loaf pan and smooth the top.

Bake in a preheated moderate oven (180°C/350°F, Gas Mark 4) for 40 minutes. Cool in the tin, then turn out onto a serving plate. Serve chilled.
Serves 4 to 6

Quick Liver Pâté

Metric/Imperial	American
100 g/4 oz continental liver sausage, skinned	¼ lb continental liver sausage or liverwurst, skinned
50 g/2 oz butter or margarine, softened	4 tablespoons butter or margarine, softened
50 g/2 oz cream cheese	¼ cup cream cheese
1 tablespoon milk	1 tablespoon milk
lemon juice	lemon juice
salt and pepper	salt and pepper

Cream the liver sausage with the butter or margarine and cream cheese. Beat in the milk, lemon juice and salt and pepper to taste. Add a little more milk if the mixture seems too stiff. Pack into four small pots and chill before serving with hot toast.
Serves 4

Devilled Stuffed Eggs

Metric/Imperial
4 hard-boiled eggs, halved
　　lengthways
2 × 75 g/3 oz packets cream
　　cheese
anchovy essence
salt and pepper
3 celery sticks, cut into
　　7.5 cm/3 inch pieces
Sauce:
3 tablespoons Worcestershire
　　sauce
2 tablespoons tomato ketchup
grated rind and juice of
　　1 lemon
few drops of Tabasco sauce
1 tablespoon tomato chutney
1 teaspoon made mustard
salt and pepper

American
4 hard-cooked eggs, halved
　　lengthwise
2 × 3 oz packages cream cheese
anchovy paste
salt and pepper
3 celery stalks, cut into
　　3 inch pieces
Sauce:
3 tablespoons Worcestershire
　　sauce
2 tablespoons tomato ketchup
grated rind and juice of
　　1 lemon
few drops of hot pepper sauce
1 tablespoon tomato chutney
1 teaspoon prepared mustard
salt and pepper

Carefully remove the yolks from the egg whites. Mash the yolks with the cream cheese, then mix in anchovy essence (paste), salt and pepper to taste. Fill the egg whites with this mixture. Arrange the stuffed eggs on a platter with the celery.

　　Mix together the sauce ingredients with salt and pepper to taste. Pour a little sauce over each egg and serve the rest separately.
Serves 4

Hot Bel Paese Bites

Metric/Imperial
5 slices of white bread,
　　crusts removed
50 g/2 oz butter or margarine
2 tablespoons oil
100 g/4 oz Bel Paese cheese,
　　thinly sliced
10 anchovy fillets, halved

American
5 slices of white bread,
　　crusts removed
4 tablespoons butter or
　　margarine
2 tablespoons oil
¼ lb Bel Paese cheese, thinly
　　sliced
10 anchovy fillets, halved

Cut each slice of bread into quarters. Melt the butter or margarine with the oil in a frying pan, add the bread squares and fry until crisp and golden brown on both sides. Drain on kitchen paper towels.

　　Cut the cheese slices into squares the same size as the bread squares, and place one on each bread square. Top with the anchovy halves.

　　Grill (broil) until the cheese has melted. Serve hot.
Makes 20

Tagliatelle with Cream Cheese and Nuts

Metric/Imperial
25 g/1 oz butter or margarine
1½ × 225 g/8 oz packets cream
    cheese
50 g/2 oz Parmesan cheese,
    grated
100 g/4 oz walnuts, chopped
1 tablespoon chopped parsley
500 g/1 lb tagliatelle
salt and pepper

American
2 tablespoons butter or
    margarine
1½ × 8 oz packages cream cheese
½ cup grated Parmesan cheese
1 cup chopped walnuts
1 tablespoon chopped parsley
1 lb tagliatelle
salt and pepper

Melt the butter or margarine in a saucepan. Add the cream cheese and heat very gently, stirring, until melted. Stir in the Parmesan cheese, walnuts and parsley and leave to heat through while you cook the pasta.
   Cook the tagliatelle in boiling salted water until just tender. Drain well and tip into a warmed serving dish. Add the cream cheese sauce and toss to coat. Season to taste with salt and pepper and serve hot.
Serves 6

Tomato Fans

Metric/Imperial
4 large tomatoes
1 teaspoon dried basil
4 hard-boiled eggs, sliced
4 tablespoons mayonnaise
2 spring onions, chopped
salt and pepper
To garnish:
green pepper strips
cucumber slices

American
4 large tomatoes
1 teaspoon dried basil
4 hard-cooked eggs, sliced
¼ cup mayonnaise
2 scallions, chopped
salt and pepper
For garnish:
green pepper strips
cucumber slices

Place the tomatoes on a surface, stalk ends down. Cut through the centre almost to the stalk, then make two similar cuts on each side of the first cut. Put a little basil in each cut. Chill well.
   Just before serving, put a slice of egg in each cut. Chop the remaining egg and mix with the mayonnaise, spring onions (scallions) and salt and pepper to taste. Spoon a little of this mixture on top of each tomato and garnish with green pepper strips and cucumber slices.
Serves 4

Asparagus Polonaise

Metric/Imperial	American
500 g/1 lb fresh or frozen asparagus spears	1 lb fresh or frozen asparagus spears
salt and pepper	salt and pepper
40 g/1½ oz butter	3 tablespoons butter
50 g/2 oz fresh breadcrumbs	1 cup soft bread crumbs
2 hard-boiled eggs, chopped	2 hard-cooked eggs, chopped

Cook the asparagus in boiling salted water until just tender.

Meanwhile melt the butter in a frying pan (skillet). Add the breadcrumbs and fry until golden. Stir in the eggs and salt and pepper to taste.

Drain the asparagus and arrange on four warmed serving plates. Top with the egg and breadcrumb mixture and serve hot.

Serves 4

Eggs in Green Sauce

Metric/Imperial	American
500 g/1 lb frozen peas, thawed	1 lb frozen peas, thawed
25 g/1 oz butter, melted	2 tablespoons butter, melted
2 tablespoons double cream	2 tablespoons heavy cream
1 tablespoon chopped fresh mint	1 tablespoon chopped fresh mint
salt and pepper	salt and pepper
4 eggs	4 eggs

Place the peas, butter, cream, mint and salt and pepper to taste in a blender or food processor and purée until smooth. Pour the sauce into a saucepan and leave to heat through gently.

Meanwhile soft-boil the eggs for 4 to 5 minutes.

Divide the sauce between four warmed ramekin dishes. Drain the eggs and shell them carefully. Place an egg in each dish and serve.

Serves 4

Cottage Cheese Mousse

Metric/Imperial	American
500 g/1 lb cottage cheese, sieved	2 cups cottage cheese, strained
150 ml/¼ pint plain yogurt	⅔ cup plain yogurt
1 tablespoon tomato purée	1 tablespoon tomato paste
squeeze of lemon juice	squeeze of lemon juice
salt and pepper	salt and pepper
100 g/4 oz peeled prawns	¼ lb cooked shelled shrimp

Mix together the cottage cheese, yogurt, tomato purée (paste), lemon juice and salt and pepper to taste. Divide between four ramekin dishes, pressing down well. Top with the prawns (shrimp). Cover and chill for 1 hour before serving.

Serves 4

Stuffed Mushrooms

Metric/Imperial	American
12 large flat mushrooms	12 large flat mushrooms
3 tablespoons olive oil	3 tablespoons olive oil
1 garlic clove, chopped	1 garlic clove, chopped
3 shallots, chopped	3 shallots, chopped
25 g/1 oz fresh breadcrumbs	½ cup soft bread crumbs
50 g/2 oz Parmesan cheese, grated	½ cup grated Parmesan cheese
2 teaspoons chopped parsley	2 teaspoons chopped parsley
1 teaspoon chopped chives	1 teaspoon chopped chives
salt and pepper	salt and pepper
25 g/1 oz butter or margarine	2 tablespoons butter or margarine

Remove the stalks from the mushrooms and chop them finely.

Heat the oil in a frying pan, add the garlic, shallots and chopped mushroom stalks and fry for 5 minutes. Remove from the heat and stir in the breadcrumbs, cheese, parsley, chives and salt and pepper to taste.

Arrange the mushroom caps, hollow sides up, in a greased flameproof dish. Fill with the cheese mixture and dot with the butter or margarine. Place under a preheated grill (broiler) and cook gently for about 5 minutes or until the stuffing is golden and bubbling and the mushrooms are tender. Serve hot.
Serves 4

Italian Eggs

Metric/Imperial	American
6 hard-boiled eggs, sliced	6 hard-cooked eggs, sliced
tomato wedges to garnish	tomato wedges for garnish
Sauce:	Sauce:
25 g/1 oz parsley, chopped	¼ cup chopped parsley
1 teaspoon chopped fresh marjoram	1 teaspoon chopped fresh marjoram
1 garlic clove, crushed	1 garlic clove, crushed
6 black olives, stoned and chopped	6 pitted ripe olives, chopped
1 shallot, finely chopped	1 shallot, finely chopped
2 anchovy fillets, chopped	2 anchovy fillets, chopped
pepper	pepper
120 ml/4 fl oz olive oil	½ cup olive oil

Put the parsley, marjoram, garlic, olives, shallot, anchovies and pepper to taste in a blender or food processor and purée until smooth. Gradually work in the oil. Alternatively, pound the ingredients together in a mortar with a pestle and beat in the oil.

Arrange the eggs on a serving plate and pour over the sauce. Garnish with tomato wedges.
Serves 4

Cheese and Mushroom Ball

Metric/Imperial
1 × 225 g/8 oz packet cream
  cheese
50 g/2 oz butter or margarine
225 g/8 oz mushrooms, sliced
75 g/3 oz smoked cheese, grated
2 tablespoons chopped parsley

American
1 × 8 oz package cream cheese
4 tablespoons butter or
  margarine
½ lb mushrooms, sliced
¾ cup grated smoked cheese
2 tablespoons chopped parsley

Beat the cream cheese with the butter or margarine until light and fluffy.
Add the mushrooms, smoked cheese and parsley and mix well. Shape
into a ball, wrap in plastic wrap and chill until firm.
  Serve with savoury biscuits (crackers).
Serves 8 to 10

Sweet and Sour Avocados

Metric/Imperial
2 ripe avocados, halved and
  stoned
4 teaspoons caster sugar
4 teaspoons mayonnaise
2 dessert apples, peeled,
  cored and grated
4 slices of cooked ham, diced
1 × 326 g/11½ oz can sweetcorn
  kernels, drained

American
2 ripe avocados, halved and
  seeded
4 teaspoons sugar
4 teaspoons mayonnaise
2 apples, peeled, cored and
  shredded
4 slices of cooked ham, diced
1 × 11½ oz can whole kernel corn,
  drained

Scoop the flesh out of the avocado halves, keeping the skins intact. Mash
the flesh with the sugar and mayonnaise. Stir in the apples, ham and
corn. Spoon the mixture into the avocado skins and serve immediately.
Serves 4

Pears with Grapes

Metric/Imperial
4 ripe pears, peeled, halved
  and cored
2 × 75 g/3 oz packets cream
  cheese
3 tablespoons mayonnaise
salt and pepper
225 g/8 oz seedless grapes,
  halved
paprika

American
4 ripe pears, peeled, halved
  and cored
2 × 3 oz packages cream cheese
3 tablespoons mayonnaise
salt and pepper
½ lb seedless grapes, halved
paprika

Place two pear halves, cut sides down, on each of four individual serving
plates. Beat the cream cheese with the mayonnaise and salt and pepper
to taste until softened. Spread all over the pears.
  Press the grapes into the cream cheese mixture and sprinkle with a
little paprika.
Serves 4

Mushroom and Egg Ramekins

Metric/Imperial
225 g/8 oz small button
  mushrooms
1 garlic clove, crushed
150 ml/¼ pint beef stock
4 eggs
1 tablespoon chopped parsley
salt and pepper

American
½ lb small mushrooms
1 garlic clove, crushed
⅔ cup beef stock or broth
4 eggs
1 tablespoon chopped parsley
salt and pepper

Place the mushrooms, garlic and stock in a saucepan. Bring to the boil
and simmer for 10 minutes.

Meanwhile break an egg into each of four greased ramekin dishes.
Place on a baking sheet and cook in a preheated moderate oven
(180°C/350°F, Gas Mark 4) for 8 to 10 minutes or until the eggs are set.

Stir the parsley and salt and pepper to taste into the mushroom mixture
and spoon on top of the eggs. Serve hot.
Serves 4

Noodles with Mushrooms and Cream

Metric/Imperial
3 tablespoons oil
1 small onion, chopped
1 garlic clove, crushed
225 g/8 oz mushrooms, sliced
100 g/4 oz prosciutto ham,
  shredded
300 ml/½ pint single cream
salt and pepper
500 g/1 lb egg noodles

American
3 tablespoons oil
1 small onion, chopped
1 garlic clove, crushed
½ lb mushrooms, sliced
¼ lb prosciutto ham, shredded
1¼ cups light cream
salt and pepper
1 lb egg noodles

Heat the oil in a saucepan. Add the onion and garlic and fry until softened.
Stir in the mushrooms and prosciutto and cook for a further 3 minutes.
Add the cream and salt and pepper to taste, mix well and leave to cook
gently while you cook the pasta.

Cook the noodles in boiling salted water until just tender. Drain well and
return to the pan. Pour over the sauce and toss to coat. Serve hot.
Serves 4 to 6

Stuffed Lemons

Metric/Imperial
6 large lemons
1 × 200 g/7 oz can tuna fish
  or other fish, drained and
  flaked
1 teaspoon French mustard
6 tablespoons mayonnaise
pinch of paprika
pepper
1 egg white
parsley sprigs to garnish

American
6 large lemons
1 × 7 oz can tuna fish or
  other fish, drained and
  flaked
1 teaspoon Dijon-style mustard
6 tablespoons mayonnaise
pinch of paprika
pepper
1 egg white
parsley sprigs for garnish

Cut the pointed ends off the lemons to make a flat surface so they can stand upright. Cut off the stalk ends and scoop out the flesh. Discard all pith, pips and membrane and chop the flesh.

Mix the lemon flesh with the fish, mustard, mayonnaise, paprika and pepper to taste. Beat the egg white until stiff and fold into the mixture.

Fill the lemon shells with the fish mixture, piling it up. Chill well before serving, garnished with parsley sprigs.
Serves 6

Tarragon Cream Pears

Metric/Imperial
2 ripe pears, peeled, halved
  and cored
lettuce leaves
paprika
Dressing:
1 egg
2 tablespoons tarragon vinegar
2 teaspoons caster sugar
4 tablespoons double cream,
  whipped

American
2 ripe pears, peeled, halved
  and cored
lettuce leaves
paprika
Dressing:
1 egg
2 tablespoons tarragon vinegar
2 teaspoons sugar
¼ cup heavy cream, whipped

First make the dressing: place the egg, vinegar and sugar in a heavy-based saucepan and heat gently, stirring, until the mixture thickens. Do not allow to boil. Remove from the heat and dip the bottom of the pan in cold water to cool quickly. Fold in the cream.

Place a pear half on four individual plates lined with lettuce leaves. Pour over the dressing and sprinkle with a little paprika.
Serves 4

Sardine-Stuffed Eggs

Metric/Imperial
4 hard-boiled eggs, halved
   lengthways
1 × 150 g/5 oz can sardines,
   drained
1 teaspoon chopped parsley
2 teaspoons quick-cook oats
2 tablespoons single cream
pinch of cayenne pepper
salt and pepper
parsley sprigs to garnish

American
4 hard-cooked eggs, halved
   lengthwise
1 × 5 oz can sardines, drained
1 teaspoon chopped parsley
2 teaspoons quick-cook oats
2 tablespoons light cream
pinch of cayenne
salt and pepper
parsley sprigs for garnish

Scoop the yolks out of the egg halves, keeping the whites intact. Mash the yolks with the sardines, parsley, oats, cream, cayenne and salt and pepper to taste.

Spoon or pipe the sardine mixture into the egg whites and garnish each with a parsley sprig.

Serves 4

Avocado, Grapefruit and Sesame Salad

Metric/Imperial
2 large avocados, peeled,
   stoned and sliced
juice of 1 lemon
2 grapefruit, peeled and
   segmented
1 tablespoon chopped fresh
   mint
lettuce leaves
2 tablespoons sesame seeds

American
2 avocados, peeled, seeded
   and sliced
juice of 1 lemon
2 grapefruit, peeled and
   segmented
1 tablespoon chopped fresh
   mint
lettuce leaves
2 tablespoons sesame seeds

Toss the avocado slices with the lemon juice to prevent discoloration. Mix the avocado with the grapefruit and mint.

Place a few lettuce leaves on four serving plates and pile the avocado mixture on top. Sprinkle over the sesame seeds and serve.

Serves 4

Strawberry and Asparagus Salad

Metric/Imperial	American
1 × 350 g/12 oz can asparagus spears, drained	1 × 12 oz can asparagus spears, drained
500 g/1 lb strawberries, sliced	1 lb strawberries, sliced
50 g/2 oz walnut halves	½ cup walnut halves
½ cucumber, sliced	½ cucumber, sliced
1 egg white	1 egg white
150 ml/¼ pint mayonnaise	⅔ cup mayonnaise

Arrange the asparagus spears on a serving plate to resemble the spokes of a wheel. Place the strawberries, walnuts and cucumber in a decorative pattern on top.

Beat the egg white until stiff and fold into the mayonnaise. Spoon a little of this dressing into the centre of the salad and serve the rest separately.
Serves 4 to 6

Cheesy Orange Cups

Metric/Imperial	American
4 oranges	4 oranges
1 × 75 g/3 oz packet cream cheese	1 × 3 oz package cream cheese
1 green pepper, cored, seeded and diced	1 green pepper, seeded and diced
25 g/1 oz walnuts, chopped	¼ cup chopped walnuts
salt and pepper	salt and pepper
cucumber slices to garnish	cucumber slices for garnish

Cut about one-third off the end of each orange. Scoop out the flesh and chop it. Set the orange skin shells aside.

Mix the orange flesh into the cream cheese, then mix in the green pepper, walnuts and salt and pepper to taste. Fill the orange shells with the mixture and garnish with cucumber slices.
Serves 4

Avocados with Corn

Metric/Imperial	American
1 × 326 g/11½ oz can sweetcorn kernels, drained	1 × 11½ oz can whole kernel corn, drained
225 g/8 oz cottage cheese	1 cup cottage cheese
2 tablespoons chopped chives	2 tablespoons chopped chives
salt and pepper	salt and pepper
4 ripe avocados, halved and stoned	4 ripe avocados, halved and seeded
lemon juice	lemon juice

Mix together the corn, cottage cheese, chives and salt and pepper to taste. Rub the cut surfaces of the avocado halves with lemon juice to prevent discoloration, then fill the hollows with the corn mixture.
Serves 8

Strawberry and Melon Appetizer

Metric/Imperial
1 small ripe honeydew or
  cantaloup melon, halved and
  seeded
100 g/4 oz strawberries, sliced
1 × 5 cm/2 inch piece of
  cucumber, chopped
grated rind and juice of
  1 orange
2 tablespoons chopped fresh
  mint
shredded lettuce
mint sprigs to garnish

American
1 small ripe honeydew or
  cantaloup melon, halved and
  seeded
¼ lb strawberries, sliced
1 × 2 inch piece of cucumber,
  chopped
grated rind and juice of
  1 orange
2 tablespoons chopped fresh
  mint
shredded lettuce
.mint sprigs for garnish

Scoop the melon flesh out of the shells with a melon baller, or cut it into cubes. Mix with the strawberries, cucumber, orange rind and juice and mint. Chill lightly.

Place a little shredded lettuce in four to six serving glasses and spoon the melon mixture on top. Garnish with mint sprigs.
Serves 4 to 6

Pasta with Avocado Dressing

Metric/Imperial
350 g/12 oz pasta shells
salt and pepper
4 spring onions, chopped
2 tablespoons chopped parsley
Dressing:
1 ripe avocado, halved and
  stoned
juice of 1 lemon
1 garlic clove, crushed
1 teaspoon caster sugar
150 ml/¼ pint single cream

American
¾ lb pasta shells
salt and pepper
4 scallions, chopped
2 tablespoons chopped parsley
Dressing:
1 ripe avocado, halved and
  seeded
juice of 1 lemon
1 garlic clove, crushed
1 teaspoon sugar
⅔ cup light cream

Cook the pasta shells in boiling salted water until just tender. Drain and cool.

To make the dressing: scoop the avocado flesh out of the skins and place in a blender or food processor with the remaining dressing ingredients. Purée until smooth. Season to taste with salt and pepper.

Add the avocado dressing to the pasta shells with the spring onions (scallions) and parsley. Toss well together. Serve lightly chilled.
Serves 6 to 8

Avocado Crab Cocktail

Metric/Imperial
2 ripe avocados, peeled and
  stoned
1 tablespoon lemon juice
3 tablespoons mayonnaise
1 × 200 g/7 oz can crabmeat,
  drained and flaked
1 green pepper, cored, seeded
  and diced
salt and pepper
shredded lettuce
lemon wedges to garnish

American
2 ripe avocados, peeled and
  seeded
1 tablespoon lemon juice
3 tablespoons mayonnaise
1 × 7 oz can crabmeat, drained
  and flaked
1 green pepper, seeded
  and diced
salt and pepper
shredded lettuce
lemon wedges for garnish

Mash the avocados with the lemon juice until smooth, then beat in the mayonnaise. Fold in the crabmeat and green pepper and season to taste with salt and pepper.

Half fill four glasses or individual dishes with shredded lettuce and pile the avocado mixture on top. Garnish with lemon wedges.

Serves 4

Cottage Kipper Mousse

Metric/Imperial
1 × 225 g/8 oz frozen boil-in-
  the-bag kipper fillets
15 g/½ oz butter or margarine
1 onion, finely chopped
225 g/8 oz cottage cheese,
  sieved
7 g/¼ oz powdered gelatine
150 ml/¼ pint hot water
salt and pepper
cucumber slices to garnish

American
1 × 8 oz frozen boil-in-the-bag
  kipper fillets
1 tablespoon butter or
  margarine
1 onion, finely chopped
1 cup cottage cheese, strained
1 envelope (1 tablespoon)
  unflavored gelatin
⅔ cup hot water
salt and pepper
cucumber slices for garnish

Cook the kipper fillets according to the instructions on the packet. Cool and flake.

Melt the butter or margarine in a frying pan (skillet), add the onion and fry until softened. Add to the kippers with the cottage cheese and mash together well.

Dissolve the gelatine in the hot water. Beat into the kipper mixture with salt and pepper to taste. Pour into a dampened decorative mould and chill until set.

Turn out of the mould onto a serving plate and garnish with cucumber slices.

Serves 4 to 6

Avocado Prosciutto

Metric/Imperial
2 ripe avocados, peeled, stoned
   and sliced
juice of 1 orange
100 g/4 oz prosciutto ham
2 oranges, peeled and segmented
watercress to garnish

American
2 ripe avocados, peeled, seeded
   and sliced
juice of 1 orange
¼ lb prosciutto ham
2 oranges, peeled and segmented
watercress for garnish

Toss the avocado slices in the orange juice to prevent discoloration, then arrange on four individual serving plates. Cut the ham into strips and roll them up. Arrange on the avocado slices with the orange segments. Garnish with watercress and serve.
Serves 4

Crab and Grapefruit Appetizer

Metric/Imperial
225 g/8 oz canned or fresh
   crabmeat, flaked
6 tablespoons mayonnaise
lettuce leaves
2 grapefruit, peeled and
   segmented
paprika

American
½ lb canned or fresh crabmeat,
   flaked
6 tablespoons mayonnaise
lettuce leaves
2 grapefruit, peeled and
   segmented
paprika

Mix together the crabmeat and mayonnaise. Make a bed of lettuce leaves on each of four serving plates and pile the crabmeat mixture in the centre. Surround with the grapefruit segments and sprinkle over a little paprika.
Serves 4

Peaches with Cheese Balls

Metric/Imperial
4 tablespoons sultanas
1 × 225 g/8 oz packet cream
   cheese
2 tablespoons milk
25 g/1 oz walnuts, chopped
lettuce leaves
8 canned peach halves
watercress to garnish

American
¼ cup golden raisins
1 × 8 oz package cream cheese
2 tablespoons milk
¼ cup chopped walnuts
lettuce leaves
8 canned peach halves
watercress for garnish

Cover the sultanas (raisins) with boiling water and leave them to soak for 5 minutes.

Meanwhile cream the cream cheese with the milk until softened. Drain the sultanas (raisins) and mix into the cream cheese with the walnuts. Divide the mixture into eight portions and shape into balls.

Make a bed of lettuce leaves on a serving platter. Arrange the peach halves on top, cut sides up, and place a cheese ball in the hollow of each half. Garnish with watercress. Chill lightly before serving.
Serves 4

Potted Mushrooms

Metric/Imperial	American
75 g/3 oz butter or margarine	6 tablespoons butter or
500 g/1 lb mushrooms, chopped	margarine
1 teaspoon chopped fresh thyme	1 lb mushro ms, chopped
1 teaspoon chopped parsley	1 teaspoon chopped fresh thyme
salt and pepper	1 teaspoo chopped parsley
	salt and pepper

Melt 25 g/1 oz (2 tablespoons) of the butter or margarine in a saucepan. Add the mushrooms, herbs and salt and pepper to taste. Cover and cook gently for 10 minutes, shaking the pan occasionally to prevent sticking.

Using a slotted spoon, lift out the mushrooms and chop them very finely. Boil the liquid in the pan until reduced to 2 tablespoons. Stir in the mushrooms, and taste and adjust the seasoning.

Pack the mushroom mixture into four ramekin dishes and smooth the tops. Chill well.

Melt the remaining butter or margarine and pour over the mushroom mixture in the ramekins. Chill until set.

Serves 4

Neptune's Tomatoes

Metric/Imperial	American
12 medium tomatoes, skinned	12 medium tomatoes, peeled
225 g/8 oz cooked peeled prawns	½ lb cooked shelled tiny shrimp
3 celery sticks, diced	3 celery stalks, diced
1 dessert apple, cored and diced	1 apple, cored and diced
1 green pepper, cored, seeded	1 green pepper, seeded
and diced	and diced
1 large ripe avocado, peeled,	1 large ripe avocado, peeled,
stoned and diced	seeded and diced
1 tablespoon lemon juice	1 tablespoon lemon juice
250 ml/8 fl oz soured cream	1 cup sour cream
salt and pepper	salt and pepper

Cut a lid off the rounded end of each tomato and scoop out the insides. Discard the seeds and chop the pulp. Mix the tomato pulp with the prawns (shrimp), celery, apple and green pepper. Toss the avocado in the lemon juice to prevent discoloration and add to the mixture with the sour cream and salt and pepper to taste.

Season the insides of the tomato shells with salt and pepper, then fill with the prawn (shrimp) mixture. Replace the lids and chill lightly before serving.

Serves 6

Devilled Cottage Eggs

Metric/Imperial
4 hard-boiled eggs, halved
   lengthways
¼ teaspoon dry mustard
2 teaspoons vinegar
1 tablespoon chutney
pinch of cayenne pepper
1 teaspoon chopped chives
salt
225 g/8 oz cottage cheese

American
4 hard-cooked eggs, halved
   lengthwise
¼ teaspoon dry mustard
2 teaspoons vinegar
1 tablespoon chutney
pinch of cayenne
1 teaspoon chopped chives
salt
1 cup cottage cheese

Scoop the yolks out of the egg halves, keeping the whites intact. Mash the yolks with the mustard, vinegar, chutney, cayenne, chives and salt to taste. Beat in the cottage cheese.
   Fill the egg whites with the cheese mixture. Chill lightly before serving.
Serves 4

Prune-Stuffed Tomatoes

Metric/Imperial
4 large tomatoes
1 × 75 g/3 oz packet cream
   cheese
50 g/2 oz butter or margarine
10 canned prunes, stoned and
   chopped
salt and pepper
4 walnut halves

American
4 large tomatoes
1 × 3 oz package cream cheese
4 tablespoons butter or
   margarine
10 canned prunes, pitted and
   chopped
salt and pepper
4 walnut halves

Cut a lid from the top of each tomato and reserve. Scoop out the insides of the tomatoes, then place them upside-down on kitchen paper towels to drain.
   Beat the cream cheese and butter or margarine together, then mix in the prunes. Season the insides of the tomatoes with salt and pepper and fill with the prune mixture. Place a walnut half on top of each, then add the tomato lids. Chill lightly before serving.
Serves 4

Spiced Grapefruit

Metric/Imperial
2 grapefruit, halved
25 g/1 oz dark brown sugar
pinch of ground ginger
pinch of ground cinnamon

American
2 grapefruit, halved
3 tablespoons dark brown sugar
pinch of ground ginger
pinch of ground cinnamon

Loosen the grapefruit segments. Mix together the sugar and spices and sprinkle over the grapefruit. Cover and chill overnight.
Serves 4

Tuna-Stuffed Peppers

Metric/Imperial
4 large red or green peppers
4 medium potatoes
1 × 200 g/7 oz can tuna fish,
  drained and flaked
2 pickled onions, chopped
½ teaspoon made mustard
1 tablespoon lemon juice
3 tablespoons oil
salt and pepper

American
4 large red or green peppers
4 medium potatoes
1 × 7 oz can tuna fish, drained
  and flaked
4 cocktail onions, chopped
½ teaspoon prepared mustard
1 tablespoon lemon juice
3 tablespoons oil
salt and pepper

Cut the tops off the peppers and scoop out the core and seeds. Blanch the pepper tops and shells in boiling water for 3 minutes. Drain and leave to cool.

Cook the potatoes in boiling water until tender. Drain well, then cool. Dice the potatoes.

Mix together the potatoes, tuna fish, onions, mustard, lemon juice, oil and salt and pepper to taste. Use to stuff the pepper shells and replace the tops. Chill well before serving.
Serves 4

Savoury Pears

Metric/Imperial
225 g/8 oz Cheddar cheese,
  grated
2 red dessert apples, cored
  and grated
50 g/2 oz walnuts, chopped
50 g/2 oz raisins
150 ml/¼ pint milk
few drops of Worcestershire
  sauce
salt and pepper
4 pears, halved and cored
lemon juice
tomato wedges to garnish

American
2 cups grated Cheddar cheese
2 red-skinned apples, cored
  and grated
½ cup chopped walnuts
⅓ cup raisins
⅔ cup milk
few drops of Worcestershire
  sauce
salt and pepper
4 pears, halved and cored
lemon juice
tomato wedges for garnish

Mix together the cheese, apples, walnuts, raisins, milk, Worcestershire sauce and salt and pepper to taste.

Brush the cut surfaces of the pears with lemon juice to prevent discoloration, then pile the cheese mixture on top. Arrange two halves on each of four individual serving plates and garnish with tomato wedges.
Serves 4

Marinated Mushrooms

Metric/Imperial
750 g/1½ lb small button
  mushrooms
300 ml/½ pint dry white wine
2 teaspoons lemon juice
3 tablespoons olive oil
½ teaspoon paprika
salt and pepper
chopped parsley to garnish

American
1½ lb small button mushrooms
1¼ cups dry white wine
2 teaspoons lemon juice
3 tablespoons olive oil
½ teaspoon paprika
salt and pepper
chopped parsley for garnish

Put the mushrooms into a saucepan and add the wine and lemon juice. Simmer for 5 minutes. Drain the mushrooms, reserving the wine, and leave to cool.

Mix the wine with the oil, paprika and salt and pepper to taste. Add the mushrooms and stir well to coat. Chill and serve, sprinkled with parsley.
Serves 6

Salted Nuts

Metric/Imperial
75 g/3 oz butter or margarine
6 tablespoons oil
500 g/1 lb shelled mixed nuts
1 teaspoon cayenne pepper
salt

American
6 tablespoons butter or
  margarine
6 tablespoons oil
1 lb shelled mixed nuts
1 teaspoon cayenne
salt

Melt the butter or margarine with the oil in a large frying pan (skillet). Add the nuts and fry for about 5 minutes or until browned all over. Shake the pan frequently to prevent the nuts sticking.

Tip the nuts onto kitchen paper towels to drain. Sprinkle with the cayenne and salt to taste and toss to coat. Cool before serving.
Makes 500 g/1 lb

Pepper Cheese Slices

Metric/Imperial
500 g/1 lb cottage cheese
1 × 225 g/8 oz packet cream
  cheese
4 tablespoons chopped parsley
  or chives
4 green or red peppers, cored
  and seeded
paprika

American
2 cups cottage cheese
1 × 8 oz package cream cheese
¼ cup chopped parsley or
  chives
4 green or red peppers,
  seeded
paprika

Mix together the cottage cheese, cream cheese and herbs. Fill the peppers with the cheese mixture, wrap in plastic wrap and chill overnight.

The next day, slice the peppers thickly crosswise and sprinkle each cheese-filled slice with paprika.
Serves 4 to 6

Soured Cream Mushrooms

Metric/Imperial
2 x 210 g/7½ oz cans small
   whole mushrooms in brine,
   drained
150 ml/¼ pint soured cream
2 tablespoons mayonnaise
1 teaspoon dried tarragon
salt and pepper
lettuce leaves
chopped parsley to garnish

American
2 x 7½ oz cans small whole
   mushrooms in brine, drained
⅔ cup sour cream
2 tablespoons mayonnaise
1 teaspoon dried tarragon
salt and pepper
lettuce leaves
chopped parsley for garnish

Mix together the mushrooms, sour cream, mayonnaise, tarragon and salt and pepper to taste. Chill for about 20 minutes.

Place two or three lettuce leaves on each of four individual serving plates and spoon the mushroom mixture on top. Sprinkle with chopped parsley.
Serves 4

Piquant Pears

Metric/Imperial
shredded lettuce
1 x 750 g/1½ lb can pear halves,
   drained
25 g/1 oz walnuts, chopped
Dressing:
175 g/6 oz blue cheese,
   crumbled
120 ml/4 fl oz mayonnaise
120 ml/4 fl oz soured cream
pinch of cayenne pepper
salt and pepper

American
shredded lettuce
1 x 1½ lb can pear halves,
   drained
¼ cup chopped walnuts
Dressing:
1½ cups crumbled blue cheese
½ cup mayonnaise
½ cup sour cream
pinch of cayenne
salt and pepper

Make a bed of shredded lettuce on six individual serving plates and arrange the pear halves on top, cut sides down. Chill.

To make the dressing, mix together all the ingredients with salt and pepper to taste. Spoon the dressing over the pears and sprinkle the walnuts on top.
Serves 6

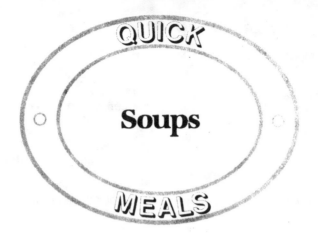

Scottish Mushroom Soup

Metric/Imperial
2 × 300 g/11½ oz cans
  condensed cream of mushroom
  soup
milk
3 tablespoons whiskey
4 tablespoons single cream

American
2 × 11½ oz cans condensed
  cream of mushroom soup
milk
3 tablespoons whiskey
¼ cup light cream

Make up the soup with milk as directed on the can and heat in a
saucepan. Stir in the whiskey and serve immediately, topped with a swirl
of cream.
Serves 4

Salmon Chowder

Metric/Imperial
600 ml/1 pint milk
1 × 225 g/8 oz can
  cream-style sweetcorn
1 × 200 g/7 oz can sweetcorn
  kernels, drained
1 × 350 g/12 oz can salmon,
  drained and flaked
25 g/1 oz butter or margarine
1 tablespoon chopped parsley
salt and pepper

American
2½ cups milk
1 × 8 oz can cream-style corn
1 × 7 oz can whole kernel corn,
  drained
1 × 12 oz can salmon, drained
  and flaked
2 tablespoons butter or margarine
1 tablespoon chopped parsley
salt and pepper

Pour the milk into a saucepan and bring almost to the boil. Stir in the
cream-style corn and corn kernels and heat through. Stir in the salmon,
butter or margarine, parsley and salt and pepper to taste and continue
cooking gently until the soup is piping hot.
Serves 4

Chicken Liver Soup

Metric/Imperial
25 g/1 oz butter or margarine
1 onion, chopped
1 garlic clove, crushed
100 g/4 oz chicken livers,
    chopped
350 g/12 oz frozen peas
1.2 litres/2 pints chicken
    stock
50 g/2 oz small pasta shapes
salt and pepper
1 tablespoon chopped parsley
2 tablespoons grated Parmesan
    cheese

American
2 tablespoons butter or margarine
1 onion, chopped
1 garlic clove, crushed
1 cup chopped chicken livers
3 cups frozen peas
5 cups chicken stock or
    broth
½ cup small pasta shapes
salt and pepper
1 tablespoon chopped parsley
2 tablespoons grated Parmesan
    cheese

Melt the butter or margarine in a saucepan. Add the onion and garlic and fry until softened. Stir in the chicken livers and fry, stirring, until lightly browned. Add the peas, stock, pasta shapes and salt and pepper to taste and bring to the boil. Simmer for about 12 minutes or until the pasta is just tender.
    Stir in the parsley and cheese and serve hot.
Serves 4 to 6

Country Vegetable Soup

Metric/Imperial
50 g/2 oz butter or margarine
1 onion, chopped
500 g/1 lb frozen mixed chopped
    vegetables (carrots, celery,
    cauliflower, potatoes, etc.)
300 ml/½ pint chicken stock
1 bay leaf
½ teaspoon dried rosemary
¼ teaspoon dried sage
salt and pepper
600 ml/1 pint milk

American
4 tablespoons butter or margarine
1 onion, chopped
1 lb frozen mixed chopped
    vegetables (carrots, celery,
    cauliflower, potatoes, etc.)
1¼ cups chicken stock or broth
1 bay leaf
½ teaspoon dried rosemary
¼ teaspoon dried sage
salt and pepper
2½ cups milk

Melt the butter or margarine in a saucepan. Add the onion and mixed vegetables and fry gently for 5 minutes, stirring occasionally. Add the stock, herbs and salt and pepper to taste and bring to the boil. Cover and simmer for 15 minutes. Discard the bay leaf.
    Purée the soup in a blender or food processor, then return to the pan. Stir in the milk and heat through gently. Taste and adjust the seasoning, then serve hot.
Serves 4

Mediterranean Rice Soup

Metric/Imperial
1.2 litres/2 pints chicken or
  beef stock
65 g/2½ oz long-grain rice
2 egg yolks
juice of 1 lemon
50 g/2 oz Parmesan cheese,
  grated
2 tablespoons water

American
5 cups chicken or beef stock
  or broth
⅓ cup rice
2 egg yolks
juice of 1 lemon
½ cup grated Parmesan cheese
2 tablespoons water

Place the stock in a saucepan and bring to the boil. Stir in the rice and simmer for 15 to 20 minutes or until the rice is tender.

Lightly beat the egg yolks with the lemon juice, cheese and water. Pour into a warmed soup tureen. Gradually stir in the boiling rice soup and serve immediately.
Serves 6

Tomato Cream Cheese Soup

Metric/Imperial
3 tablespoons oil
1 onion, sliced
1 garlic clove, crushed
1 × 400 g/14 oz can tomatoes,
  drained and chopped
2 tablespoons tomato purée
1 teaspoon caster sugar
1.2 litres/2 pints chicken
  stock
salt and pepper
50 g/2 oz vermicelli, broken
  into short lengths
1 × 75 g/3 oz packet cream
  cheese, chopped

American
3 tablespoons oil
1 onion, sliced
1 garlic clove, crushed
1 × 16 oz can tomatoes, drained
  and chopped
2 tablespoons tomato paste
1 teaspoon sugar
5 cups chicken stock or
  broth
salt and pepper
½ cup broken up vermicelli
1 × 3 oz package cream cheese,
  chopped

Heat the oil in a saucepan. Add the onion and garlic and fry until softened. Stir in the tomatoes, tomato purée (paste), sugar, stock and salt and pepper to taste and bring to the boil. Simmer for 30 minutes.

Stir in the vermicelli and simmer for a further 5 minutes or until it is tender. Add the cream cheese in pieces and stir until melted. Serve hot.
Serves 4 to 6

Bacon and Cheese Soup

Metric/Imperial
4 streaky bacon rashers,
    derinded and chopped
1 large onion, chopped
25 g/1 oz plain flour
300 ml/½ pint chicken stock
300 ml/½ pint milk
2 carrots, thinly sliced
salt and pepper
100 g/4 oz Cheddar cheese,
    grated

American
4 bacon slices, chopped
1 large onion, chopped
¼ cup all-purpose flour
1¼ cups chicken stock or broth
1¼ cups milk
2 carrots, thinly sliced
salt and pepper
1 cup grated Cheddar cheese

Fry the bacon with the onion in a saucepan until the bacon is crisp and the onion softened. Stir in the flour and cook for 2 minutes, then gradually stir in the stock and milk. Bring to the boil, stirring. Add the carrots and salt and pepper to taste, cover and simmer for 20 minutes.
    Stir in the cheese until melted and serve hot.
Serves 4

Mushroom and Pasta Chowder

Metric/Imperial
2 tablespoons oil
1 onion, chopped
6 streaky bacon rashers,
    derinded and chopped
1 garlic clove, crushed
1 tablespoon plain flour
600 ml/1 pint beef stock
300 ml/½ pint milk
50 g/2 oz small pasta shapes
100 g/4 oz mushrooms, sliced
salt and pepper

American
2 tablespoons oil
1 onion, chopped
6 bacon slices, chopped
1 garlic clove, crushed
1 tablespoon all-purpose flour
2½ cups beef stock or broth
1¼ cups milk
½ cup small pasta shapes
1 cup sliced mushrooms
salt and pepper

Heat the oil in a saucepan. Add the onion, bacon and garlic and fry until the onion is softened. Stir in the flour and cook for 1 minute, then gradually stir in the stock and milk. Bring to the boil, stirring.
    Add the pasta, mushrooms and salt and pepper to taste. Simmer for 20 minutes. Serve hot.
Serves 4

Sausage Soup

Metric/Imperial
25 g/1 oz butter or margarine
1 large onion, sliced
1 garlic clove, crushed
1 tablespoon gravy powder
900 ml/1½ pints water
1 teaspoon made mustard
salt and pepper
4 pork and beef sausages,
   cut into chunks
100 g/4 oz Cheddar cheese,
   grated

American
2 tablespoons butter or margarine
1 large onion, sliced
1 garlic clove, crushed
1 tablespoon gravy powder
3½ cups water
1 teaspoon prepared mustard
salt and pepper
4 pork and beef sausages,
   cut into chunks
1 cup grated Cheddar cheese

Melt the butter or margarine in a saucepan. Add the onion and garlic and fry until softened. Dissolve the gravy powder in a little of the water, then add to the pan with the remaining water, the mustard and salt and pepper to taste. Bring to the boil and simmer for 30 minutes.

Add the sausage chunks and simmer for a further 10 minutes. Stir in the cheese until melted, then serve hot.
Serves 4

Cream of Spinach Soup

Metric/Imperial
50 g/2 oz butter or margarine
1 × 175 g/6 oz packet frozen
   chopped spinach, thawed
1 onion, chopped
25 g/1 oz plain flour
pinch of grated nutmeg
600 ml/1 pint milk
300 ml/½ pint chicken stock
salt and pepper
2 tablespoons double cream

American
4 tablespoons butter or margarine
1 × 6 oz package frozen chopped
   spinach, thawed
1 onion, chopped
¼ cup all-purpose flour
pinch of grated nutmeg
2½ cups milk
1¼ cups chicken stock or broth
salt and pepper
2 tablespoons heavy cream

Melt the butter or margarine in a saucepan. Add the spinach and onion and cook gently for 5 minutes, stirring occasionally. Mix the flour and nutmeg with the milk, then add to the pan with the stock and salt and pepper to taste. Bring to the boil, stirring, then cover and simmer for 15 minutes.

Swirl in the cream and serve hot.
Serves 4 to 6

Bean and Bacon Chowder

Metric/Imperial	American
25 g/1 oz butter or margarine	2 tablespoons butter or
6 streaky bacon rashers,	margarine
derinded and chopped	6 bacon slices, chopped
2 leeks, thinly sliced	2 leeks, thinly sliced
2 carrots, chopped	2 carrots, chopped
600 ml/1 pint water	2½ cups water
1 × 400 g/14 oz can tomatoes	1 × 16 oz can tomatoes
1 × 425 g/15 oz can baked	1 × 16 oz can baked beans in
beans in tomato sauce	tomato sauce
1 teaspoon dried mixed herbs	1 teaspoon dried mixed herbs
salt and pepper	salt and pepper

Melt the butter or margarine in a saucepan. Add the bacon, leeks and
carrots and fry gently for 5 minutes, stirring occasionally. Add the
remaining ingredients with salt and pepper to taste and bring to the boil.
Cover and simmer for 30 minutes. Serve hot.
Serves 6

Olive Soup

Metric/Imperial	American
25 g/1 oz butter or margarine	2 tablespoons butter or
1 onion, chopped	margarine
1 celery stick, chopped	1 onion, chopped
750 ml/1¼ pints beef stock	1 celery stalk, chopped
100 g/4 oz stuffed olives	3 cups beef stock or broth
salt and pepper	¾ cup pimiento-stuffed olives
50 g/2 oz Gruyère cheese,	salt and pepper
grated	½ cup grated Gruyère cheese

Melt the butter or margarine in a saucepan. Add the onion and celery and
fry until softened. Stir in the stock, olives and salt and pepper to taste.
Bring to the boil and simmer for 15 minutes.

Purée the soup in a blender or food processor and return to the
saucepan. Reheat, then taste and adjust the seasoning. Serve hot,
topped with the cheese.
Serves 4

Cheesy Peanut Chowder

Metric/Imperial
3 tablespoons smooth peanut
  butter
50 g/2 oz soft brown sugar
300 ml/½ pint milk
25 g/1 oz butter or margarine
1 onion, chopped
450 ml/¾ pint chicken stock
150 g/5 oz salted peanuts
1 × 200 g/7 oz can sweetcorn
  kernels, drained
salt and pepper
225 g/8 oz Gouda cheese,
  grated

American
3 tablespoons smooth peanut
  butter
⅓ cup firmly packed brown
  sugar
1¼ cups milk
2 tablespoons butter or
  margarine
1 onion, chopped
2 cups chicken stock or broth
¾ cup salted peanuts
1 × 7 oz can whole kernel corn,
  drained
salt and pepper
2 cups grated Gouda cheese

Put the peanut butter, sugar and milk in a saucepan and heat, stirring until smooth.

In another saucepan, melt the butter or margarine, add the onion and fry until softened. Stir in the peanut mixture from the other pan and the stock and bring to the boil. Add the salted peanuts and corn and season to taste with salt and pepper. Cook gently for 5 minutes.

Stir in the cheese until melted, then serve hot.

Serves 6

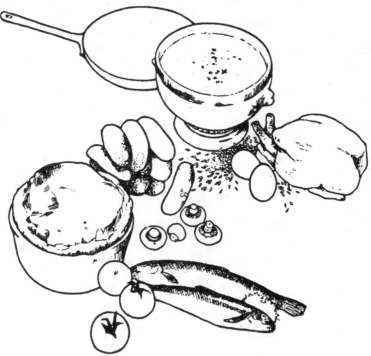

Chinese Pork Soup

Metric/Imperial
100 g/4 oz lean pork, very
  thinly sliced
1 tablespoon soy sauce
1 tablespoon sesame seed oil
1 teaspoon cornflour
225 g/8 oz carrots, sliced
1.2 litres/2 pints chicken
  stock
salt

American
¼ lb lean pork, very thinly
  sliced
1 tablespoon soy sauce
1 tablespoon sesame seed oil
1 teaspoon cornstarch
½ lb carrots, sliced
5 cups chicken stock or
  broth
salt

Place the pork in a bowl and add the soy sauce, oil and cornflour
(cornstarch). Stir well, then marinate for 10 minutes.
  Meanwhile put the carrots, stock and salt to taste in a saucepan and
bring to the boil. Simmer for 5 minutes
  Add the pork mixture to the saucepan, stir and simmer for 8 to 10
minutes longer or until the pork and carrots are tender. Serve hot.
Serves 4

Chinese Crab and Sweetcorn Soup

Metric/Imperial
900 ml/1½ pints chicken stock
  (made with 2 stock cubes)
225 g/8 oz frozen sweetcorn
  kernels
2 thin slices of fresh root
  ginger, peeled
1 × 200 g/7 oz can crabmeat,
  drained and flaked
2 tablespoons dry sherry
1 tablespoon soy sauce
2 teaspoons chopped chives
salt and pepper
1 tablespoon cornflour
2 tablespoons water

American
4 cups chicken stock or broth
½ lb frozen whole kernel corn
2 thin slices of fresh
  ginger root, peeled
1 × 7 oz can crabmeat, drained
  and flaked
2 tablespoons dry sherry
1 tablespoon soy sauce
2 teaspoons chopped chives
salt and pepper
1 tablespoon cornstarch
2 tablespoons water

Bring the stock to the boil. Add the corn and ginger and simmer for 3
minutes.
  Stir in the crabmeat, sherry, soy sauce, chives and salt and pepper to
taste and simmer for a further 3 minutes.
  Discard the ginger. Blend the cornflour (cornstarch) with the water and
add to the pan. Simmer, stirring, until thickened. Serve hot.
Serves 4 to 6

Dutch Pepper Soup

Metric/Imperial
25 g/1 oz butter or margarine
225 g/8 oz streaky bacon
  rashers, derinded and diced
2 onions, chopped
75 g/3 oz long-grain rice
1.2 litres/2 pints beef stock
4 tomatoes, chopped
1 green pepper, cored, seeded
  and cut into rings
1 red pepper, cored, seeded
  and cut into rings
salt and pepper

American
2 tablespoons butter or
  margarine
½ lb bacon slices, diced
2 onions, chopped
½ cup rice
5 cups beef stock or broth
4 tomatoes, chopped
1 green pepper, seeded and
  cut into rings
1 red pepper, seeded
  and cut into rings
salt and pepper

Melt the butter or margarine in a saucepan. Add the bacon and onions and fry until golden. Stir in the rice and continue frying until it is transparent. Add the stock and bring to the boil. Cover and simmer for 20 minutes or until the rice is tender.

Stir in the tomatoes, pepper rings and salt and pepper to taste. Continue simmering for 5 minutes. Serve hot.
Serves 4 to 6

French Onion Soup

Metric/Imperial
75 g/3 oz butter or margarine
750 g/1½ lb onions, sliced
1 garlic clove, crushed
1 tablespoon plain flour
1.2 litres/2 pints beef stock
salt and pepper
4 slices of French bread
50 g/2 oz Cheddar cheese
  grated

American
6 tablespoons butter or
  margarine
1½ lb onions, sliced
1 garlic clove, crushed
1 tablespoon all-purpose flour
5 cups beef stock or broth
salt and pepper
4 slices of French bread
½ cup grated Cheddar cheese

Melt the butter or margarine in a saucepan. Add the onions and fry gently until they are soft and golden brown. Stir in the garlic and flour and cook for 2 minutes, then gradually stir in the stock. Bring to the boil, stirring. Add salt and pepper to taste, then cover and simmer for 20 minutes.

Meanwhile place the bread slices under a preheated grill (broiler) and toast on both sides. Sprinkle the cheese on the bread and grill (broil) until melted.

Ladle the soup into warmed bowls and float a slice of toasted cheese in each one. Serve hot.
Serves 4

Watercress and Vermicelli Soup

Metric/Imperial
2 tablespoons oil
2 onions, sliced
2 bunches of watercress,
  chopped
1.5 litres/2½ pints chicken
  stock
salt and pepper
75 g/3 oz vermicelli,
  broken into short lengths
1 hard-boiled egg, finely
  chopped

American
2 tablespoons oil
2 onions, sliced
2 bunches of watercress,
  chopped
6 cups chicken stock or
  broth
salt and pepper
¾ cup broken up vermicelli
1 hard-cooked egg, finely
  chopped

Heat the oil in a saucepan. Add the onions and watercress and fry gently for 5 minutes. Add the stock and salt and pepper to taste and bring to the boil. Simmer for 20 minutes.

Stir in the vermicelli and simmer for a further 5 minutes or until it is tender. Sprinkle the chopped egg on top and serve hot.
Serves 4 to 6

Greek Vegetable Soup

Metric/Imperial
450 ml /¾ pint beef stock
100 g/4 oz frozen mixed
  vegetables
1 egg yolk
300 ml/½ pint plain yogurt
salt and pepper
1 tablespoon chopped fresh
  mint
grated rind of 1 lemon

American
2 cups beef stock or broth
¼ lb (1 cup) frozen mixed
  vegetables
1 egg yolk
1¼ cups plain yogurt
salt and pepper
1 tablespoon chopped fresh
  mint
grated rind of 1 lemon

Place the stock in a saucepan and bring to the boil. Add the vegetables and simmer for 5 minutes.

Lightly beat the egg yolk with the yogurt in a bowl. Add about 6 tablespoons of the hot stock and mix well, then stir this into the soup in the saucepan. Heat through gently without boiling. Season to taste with salt and pepper.

Ladle the soup into four bowls and sprinkle the mint and lemon rind on top. Serve hot.
Serves 4

Curried Apple Bisque

Metric/Imperial
25 g/1 oz butter or margarine
1 onion, chopped
2 Golden Delicious apples,
  peeled, cored and chopped
1 teaspoon curry powder
450 ml/¾ pint chicken stock
salt and pepper
150 ml/¼ pint double cream
toasted flaked almonds to
  garnish

American
2 tablespoons butter or
  margarine
1 onion, chopped
2 Golden Delicious apples,
  peeled, cored and chopped
1 teaspoon curry powder
2 cups chicken stock or broth
salt and pepper
⅔ cup heavy cream
toasted sliced almonds
  for garnish

Melt the butter or margarine in a saucepan. Add the onion and apples and fry until the onion is softened. Stir in the curry powder and cook for 1 minute, then stir in the stock.

Purée the mixture in a blender or food processor and return to the pan. Season to taste with salt and pepper and bring to the boil. Stir in the cream and heat through gently. Serve hot, sprinkled with almonds.
Serves 4

Swedish Tomato Soup

Metric/Imperial
40 g/1½ oz butter or margarine
2 onions, chopped
1 garlic clove, crushed
1 × 400 g/14 oz can tomatoes
250 ml/8 fl oz chicken stock
1 teaspoon dried dill
salt and pepper
3 tablespoons mayonnaise

American
3 tablespoons butter or
  margarine
2 onions, chopped
1 garlic clove, crushed
1 × 16 oz can tomatoes
1 cup chicken stock or broth
1 teaspoon dried dill
salt and pepper
3 tablespoons mayonnaise

Melt the butter or margarine in a saucepan. Add the onions and garlic and fry until softened. Stir in the tomatoes with their juice, the stock, dill and salt and pepper to taste. Bring to the boil and simmer for 10 minutes.

Purée the mixture in a blender or food processor. Whisk in the mayonnaise. Chill before serving.
Serves 4 to 6

Iced Plum Soup

Metric/Imperial
1 × 400 g/14 oz can plums
120 ml/4 fl oz water
75 g/3 oz sugar
½ teaspoon ground cinnamon
salt and pepper
1 tablespoon cornflour
120 ml/4 fl oz red wine
grated rind and juice of
   1 lemon
150 ml/¼ pint soured cream

American
1 × 16 oz can plums
½ cup water
6 tablespoons sugar
½ teaspoon ground cinnamon
salt and pepper
1 tablespoon cornstarch
½ cup red wine
grated rind and juice of
   1 lemon
⅔ cup sour cream

Drain the plums, reserving the syrup, and remove the stones (pits). Put the plums and reserved syrup into a saucepan and add the water, sugar, cinnamon and salt and pepper to taste. Bring to the boil and simmer for 5 minutes.

Blend the cornflour (cornstarch) with the wine and add to the pan. Simmer, stirring, until thickened. Stir in the lemon rind and juice.

Purée the soup in a blender or food processor. Cool, then stir in the sour cream. Chill well before serving.
Serves 4

Chilled Tomato Soup

Metric/Imperial
1 × 400 g/14 oz can tomatoes,
   drained
100 g/4 oz cucumber, peeled
   and chopped
1 garlic clove, crushed
1 green pepper, cored, seeded
   and chopped
2 teaspoons Worcestershire
   sauce
pinch of cayenne pepper
salt
150 ml/¼ pint plain yogurt

American
1 × 16 oz can tomatoes, drained
1 cup peeled chopped cucumber
1 garlic clove, crushed
1 green pepper, seeded and
   chopped
2 teaspoons Worcestershire
   sauce
pinch of cayenne
salt
⅔ cup plain yogurt

Put the tomatoes, cucumber, garlic, half the green pepper, the Worcestershire sauce, cayenne and salt to taste in a blender or food processor. Purée until smooth.

Stir the yogurt and remaining green pepper into the soup and chill well before serving.
Serves 4

Quick Gazpacho

Metric/Imperial
1 × 400 g/14 oz can tomatoes
3 tablespoons olive oil
3 tablespoons red wine
  vinegar
1 onion, finely chopped
½ cucumber, diced
1 green pepper, cored, seeded
  and diced
150 ml/¼ pint tomato juice
salt and pepper

American
1 × 16 oz can tomatoes
3 tablespoons olive oil
3 tablespoons red wine
  vinegar
1 onion, finely chopped
½ cucumber, diced
1 green pepper, seeded
  and diced
⅔ cup tomato juice
salt and pepper

Purée the tomatoes with the oil and vinegar in a blender or food processor or by rubbing through a sieve. Stir in the remaining ingredients with salt and pepper to taste. Chill well before serving.
Serves 4

Iced Beetroot (Beet) Soup

Metric/Imperial
2 cooked beetroot, chopped
600 ml/1 pint chicken stock
2 tablespoons white wine
  vinegar
grated rind and juice of
  1 large orange
salt and pepper
300 ml/½ pint single cream

American
2 cooked beets, chopped
2½ cups chicken stock or broth
2 tablespoons white wine
  vinegar
grated rind and juice of
  1 large orange
salt and pepper
1¼ cups light cream

Place the beetroot (beets), stock, vinegar, orange rind and juice and salt and pepper to taste in a blender or food processor. Purée until smooth.
    Stir the cream into the soup and chill well before serving.
Serves 4

Chilled Cucumber Soup

Metric/Imperial
2 cucumbers, chopped
225 g/8 oz Gouda cheese, cubed
2 tablespoons lemon juice
300 ml/½ pint chicken stock
1 teaspoon dried mixed herbs
salt and pepper

American
2 cucumbers, chopped
½ lb Gouda cheese, cubed
2 tablespoons lemon juice
1¼ cups chicken stock or broth
1 teaspoon dried mixed herbs
salt and pepper

Put all the ingredients, with salt and pepper to taste, in a blender or food processor and process until smooth. Pour into a bowl and chill well before serving.
Serves 6

Chilled Prawn (Shrimp) and Cucumber Soup

Metric/Imperial
1 large cucumber, peeled,
  seeded and chopped
6 spring onions, chopped
1 teaspoon dried dill
900 ml/1½ pints chicken stock
25 g/1 oz cornflour
3 tablespoons water
salt and pepper
few drops of green food
  colouring
50 g/2 oz cooked peeled
  prawns
4 tablespoons single cream

American
1 large cucumber, peeled,
  seeded and chopped
6 scallions, chopped
1 teaspoon dried dill
3½ cups chicken stock or broth
¼ cup cornstarch
3 tablespoons water
salt and pepper
few drops of green food
  coloring
½ cup cooked shelled shrimp
¼ cup light cream

Place the cucumber, spring onions (scallions), dill and stock in a
saucepan and bring to the boil. Simmer for 10 minutes or until the
vegetables are tender. Cool slightly, then purée in a blender or food
processor and return to the pan.

Mix the cornflour (cornstarch) with the water and add to the pan. Bring
back to the boil, stirring, and simmer until thickened. Add salt and pepper
to taste and a few drops of food colouring. Cool, then stir in the prawns
(shrimp).

Chill well before serving, swirled with the cream.
Serves 4

Uncooked Pepper Soup

Metric/Imperial
2 large green or red peppers,
  cored, seeded and chopped
450 ml/¾ pint chicken stock
2 tablespoons lemon juice
¼ teaspoon Worcestershire sauce
1 garlic clove, chopped
salt and pepper
soured cream to serve

American
2 large green or red peppers,
  seeded and chopped
2 cups chicken stock or broth
2 tablespoons lemon juice
¼ teaspoon Worcestershire sauce
1 garlic clove, chopped
salt and pepper
sour cream to serve

Place the peppers in a blender or food processor with half the stock, the
lemon juice, Worcestershire sauce and garlic. Process until smooth. Stir
in the remaining stock and season to taste with salt and pepper.

Pour into a bowl, cover and chill well. Serve topped with sour cream.
Serves 4

Minted Pea Soup

Metric/Imperial
40 g/1½ oz butter or
  margarine
1 onion, chopped
350 g/12 oz frozen peas
450 ml/¾ pint chicken stock
2 tablespoons chopped fresh
  mint
25 g/1 oz plain flour
150 ml/¼ pint milk
salt and pepper

American
3 tablespoons butter or
  margarine
1 onion, chopped
¾ lb frozen peas
2 cups chicken stock or broth
2 tablespoons chopped fresh
  mint
¼ cup all-purpose flour
⅔ cup milk
salt and pepper

Melt 15 g/½ oz (1 tablespoon) of the butter or margarine in a saucepan.
Add the onion and peas and cook gently for 5 minutes, stirring
occasionally. Add the stock and half the mint and bring to the boil.
Simmer for 10 minutes, then purée in a blender or food processor.
  Melt the remaining butter or margarine in the cleaned pan. Stir in the
flour and cook for 2 minutes. Gradually stir in the puréed pea mixture and
bring to the boil, stirring. Simmer until thickened. Stir in the milk and
season to taste with salt and pepper. Cool, then chill.
  Serve cold, sprinkled with the remaining mint.
Serves 4 to 6

Iced Avocado Soup

Metric/Imperial
2 ripe avocados, peeled and
  stoned
450 ml/¾ pint chicken stock
½ teaspoon grated onion
1 teaspoon lemon juice
½ teaspoon Worcestershire
  sauce
300 ml/½ pint plain yogurt
150 ml/¼ pint single cream
salt and pepper
chopped chives to garnish

American
2 ripe avocados, peeled and
  seeded
2 cups chicken stock or broth
½ teaspoon grated onion
1 teaspoon lemon juice
½ teaspoon Worcestershire
  sauce
1¼ cups plain yogurt
⅔ cup light cream
salt and pepper
chopped chives for garnish

Put all the ingredients, with salt and pepper to taste, into a blender or food
processor and purée until smooth. Taste and adjust the seasoning, and
dilute with more stock if the soup is too thick. Chill well and serve
sprinkled with chives.
Serves 4 to 6

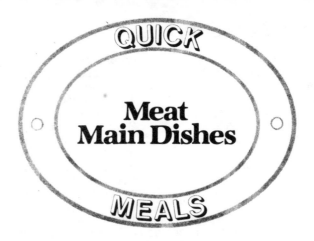

Hamburger Casserole

Metric/Imperial
500 g/1 lb lean minced beef
50 g/2 oz fresh breadcrumbs
1 small onion, grated
1 egg, beaten
salt and pepper
25 g/1 oz butter or margarine
1 tablespoon oil
50 g/2 oz pasta shells
Sauce:
1 large onion, sliced
100 g/4 oz mushrooms, sliced
1 tablespoon plain flour
300 ml/½ pint beef stock
1 tablespoon tomato purée

American
1 lb lean ground beef
1 cup soft bread crumbs
1 small onion, grated
1 egg, beaten
salt and pepper
2 tablespoons butter or
   margarine
1 tablespoon oil
1 cup pasta shells
Sauce:
1 large onion, sliced
1 cup sliced mushrooms
1 tablespoon all-purpose flour
1¼ cups beef stock or broth
1 tablespoon tomato paste

Mix together the beef, half the breadcrumbs, the onion, egg and salt and
pepper to taste. Form into eight patties and coat with the remaining
breadcrumbs. Melt the butter or margarine with the oil in a frying pan
(skillet). Add the patties and brown on both sides.

Meanwhile cook the pasta in boiling salted water until just tender. Drain
well. Spread the pasta over the bottom of a greased ovenproof dish and
arrange the burgers on top.

Add the onion to the frying pan (skillet) and fry until softened. Add the
mushrooms and fry for a further 2 minutes. Sprinkle over the flour and stir
in well, then stir in the stock and tomato purée (paste). Bring to the boil,
stirring.

Pour the sauce over the burgers. Cook in a preheated moderate oven
(180°C/350°F, Gas Mark 4) for 30 minutes. Serve hot.
Serves 4

Burger Roll

Metric/Imperial	American
750 g/1½ lb lean minced beef	1½ lb lean ground beef
75 g/3 oz fresh breadcrumbs	1½ cups soft bread crumbs
2 eggs, beaten	2 eggs, beaten
2 teaspoons dry mustard	2 teaspoons dry mustard
1 onion, finely chopped	1 onion, finely chopped
2 tablespoons chopped parsley	2 tablespoons chopped parsley
salt and pepper	salt and pepper
1 tablespoon plain flour	1 tablespoon all-purpose flour
100 g/4 oz cheese, grated	1 cup grated cheese
25 g/1 oz butter or margarine, melted	2 tablespoons butter or margarine, melted

Mix together the beef, breadcrumbs, eggs, mustard, onion, parsley and salt and pepper to taste. Sprinkle the flour on a 25 × 38 cm/10 × 15 inch piece of foil. Spread the beef mixture on the foil, almost to the edges. Chill for 30 minutes

Sprinkle the cheese over the beef rectangle. Roll up from one short side, using the foil to lift the meat. Place the roll on a baking sheet, with the join underneath, and brush with the melted butter or margarine.

Cook in a preheated moderate oven (180°C/350°F, Gas Mark 4) for 1 hour. Cut into slices to serve.
Serves 4

Cheesy Corn Burgers

Metric/Imperial	American
750 g/1½ lb lean minced beef	1½ lb lean ground beef
salt and pepper	salt and pepper
1 × 200 g/7 oz can sweetcorn kernels, drained	1 × 7 oz can whole kernel corn, drained
1 large dessert apple, cored and grated	1 large apple, cored and grated
225 g/8 oz Gouda cheese, grated	2 cups grated Gouda cheese
2 teaspoons chilli sauce	2 teaspoons chili sauce
4 hamburger buns, split	4 hamburger buns, split

Season the beef with salt and pepper, then shape into eight thin patties. Grill (broil) until browned on both sides and cooked to your liking.

Meanwhile mix together the corn, apple, cheese, chilli sauce and salt and pepper to taste. Toast the cut sides of the buns under the grill (broiler).

Place a burger on each bun half and top with the corn mixture. Continue grilling (broiling) until melted and golden. Serve hot.
Serves 4

Corned Beef Hotpot

Metric/Imperial
2 tablespoons oil
2 onions, sliced
2 celery sticks, chopped
100 g/4 oz runner beans, sliced
300 ml/½ pint beef stock
2 tablespoons tomato ketchup
salt and pepper
1 × 350 g/12 oz can corned
  beef, chopped

American
2 tablespoons oil
2 onions, sliced
2 celery stalks, chopped
¼ lb green beans, sliced
1¼ cups beef stock or broth
2 tablespoons tomato ketchup
salt and pepper
1 × 12 oz can corned beef,
  chopped

Heat the oil in a saucepan. Add the onions and celery and fry until the onions are softened. Stir in the beans, then add the stock and bring to the boil. Simmer for 15 minutes.

Stir in the ketchup and salt and pepper to taste, then fold in the corned beef. Simmer for a further 5 minutes. Serve hot.
Serves 4

Chilli con Carne

Metric/Imperial
1 tablespoon oil
1 onion, chopped
500 g/1 lb lean minced beef
1 × 400 g/14 oz can tomatoes,
  drained and chopped
1 × 450 g/16 oz can chilli
  beans
1 teaspoon chilli seasoning
salt and pepper

American
1 tablespoon oil
1 onion, chopped
1 lb lean ground beef
1 × 16 oz can tomatoes,
  drained and chopped
1 × 16 oz can chili beans
1 teaspoon chili seasoning
salt and pepper

Heat the oil in a frying pan (skillet). Add the onion and fry until softened. Add the beef and fry until it is browned and crumbly. Pour off all excess fat from the pan, then stir in the tomatoes. Simmer gently for 10 minutes.

Stir in the beans with their sauce, the chilli seasoning and salt and pepper to taste. Cook gently for a further 5 minutes or until piping hot.
Serves 4

Variation:
Substitute 1 × 450 g/16 oz can baked beans in tomato sauce for the chilli beans and increase the chilli seasoning to 1 tablespoon.

Steak with Green Peppercorns

Metric/Imperial	American
4 fillet or rump steaks	4 boneless sirloin steaks
1 tablespoon coarsely crushed green peppercorns	1 tablespoon coarsely crushed green peppercorns
25 g/1 oz butter or margarine	2 tablespoons butter or margarine
1 tablespoon oil	1 tablespoon oil
juice of ½ lemon	juice of ½ lemon
2 tablespoons brandy	2 tablespoons brandy

Trim any fat from the steaks. Press the peppercorns into both sides of the steaks. Cover and leave for 30 minutes.

Melt the butter or margarine with the oil in a large frying pan (skillet). Add the steaks, two at a time if necessary, and fry for 3 to 4 minutes on each side or until cooked to your liking.

Transfer the steaks to a warmed serving platter and sprinkle over the lemon juice. Warm the brandy in a ladle, set alight and pour over the steaks. Serve flaming.
Serves 4

Variation:
For a creamy sauce, stir the lemon juice into the pan juices, then add 2 tablespoons cream. Heat through quickly and pour over the steaks. Add the brandy and serve.

Beef and Green Pepper Curry

Metric/Imperial	American
4 tablespoons oil	¼ cup oil
1 green pepper, cored, seeded and sliced	1 green pepper, seeded and sliced
2 onions, chopped	2 onions, chopped
½ teaspoon ground cumin	½ teaspoon ground cumin
2 teaspoons garam masala	2 teaspoons garam masala
¼ teaspoon ground cinnamon	¼ teaspoon ground cinnamon
1 teaspoon chilli powder	1 teaspoon chili powder
salt and pepper	salt and pepper
750 g/1½ lb lean minced beef	1½ lb lean ground beef

Heat the oil in a frying pan (skillet). Add the green pepper and fry for 1 minute. Remove from the pan with a slotted spoon and reserve.

Add the onions to the pan and fry until golden brown. Stir in the spices and salt and pepper to taste and fry for 1 minute longer. Add the beef and fry until it is browned and crumbly.

Return the green pepper to the pan and mix well. Cover and cook for a further 15 minutes, stirring occasionally. Serve hot.
Serves 4

Meatball Curry

Metric/Imperial
500 g/1 lb lean minced beef
  or lamb
1 onion, finely chopped
2 teaspoons curry powder
1 egg, beaten
salt and pepper
oil for frying
Sauce:
1 onion, chopped
1 × 225 g/8 oz can tomatoes,
  drained and chopped
2 tablespoons curry powder
1 tablespoon plain flour
150 ml/¼ pint beef stock
salt and pepper

American
1 lb lean ground beef or
  lamb
1 onion, finely chopped
2 teaspoons curry powder
1 egg, beaten
salt and pepper
oil for frying
Sauce:
1 onion, chopped
1 × 8 oz can tomatoes, drained
  and chopped
2 tablespoons curry powder
1 tablespoon all-purpose flour
⅔ cup beef stock or broth
salt and pepper

Combine the meat, onion, curry powder, egg and salt and pepper to taste.
Divide into 16 portions and shape into balls with floured hands.

Heat enough oil in a frying pan (skillet) to cover the bottom thinly. Add
the meatballs and fry until browned on all sides. Remove from the pan
with a slotted spoon.

Pour off all but 2 tablespoons of the oil from the pan. Add the onion and
fry until softened. Stir in the tomatoes, curry powder and flour and cook
for 2 minutes, then stir in the stock and salt and pepper to taste. Bring to
the boil.

Return the meatballs to the pan and turn to coat with the sauce. Cover
and simmer gently for 30 minutes, stirring occasionally. Serve hot.
Serves 4

Steak Kebabs

Metric/Imperial
500 g/1 lb rump steak, cut
  1 cm/½ inch thick, cut into
  2.5 cm/1 inch squares
8 small tomatoes
8 button onions, parboiled
8 button mushrooms
8 thick cucumber slices
4 streaky bacon rashers,
  derinded, halved crossways
  and rolled up
oil

American
1 lb boneless sirloin steak, cut
  ½ inch thick, cut into 1 inch
  squares
8 cherry tomatoes
8 pearl onions, parboiled
8 button mushrooms
8 thick cucumber slices
4 bacon slices, halved
  crosswise and rolled up
oil

Thread the steak cubes, vegetables and bacon rolls alternately onto four
or eight skewers. Brush with a little oil, then place under a preheated grill
(broiler) and cook for about 8 minutes, turning frequently. Serve hot.
Serves 4

Keema Curry

Metric/Imperial	American
2 tablespoons oil	2 tablespoons oil
1 onion, chopped	1 onion, chopped
1 garlic clove, crushed	1 garlic clove, crushed
2 teaspoons ground ginger	2 teaspoons ground ginger
1 tablespoon garam masala	1 tablespoon garam masala
½ teaspoon chilli powder	½ teaspoon chili powder
750 g/1½ lb lean minced beef	1½ lb lean ground beef
1 × 225 g/8 oz can tomatoes	1 × 8 oz can tomatoes
2 tablespoons tomato purée	2 tablespoons tomato paste
150 ml/¼ pint beef stock	⅔ cup beef stock or broth
300 ml/½ pint plain yogurt	1¼ cups plain yogurt
salt and pepper	salt and pepper

Heat the oil in a saucepan. Add the onion and garlic and fry until softened. Stir in the spices and cook for 1 minute, then add the beef. Fry until the beef is browned and crumbly.

Add the tomatoes, tomato purée (paste), stock, half the yogurt and salt and pepper to taste and stir well. Cover and cook gently for 40 minutes.

Stir in the remaining yogurt, heat through and serve hot.
Serves 4

Beef Crumble

Metric/Imperial	American
500 g/1 lb minced beef	1 lb ground beef
4 teaspoons gravy powder	4 teaspoons gravy powder
600 ml/1 pint water	2½ cups water
50 g/2 oz plain flour	½ cup all-purpose flour
50 g/2 oz dry sage and onion stuffing mix	1 cup dry herb stuffing mix
100 g/4 oz butter or margarine	½ cup butter or margarine
100 g/4 oz Cheddar cheese, grated	1 cup grated Cheddar cheese
salt and pepper	salt and pepper

Fry the beef in a frying pan (skillet) until it is browned and crumbly. (If the beef is very lean, you may need to add a little oil to the pan.) Drain off all excess fat. Dissolve the gravy powder in a little of the water, then add to the pan with the remaining water. Bring to the boil, stirring, and simmer until thickened. Pour into an ovenproof dish.

Sift the flour into a bowl and stir in the stuffing mix. Rub in the butter or margarine until the mixture resembles breadcrumbs. Stir in the cheese and salt and pepper to taste. Sprinkle the mixture over the meat.

Cook in a preheated moderately hot oven (190°C/375°F, Gas Mark 5) for 40 minutes or until the top is browned. Serve hot.
Serves 4

Beef and Mushroom Burgers

Metric/Imperial
25 g/1 oz butter or margarine
1 tablespoon oil
1 onion, finely chopped
1 garlic clove, crushed
225 g/8 oz mushrooms, chopped
750 g/1½ lb lean minced beef
½ teaspoon dried sage
salt and pepper

American
2 tablespoons butter or
  margarine
1 tablespoon oil
1 onion, finely chopped
1 garlic clove, crushed
½ lb mushrooms, chopped
1½ lb lean ground beef
½ teaspoon dried sage
salt and pepper

Melt the butter or margarine with the oil in a frying pan (skillet). Add the onion and garlic and fry until softened. Add the mushrooms and fry for a further 3 to 4 minutes, stirring frequently. Drain off the excess fat from the pan, then tip the vegetables into a bowl. Add the beef, sage and salt and pepper to taste and mix together thoroughly with your hands. Shape the mixture into eight patties.

Grill (broil) the burgers for about 4 minutes on each side or until cooked to your liking.
Serves 4

Shepherds' Pie

Metric/Imperial
500 g/1 lb minced beef
1 packet dry minestrone soup
  mix
300 ml/½ pint water
100 g/4 oz frozen mixed
  vegetables
500 g/1 lb potatoes
2 tablespoons milk
25 g/1 oz butter or margarine
salt and pepper
25 g/1 oz Parmesan cheese,
  grated

American
1 lb ground beef
1 package dry minestrone soup
  mix
1¼ cups water
¾ cup frozen mixed vegetables
1 lb potatoes
2 tablespoons milk
2 tablespoons butter or
  margarine
salt and pepper
¼ cup grated Parmesan cheese

Fry the beef in a frying pan (skillet) until it is browned and crumbly. Pour off all excess fat from the pan, then stir in the soup mix and water. Bring to the boil and simmer for 15 minutes. Stir in the vegetables and simmer for a further 5 minutes.

Meanwhile cook the potatoes in boiling water until tender. Drain well and mash until smooth. Beat in the milk, butter or margarine and salt and pepper to taste. Keep hot.

Pour the beef and vegetable mixture into a greased ovenproof dish. Spread the potatoes over the top and sprinkle over the cheese. Grill (broil) for about 5 minutes or until the top is golden brown.
Serves 4

Herby Burgers with Blue Cheese Sauce

Metric/Imperial
500 g/1 lb lean minced beef
1 onion, finely chopped
1 egg, beaten
1 garlic clove, crushed
1 teaspoon chopped parsley
½ teaspoon dried mixed herbs
½ teaspoon dried basil
¼ teaspoon dry mustard
1 tablespoon Worcestershire
  sauce
salt and pepper
25 g/1 oz butter or margarine
Sauce:
50 g/2 oz butter or margarine
50 g/2 oz plain flour
600 ml/1 pint milk
100 g/4 oz blue cheese,
  crumbled
salt and pepper

American
1 lb lean ground beef
1 onion, finely chopped
1 egg, beaten
1 garlic clove, crushed
1 teaspoon chopped parsley
½ teaspoon dried mixed herbs
½ teaspoon dried basil
¼ teaspoon dry mustard
1 tablespoon Worcestershire
  sauce
salt and pepper
2 tablespoons butter or
  margarine
Sauce:
4 tablespoons butter or
  margarine
½ cup all-purpose flour
2½ cups milk
1 cup crumbled blue cheese
salt and pepper

Mix together the beef, onion, egg, garlic, herbs, mustard, Worcestershire sauce and salt and pepper to taste. Shape into eight patties. Melt the butter or margarine in a frying pan (skillet), add the patties and brown on both sides. Transfer to an ovenproof dish.

To make the sauce, melt the butter or margarine in a saucepan. Stir in the flour and cook for 2 minutes. Gradually stir in the milk and bring to the boil, stirring. Simmer until thickened. Add the cheese and salt and pepper to taste and stir until the sauce is smooth.

Pour the sauce over the burgers. Cook in a preheated hot oven (220°C/425°F, Gas Mark 7) for 20 minutes. Serve hot.
Serves 4

Stir-Fried Beef with Broccoli

Metric/Imperial	American
225 g/8 oz rump steak, thinly sliced	½ lb flank or round steak, thinly sliced
2 teaspoons salt	2 teaspoons salt
1 teaspoon dry sherry	1 teaspoon dry sherry
1 tablespoon cornflour	1 tablespoon cornstarch
4 tablespoons oil	¼ cup oil
225 g/8 oz broccoli, broken into small florets	½ lb broccoli, broken into small florets
2 spring onions, cut into 2.5 cm/1 inch pieces	2 scallions, cut into 1 inch pieces
100 g/4 oz mushrooms, sliced	1 cup sliced mushrooms
1 tablespoon soy sauce	1 tablespoon soy sauce

Place the steak in a bowl with ½ teaspoon of the salt, the sherry and cornflour (cornstarch). Mix well, then leave to marinate for about 20 minutes.

Heat 2 tablespoons of the oil in a wok or frying pan (skillet). Add the broccoli and remaining salt and stir-fry for a few minutes or until just tender. Remove from the pan with a slotted spoon and keep hot.

Heat the remaining oil in the wok or frying pan (skillet). Add the spring onions (scallions) and stir-fry for 10 seconds, then add the steak and stir-fry until evenly browned. Add the mushrooms, soy sauce and broccoli and stir-fry for a further 30 seconds. Serve hot.
Serves 4

Corned Beef Hash

Metric/Imperial	American
50 g/2 oz butter or margarine	4 tablespoons butter or margarine
1 onion, chopped	1 onion, chopped
1 x 350 g/12 oz can corned beef, diced	1 x 12 oz can corned beef, diced
1 x 450 g/16 oz can potatoes, drained and diced	1 x 16 oz can potatoes, drained and diced
2 cooking apples, peeled, cored and chopped	2 tart apples, peeled, cored and chopped
1 tablespoon Worcestershire sauce	1 tablespoon Worcestershire sauce
salt and pepper	salt and pepper

Melt the butter or margarine in a frying pan (skillet). Add the onion and fry until softened. Stir in the remaining ingredients with salt and pepper to taste and press to a flat cake. Fry until the underside is crisp and browned.

Invert the cake onto a plate, then slide it back into the pan to cook the other side. Alternatively, brown the other side under the grill (broiler). Serve hot.
Serves 4

Stir-Fried Beef with Green Peppers

Metric/Imperial	American
225 g/8 oz rump steak, thinly sliced	½ lb flank or round steak, thinly sliced
2 teaspoons salt	2 teaspoons salt
2 teaspoons caster sugar	2 teaspoons sugar
1 tablespoon dry sherry	1 tablespoon dry sherry
1 tablespoon cornflour	1 tablespoon cornstarch
½ teaspoon chilli sauce (optional)	½ teaspoon chili sauce (optional)
pepper	pepper
3 tablespoons oil	3 tablespoons oil
1 large green pepper, cored, seeded and thinly sliced	1 large green pepper, seeded and thinly sliced
1 large tomato, cut into 6 wedges	1 large tomato, cut into 6 wedges
2 spring onions, chopped	2 scallions, chopped
1 slice of fresh root ginger peeled and finely chopped	1 slice of fresh ginger root, peeled and finely chopped
1 tablespoon soy sauce	1 tablespoon soy sauce

Place the steak in a bowl with ½ teaspoon of the salt, the sugar, sherry, cornflour (cornstarch), chilli sauce if using and pepper to taste. Mix well, then leave to marinate for about 20 minutes.

Heat 1 tablespoon of the oil in a wok or frying pan (skillet). Add the green pepper, tomato and remaining salt and stir-fry for 30 seconds. Remove from the pan with a slotted spoon.

Heat the remaining oil in the wok or frying pan (skillet). Add the spring onions (scallions) and ginger, then the steak. Stir-fry for 30 seconds, then add the soy sauce. Return the green pepper mixture to the pan and stir-fry together for a further 1 minute. Serve hot.
Serves 4

Spicy Meatballs

Metric/Imperial
750 g/1½ lb lean minced beef
2 onions, finely chopped
50 g/2 oz fresh breadcrumbs
2 green chillies, seeded and
  finely chopped
pinch of ground cinnamon
pinch of ground cloves
1 egg, beaten
salt and pepper
oil for deep frying
Sauce:
25 g/1 oz butter or margarine
25 g/1 oz plain flour
2 teaspoons curry powder
300 ml/½ pint beef stock
150 ml/¼ pint single cream

American
1½ lb lean ground beef
2 onions, finely chopped
1 cup soft bread crumbs
2 green chili peppers, seeded
  and finely chopped
pinch of ground cinnamon
pinch of ground cloves
1 egg, beaten
salt and pepper
oil for deep frying
Sauce:
2 tablespoons butter or
  margarine
¼ cup all-purpose flour
2 teaspoons curry powder
1¼ cups beef stock or broth
⅔ cup light cream

Combine the beef, onions, breadcrumbs, chillies (chili peppers), spices, egg and salt and pepper to taste. Form into small balls. Deep fry the meatballs until they are golden brown. Drain on kitchen paper towels.

For the sauce, melt the butter or margarine in a large saucepan. Stir in the flour and curry powder and cook for 2 minutes, then gradually stir in the stock. Bring to the boil, stirring, and simmer until thickened. Stir in the cream.

Add the meatballs to the sauce and simmer gently for 10 minutes, stirring occasionally. Season to taste with salt and pepper and serve hot.
Serves 4 to 6

Meat Loaf

Metric/Imperial
350 g/12 oz lean minced beef
100 g/4 oz minced pork
1 small onion, finely chopped
1 teaspoon chopped parsley
½ teaspoon dried sage
grated rind of 1 lemon
1 tablespoon lemon juice
3 tablespoons red wine
1 egg, beaten
salt and pepper

American
¾ lb lean ground beef
¼ lb ground pork
1 small onion, finely chopped
1 teaspoon chopped parsley
½ teaspoon dried sage
grated rind of 1 lemon
1 tablespoon lemon juice
3 tablespoons red wine
1 egg, beaten
salt and pepper

Mix together all the ingredients, with salt and pepper to taste. Spoon into a 500 g/1 lb loaf pan and smooth the top.

Bake in a preheated moderate oven (160°C/325°F, Gas Mark 3) for 1 hour. Cool in the tin and serve cold.
Serves 4

Curried Burgers

Metric/Imperial
500 g/1 lb lean minced beef
2 tablespoons fresh breadcrumbs
1 egg, beaten
1 large onion, finely chopped
1 teaspoon chilli powder
salt and pepper
25 g/1 oz butter or margarine
1 tablespoon oil
1 large cooking apple, peeled,
  cored and sliced
2 teaspoons curry powder
1 tablespoon plain flour
600 ml/1 pint beef stock
1 tablespoon mango chutney

American
1 lb lean ground beef
2 tablespoons soft bread crumbs
1 egg, beaten
1 large onion, finely chopped
1 teaspoon chili powder
salt and pepper
2 tablespoons butter or
  margarine
1 tablespoon oil
1 large tart apple, peeled,
  cored and sliced
2 teaspoons curry powder
1 tablespoon all-purpose flour
2½ cups beef stock or broth
1 tablespoon mango chutney

Mix together the beef, breadcrumbs, egg, about one-third of the onion, the chilli powder and salt and pepper to taste. Shape into four patties.

Melt the butter or margarine with the oil in a frying pan (skillet). Add the patties and brown on both sides. Remove from the pan.

Add the remaining onion to the pan with the apple and fry until the onion is softened. Stir in the curry powder and flour and cook for 2 minutes, then gradually stir in the stock. Bring to the boil, stirring well. Stir in the chutney and salt and pepper to taste.

Return the burgers to the pan and turn to coat with the sauce. Simmer for 15 minutes. Serve hot with boiled rice.
Serves 4

Beef and Vegetable Risotto

Metric/Imperial	American
2 tablespoons oil	2 tablespoons oil
225 g/8 oz long-grain rice	1 cup rice
500 g/1 lb lean minced beef	1 lb lean ground beef
1 onion, chopped	1 onion, chopped
1 packet dry vegetable soup mix	1 package dry vegetable soup mix
900 ml/1½ pints water	4 cups water
½ small green pepper, cored, seeded and diced	½ small green pepper, seeded and diced
½ small red pepper, cored, seeded and diced	½ small red pepper, seeded and diced
100 g/4 oz mushrooms, sliced	1 cup sliced mushrooms
2 teaspoons Worcestershire sauce	2 teaspoons Worcestershire sauce
salt and pepper	salt and pepper
grated Cheddar or Parmesan cheese to serve	grated Cheddar or Parmesan cheese to serve

Heat the oil in a saucepan. Add the rice and cook, stirring, until it is transparent. Add the beef and onion and fry until they are browned. Stir in the soup mix and water and bring to the boil. Add the green and red peppers, mushrooms, Worcestershire sauce and salt and pepper to taste. Cover and simmer for 15 minutes or until the rice is tender and has absorbed all the liquid.

Serve hot, with grated cheese.

Serves 4

French-Style Veal

Metric/Imperial	American
4 veal escalopes, beaten thin	4 veal cutlets, pounded thin
3 tablespoons plain flour	3 tablespoons all-purpose flour
1 egg, beaten	1 egg, beaten
25 g/1 oz butter or margarine	2 tablespoons butter or margarine
2 tablespoons oil	2 tablespoons oil
225 g/8 oz mushrooms, sliced	½ lb mushrooms, sliced

Coat the veal with the flour, then dip in the egg. Melt the butter or margarine with the oil in a frying pan (skillet). Add the veal and cook for about 5 minutes on each side or until golden brown and cooked through. Transfer the veal to a warmed serving dish and keep hot.

Add the mushrooms to the pan and fry for 2 to 3 minutes or until just tender. Spoon over the veal and serve hot.

Serves 4.

Veal Rolls

Metric/Imperial	American
150 g/5 oz butter or margarine, softened	10 tablespoons butter or margarine, softened
2 tablespoons chopped parsley	2 tablespoons chopped parsley
½ teaspoon dried thyme	½ teaspoon dried thyme
juice of ½ lemon	juice of ½ lemon
salt and pepper	salt and pepper
4 veal escalopes, beaten thin	4 veal cutlets, pounded thin
25 g/1 oz plain flour	¼ cup all-purpose flour
450 ml/¾ pint chicken stock	2 cups chicken stock or broth
4 tablespoons single cream	¼ cup light cream

Beat 100 g/4 oz (½ cup) of the butter or margarine with the herbs, lemon juice and salt and pepper to taste. Spread over the veal and roll up. Secure the rolls with wooden cocktail sticks or string.

Melt the remaining butter or margarine in a frying pan (skillet). Add the veal rolls and brown on all sides. Remove from the pan.

Stir the flour into the fat in the pan and cook for 2 minutes, then gradually stir in the stock. Bring to the boil, stirring, and simmer until thickened. Return veal to pan. Cover and simmer for 20 minutes.

Transfer the veal rolls to a warmed serving dish and keep hot. Stir the cream into the cooking liquid, and taste and adjust the seasoning. Pour this sauce over the veal and serve hot.
Serves 4

Crumbed Lamb Chops

Metric/Imperial	American
½ teaspoon dried rosemary	½ teaspoon dried rosemary
3 tablespoons plain flour	3 tablespoons all-purpose flour
salt and pepper	salt and pepper
4 lamb chops	4 lamb chops
1 egg, beaten	1 egg, beaten
25 g/1 oz dry breadcrumbs	⅓ cup dry bread crumbs
25 g/1 oz butter or margarine	2 tablespoons butter or margarine
2 tablespoons oil	2 tablespoons oil
100 g/4 oz mushrooms, sliced	1 cup sliced mushrooms
4 tomatoes, halved	4 tomatoes, halved
watercress to garnish	watercress for garnish

Mix together the rosemary, flour and salt and pepper to taste and use to coat the chops. Dip them in the egg, then coat with the breadcrumbs, pressing the crumbs on firmly.

Melt the butter or margarine with the oil in a frying pan (skillet). Add the chops and fry for about 5 minutes on each side or until golden brown and cooked through. Halfway through the cooking time, add the mushrooms and tomatoes to the pan to cook with the chops.

Serve hot, garnished with watercress.
Serves 4

Spiced Lamb Kebabs

Metric/Imperial	American
150 ml/¼ pint plain yogurt	⅔ cup plain yogurt
2 teaspoons ground coriander	2 teaspoons ground coriander
½ teaspoon ground turmeric	½ teaspoon ground turmeric
1 teaspoon chilli powder	1 teaspoon chili powder
1 teaspoon black pepper	1 teaspoon black pepper
salt	salt
750 g/1½ lb lean lamb, cut into 2.5 cm/1 inch cubes	1½ lb lean lamb, cut into 1 inch cubes
6 button onions, quartered	6 pearl onions, quartered

Mix together the yogurt, spices and salt to taste in a shallow dish. Add the lamb cubes and turn to coat. Cover and leave to marinate in the refrigerator overnight.

The next day, thread the lamb cubes onto skewers alternately with pieces of onion. Place under a preheated grill (broiler) and cook for about 10 minutes, turning occasionally, until the lamb is cooked through and tender. Serve hot.
Serves 4

Marinated Lamb Kebabs

Metric/Imperial	American
1 kg/2 lb boned leg of lamb, cut into 2.5 cm/1 inch cubes	2 lb boned leg of lamb, cut into 1 inch cubes
16 button mushrooms	16 button mushrooms
8 small tomatoes	8 cherry tomatoes
8 spring onions, white part only	8 scallions, white part only
1 green or red pepper, cored, seeded and cut into 2.5 cm/1 inch squares	1 green or red pepper, seeded and cut into 1 inch squares
Marinade:	Marinade:
300 ml/½ pint plain yogurt	1¼ cups plain yogurt
juice of 1 lemon	juice of 1 lemon
1 onion, grated	1 onion, grated
3 bay leaves	3 bay leaves
salt and pepper	salt and pepper

Mix together the marinade ingredients in a plastic bag. Add the lamb cubes and turn to coat. Close the bag and leave to marinate in the refrigerator for 24 hours, turning occasionally.

Thread the lamb cubes onto eight skewers alternating with the vegetables. Grill (broil) for 10 to 15 minutes, turning frequently and basting with the remaining marinade. Serve hot.
Serves 4

Pitta Kebab

Metric/Imperial
1 kg/2 lb boned leg of lamb,
   cut into 2.5 cm/1 inch
   cubes
4 tablespoons oil
juice of 2 lemons
2 fresh thyme sprigs, or
   1 teaspoon dried thyme
salt and pepper
4 pitta breads, split open
To serve:
cucumber slices
tomato slices
onion rings
lettuce leaves
stoned black olives

American
2 lb boned leg of lamb, cut
   into 1 inch cubes or lamb
   for kabobs
¼ cup oil
juice of 2 lemons
2 fresh thyme sprigs, or
   1 teaspoon dried thyme
salt and pepper
4 pitta breads (Arab pocket
   bread), split open
To serve:
cucumber slices
tomato slices
onion rings
lettuce leaves
pitted ripe olives

Put the lamb cubes in a plastic bag and sprinkle over the oil and lemon juice. Add the thyme and salt and pepper to taste. Seal the bag and leave to marinate for at least 30 minutes, turning from time to time.

Thread the lamb cubes onto four skewers, reserving the marinade. Grill (broil), or barbecue, until the lamb is browned on all sides and cooked to your taste. Baste with the reserved marinade occasionally.

Meanwhile heat the pitta bread at the sides of the grill (broiler) or barbecue for about 3 minutes on each side.

Slide the lamb cubes off the skewers and stuff into the pocket in the bread. Add cucumber and tomato slices, onion rings, lettuce leaves and olives. Serve hot.
Serves 4

Lemon Lamb Chops

Metric/Imperial
4 lamb chops
2 tablespoons oil
grated rind of 1 lemon
2 tablespoons lemon juice
2 teaspoons brown sugar
1 teaspoon ground ginger
salt and pepper

American
4 lamb chops
2 tablespoons oil
grated rind of 1 lemon
2 tablespoons lemon juice
2 teaspoons brown sugar
1 teaspoon ground ginger
salt and pepper

Place the chops in a shallow dish. Mix together the remaining ingredients, with salt and pepper to taste, and pour over the chops. Cover and leave to marinate for 3 hours, turning the chops occasionally.

Place the chops on the grill (broiler) rack, reserving the marinade. Place under a preheated grill (broiler) and cook for about 7 minutes on each side, basting with the marinade occasionally. Serve hot.
Serves 4

Seekh Kebab

Metric/Imperial	American
500 g/1 lb minced lamb	1 lb ground lamb
2 onions, finely chopped	2 onions, finely chopped
1 × 1 cm/½ inch piece fresh root ginger, peeled and grated	1 × ½ inch piece fresh ginger root, peeled and grated
1 garlic clove, crushed	1 garlic clove, crushed
¼ teaspoon ground cardamom	¼ teaspoon ground cardamom
¼ teaspoon ground cumin	¼ teaspoon ground cumin
¼ teaspoon ground cloves	¼ teaspoon ground cloves
1 teaspoon ground coriander	1 teaspoon ground coriander
salt	salt
1 egg, beaten	1 egg, beaten
1 tablespoon oil	1 tablespoon oil

Mix together all the ingredients except the oil. Divide into eight portions and shape into sausages. Thread onto skewers and brush with the oil.

Place under a preheated grill (broiler) and cook for about 10 minutes, turning occasionally, until the kebabs are cooked through. Serve hot.

Serves 4

Minted Lamburgers

Metric/Imperial	American
500 g/1 lb minced lamb	1 lb ground lamb
1 onion, finely chopped	1 onion, finely chopped
1 tablespoon chopped fresh mint	1 tablespoon chopped fresh mint
1 egg	1 egg
salt and pepper	salt and pepper
3 tablespoons oil	3 tablespoons oil
4 hamburger buns, split in half	4 hamburger buns, split in half

Mix together the lamb, onion, mint, egg and salt and pepper to taste. Shape into four patties.

Heat the oil in a frying pan (skillet). Add the patties and fry for about 5 minutes on each side. Meanwhile toast the cut surfaces of the buns.

Place a burger in each bun and serve hot, with mustard.

Serves 4

Variation:

Orangy Lamburgers: Omit the mint and egg and add 2 tablespoons fresh breadcrumbs, 1 tablespoon orange juice and 1 teaspoon chopped fresh sage to the lamb and onion. Serve garnished with orange slices.

Wellington Burgers

Metric/Imperial
25 g/1 oz butter or margarine
1 onion, grated
500 g/1 lb minced lamb
½ small green pepper, cored,
 seeded and diced
1 tablespoon tomato purée
1 teaspoon dried marjoram
1 teaspoon dried thyme
75 g/3 oz fresh breadcrumbs
1 teaspoon clear honey
salt and pepper
1 × 375 g/13 oz packet frozen
 puff pastry, thawed
2 tablespoons mint sauce
beaten egg to glaze

American
2 tablespoons butter or
 margarine
1 onion, grated
1 lb ground lamb
½ small green pepper,
 seeded and diced
1 tablespoon tomato paste
1 teaspoon dried marjoram
1 teaspoon dried thyme
1½ cups soft bread crumbs
1 teaspoon honey
salt and pepper
1 × 13 oz package frozen puff
 pastry, thawed
2 tablespoons mint sauce
beaten egg to glaze

Melt the butter or margarine in a frying pan (skillet). Add the onion and fry until softened. Tip the onion into a bowl and add the lamb, green pepper, tomato purée (paste), herbs, breadcrumbs, honey and salt and pepper to taste. Mix well together, then shape into four patties. Grill (broil) or fry until browned on both sides.

Roll out the dough and cut into eight fluted rounds, larger than the patties. Place a patty on each of four dough rounds and top with the mint sauce. Place the remaining dough rounds on top and seal the edges. Brush all over with beaten egg.

Place on a baking sheet and cook in a preheated moderately hot oven (200°C/400°F, Gas Mark 6) for 25 to 30 minutes or until the pastry is puffed up and golden brown. Serve hot.
Serves 4

Indian Burgers

Metric/Imperial
50 g/2 oz margarine
1 tablespoon garam masala
500 g/1 lb minced lamb
3 tablespoons plain yogurt
salt and pepper
3 tablespoons water

American
4 tablespoons margarine
1 tablespoon garam masala
1 lb ground lamb
3 tablespoons plain yogurt
salt and pepper
3 tablespoons water

Melt 25 g/1 oz (2 tablespoons) of the margarine in a frying pan (skillet). Add the garam masala and cook gently, stirring, for 5 minutes. Tip the spice mixture into a bowl and add the lamb, yogurt and salt and pepper to taste. Mix well together, then form into 12 small patties.

Melt the remaining margarine in the frying pan (skillet) and fry the patties until browned on both sides. Add the water to the pan and continue cooking until it has evaporated. Serve hot with boiled rice.
Serves 4

Lamb Croquettes

Metric/Imperial
500 g/1 lb minced lamb
100 g/4 oz fresh breadcrumbs
1 onion, finely chopped
2 celery sticks, diced
½ red pepper, cored, seeded
  and diced
½ green pepper, cored, seeded
  and diced
grated rind of 1 lemon
2 teaspoons Worcestershire
  sauce
salt and pepper
1 egg, beaten
dry breadcrumbs for coating
oil for deep frying

American
1 lb ground lamb
2 cups soft bread crumbs
1 onion, finely chopped
2 celery stalks, diced
½ red pepper, seeded and
  diced
½ green pepper, seeded
  and diced
grated rind of 1 lemon
2 teaspoons Worcestershire
  sauce
salt and pepper
1 egg, beaten
dry bread crumbs for coating
oil for deep frying

Mix together the lamb, fresh breadcrumbs, onion, celery, red and green peppers, lemon rind, Worcestershire sauce and salt and pepper to taste. Divide into eight and shape into sausages. Dip the sausages in the egg, then coat with the dry breadcrumbs. Deep fry for 5 to 10 minutes or until golden brown. Drain on kitchen paper towels and serve hot.
Serves 4

Lamburgers

Metric/Imperial
25 g/1 oz butter or margarine
1 onion, finely chopped
500 g/1 lb minced lamb
1 celery stick, diced
50 g/2 oz fresh white
  breadcrumbs
2 tablespoons tomato ketchup
1 teaspoon dried mixed herbs
salt and pepper
To serve:
4 hamburger buns, split in half
onion rings
tomato slices
lettuce leaves

American
2 tablespoons butter or
  margarine
1 onion, finely chopped
1 lb ground lamb
1 celery stalk, diced
1 cup soft white bread
  crumbs
2 tablespoons tomato ketchup
1 teaspoon dried mixed herbs
salt and pepper
To serve:
4 hamburger buns, split in half
onion rings
tomato slices
lettuce leaves

Melt the butter or margarine in a frying pan (skillet). Add the onion and fry until softened. Tip the onion into a bowl and add the lamb, celery, breadcrumbs, ketchup, herbs and salt and pepper to taste. Work the ingredients together with your hands, then shape into four patties. Grill (broil) for about 15 minutes, turning once.

Serve the lamburgers in buns topped with onion rings, tomato slices and lettuce leaves.
Serves 4

Sweet and Sour Pork Chops

Metric/Imperial	American
4 pork chops	4 pork chops
3 tablespoons cornflour	3 tablespoons cornstarch
120 ml/4 fl oz cider	½ cup hard or apple cider
3 tablespoons brown sugar	3 tablespoons brown sugar
3 tablespoons redcurrant jelly	3 tablespoons red currant jelly
1 tablespoon soy sauce	1 tablespoon soy sauce
3 tablespoons vinegar	3 tablespoons vinegar

Place the chops under a preheated grill (broiler) and cook for about 10 minutes on each side or until browned and cooked through.

Meanwhile combine the remaining ingredients in a saucepan. Bring to the boil, stirring, and simmer for 5 minutes.

Serve the.chops hot, topped with the sauce.

Serves 4

Sweet and Sour Pork Kebabs

Metric/Imperial	American
750 g/1½ lb pork fillet, cut into cubes	1½ lb pork tenderloin, cut into cubes
3 tablespoons oil	3 tablespoons oil
1½ tablespoons soy sauce	1½ tablespoons soy sauce
1 tablespoon black treacle	1 tablespoon molasses
grated rind and juice of 1 lemon	grated rind and juice of 1 lemon
1½ tablespoons dark brown sugar	1½ tablespoons dark brown sugar
½ teaspoon Tabasco sauce	½ teaspoon hot pepper sauce
1 teaspoon ground ginger	1 teaspoon ground ginger
salt and pepper	salt and pepper

Place the pork in a plastic bag. Mix together the remaining ingredients, with salt and pepper to taste, and pour into the bag. Close the bag and leave the pork to marinate in the refrigerator for 24 hours, turning the bag over from time to time.

Thread the pork cubes onto skewers, reserving the marinade. Place under a preheated grill (broiler), or over coals on a barbecue, and cook for about 15 minutes, basting with the reserved marinade and turning frequently. Serve hot.

Serves 4

Apple-Topped Pork Chops

Metric/Imperial
4 pork chops
3 dessert apples, cored and
    grated
100 g/4 oz fresh breadcrumbs
1 teaspoon dried sage
1 egg, beaten
salt and pepper

American
4 pork chops
3 apples, cored and grated
2 cups soft bread crumbs
1 teaspoon dried sage
1 egg, beaten
salt and pepper

Place the chops on the grill (broiler) rack and grill (broil) for about 7 minutes on each side or until cooked through.
Mix together the remaining ingredients with salt and pepper to taste. Spread over the chops. Return to the grill (broiler) and cook gently for a further 4 minutes or until the topping is golden.
Serves 4

Pork with Mushrooms and Sour Cream

Metric/Imperial
750 g/1½ lb pork fillet, cut
    crossways into 2.5 cm/1 inch
    thick slices
3 tablespoons plain flour
50 g/2 oz butter or margarine
175 g/6 oz button mushrooms
2 tablespoons dry vermouth
150 ml/¼ pint soured cream
¼ teaspoon dried mixed herbs
salt and pepper
250 ml/8 fl oz chicken stock

American
1½ lb pork tenderloin, cut
    crosswise into 1 inch
    thick slices
3 tablespoons all-purpose flour
4 tablespoons butter or
    margarine
6 oz button mushrooms
2 tablespoons dry vermouth
¾ cup sour cream
¼ teaspoon dried mixed herbs
salt and pepper
1 cup chicken stock or broth

Flatten the pork slices slightly with a rolling pin. Coat with the flour. Melt the butter or margarine in a large frying pan (skillet). Add the pork slices, a few at a time, and fry until crisp and brown on both sides. Remove the pork from the pan as it is browned.
Return all the pork to the pan with the mushrooms and cook for a further 5 minutes. Stir in the vermouth and simmer, stirring to mix in the sediment from the bottom of the pan.
Stir in the sour cream, herbs and salt and pepper to taste. Add enough stock just to cover the pork mixture. Cook gently for a further 5 to 10 minutes or until the pork is tender. Serve hot.
Serves 4

Orange Pork Chops

Metric/Imperial
4 pork chops
25 g/1 oz plain flour
40 g/1½ oz butter or margarine
1 onion, sliced
1 green pepper, cored, seeded
  and sliced
3 tablespoons brown sugar
1 tablespoon made mustard
450 ml/¾ pint orange juice
salt and pepper
1 orange, peeled and sliced

American
4 pork chops
¼ cup all-purpose flour
3 tablespoons butter or
  margarine
1 onion, sliced
1 green pepper, seeded
  and sliced
3 tablespoons brown sugar
1 tablespoon prepared mustard
2 cups orange juice
salt and pepper
1 orange, peeled and sliced

Coat the pork chops with the flour. Melt the butter or margarine in a frying pan (skillet), add the chops and brown on both sides. Remove from pan.

Add the onion and green pepper to the pan and fry until softened. Stir in the sugar, mustard, orange juice and salt and pepper to taste and bring to the boil. Return the chops to the pan. Cover and simmer for 15 minutes.

Turn the chops over, arrange the orange slices over them and cook, covered, for a further 15 minutes. Serve hot.
Serves 4

Double Decker Burgers

Metric/Imperial
225 g/8 oz minced pork
225 g/8 oz pork sausagemeat
75 g/3 oz cooked rice
1 teaspoon dried sage
2 teaspoons made mustard
1 egg, beaten
salt and pepper
3 tablespoons oil
4 hamburger buns, split in half
3-4 spring onions, shredded
2 tomatoes, sliced
¼ cucumber, sliced

American
½ lb ground pork
½ lb pork sausagemeat
¾ cup cooked rice
1 teaspoon dried sage
2 teaspoons prepared mustard
1 egg, beaten
salt and pepper
3 tablespoons oil
4 hamburger buns, split in half
3-4 scallions, shredded
2 tomatoes, sliced
¼ cucumber, sliced

Mix together the pork, sausagemeat, rice, sage, mustard, egg and salt and pepper to taste. Shape into eight patties.

Heat the oil in a frying pan (skillet). Add the patties and fry for about 5 minutes on each side.

Place a burger in each of the buns and top with the spring onions (scallions), tomatoes and cucumber. Place the remaining burgers on top and cover with the bun tops. Serve hot.
Serves 4

Pork Teriyaki

Metric/Imperial
1 kg/2 lb pork fillet, thinly
  sliced
1 teaspoon grated fresh root
  ginger
1 onion, finely chopped
½ teaspoon monosodium
  glutamate (optional)
5 tablespoons soy sauce
4 tablespoons caster sugar
4 tablespoons sake or dry
  sherry

American
2 lb pork tenderloin, thinly
  sliced
1 teaspoon grated fresh ginger
  root
1 onion, finely chopped
½ teaspoon msg (optional)
5 tablespoons soy sauce
¼ cup sugar
¼ cup sake or dry sherry

Put all the ingredients into a bowl and mix well. Leave to marinate in the refrigerator for about 1 hour.

Thread the pork onto four skewers, reserving the marinade. Place under a preheated grill (broiler) and cook for about 3 minutes on each side, basting with the reserved marinade. Serve hot.
Serves 4

Ham and Leek Roll-Ups

Metric/Imperial
40 g/1½ oz butter or margarine
500 g/1 lb leeks, sliced
1 large cooking apple,
  peeled, cored and chopped
8 slices of cooked ham
1 packet white sauce mix
milk
½ teaspoon dry mustard
50 g/2 oz cheese and onion-
  flavoured potato crisps,
  crushed

American
3 tablespoons butter or
  margarine
1 lb leeks, sliced
1 large tart apple, peeled,
  cored and chopped
8 slices of cooked ham
1 package white sauce mix
milk
½ teaspoon dry mustard
1 cup crushed cheese and onion-
  flavored potato chips

Melt the butter or margarine in a saucepan. Add the leeks and apple and cook gently until softened, stirring occasionally. Divide the leeks and apple between the slices of ham and roll them up. Arrange in one layer in a greased ovenproof dish.

Make up the white sauce with milk according to the instructions on the packet. Stir in the mustard. Pour the sauce over the ham rolls and sprinkle the potato crisps (chips) on top.

Cook in a preheated moderately hot oven (190°C/375°F, Gas Mark 5) for 15 minutes. Serve hot.
Serves 4

Sausage and Bean Pizza

Metric/Imperial
500 g/1 lb pork chipolatas
1 × 425 g/15 oz can baked
  beans in tomato sauce
100 g/4 oz mushrooms, sliced
pinch of dried mixed herbs
50 g/2 oz Cheddar cheese,
  grated
Dough base:
225 g/8 oz self-raising flour
½ teaspoon salt
50 g/2 oz butter or margarine
150 ml/¼ pint milk

American
1 lb pork link sausages
1 × 15 oz can baked beans in
  tomato sauce
1 cup sliced mushrooms
pinch of dried mixed herbs
½ cup grated Cheddar cheese
Dough base:
2 cups self-rising flour
½ teaspoon salt
4 tablespoons butter or
  margarine
¾ cup milk

Grill (broil) or fry the sausages.
　　Meanwhile make the base, sift the flour and salt into a bowl. Rub in the butter or margarine until the mixture resembles crumbs, then bind to a soft dough with the milk. Roll out the dough to a round about 1 cm/½ inch thick and place it on a greased baking sheet. Pinch up the edge to make a rim.
　　Spread the baked beans over the base. Scatter over the mushrooms and sprinkle the herbs on top. Drain the sausages and arrange on top. Scatter over the cheese.
　　Cook in a preheated moderately hot oven (200°C/400°F, Gas Mark 6) for 20 to 25 minutes. Serve hot.
Serves 2 to 4

Variation:

Curried Egg and Anchovy Pizza: Roll out the dough as above and sprinkle with 25 g/1 oz (¼ cup) grated Cheddar cheese. Cook in a preheated moderately hot oven (200°C/400°F, Gas Mark 6) for 15 minutes. Drain a 50 g/2 oz can anchovy fillets and arrange on the pizza base. Cover with 4 sliced hard-boiled eggs and sprinkle with ½ to 1 teaspoon curry powder and salt and pepper to taste. Top with 4 thinly sliced tomatoes and sprinkle with a further 50 g/2 oz (½ cup) grated Cheddar cheese. Return to the oven and cook for 5 to 10 minutes longer or until the cheese has melted and is golden brown. Serve hot.

Devilled Sausages

Metric/Imperial
25 g/1 oz butter or margarine
1 onion, thinly sliced
4 back bacon rashers, derinded
 and diced
500 g/1 lb chipolata sausages,
 cut into chunks
4 tomatoes, quartered
½ teaspoon curry powder
1 teaspoon made mustard
1 tablespoon tomato ketchup
1 tablespoon chutney
¼ teaspoon cayenne pepper
salt and pepper

American
2 tablespoons butter or
 margarine
1 onion, thinly sliced
4 slices of Canadian bacon,
 diced
1 lb pork link sausages, cut
 into chunks
4 tomatoes, quartered
½ teaspoon curry powder
1 teaspoon prepared mustard
1 tablespoon tomato ketchup
1 tablespoon chutney
¼ teaspoon cayenne
salt and pepper

Melt the butter or margarine in a frying pan (skillet). Add the onion, bacon and sausages and fry until golden brown. Stir in the remaining ingredients with salt and pepper to taste and cook for a further 5 minutes, stirring frequently. Serve hot.
Serves 4

Gammon (Ham) with Raisin Sauce

Metric/Imperial
4 gammon steaks
15 g/½ oz butter or margarine,
 melted
Sauce:
50 g/2 oz raisins
2 cloves
25 g/1 oz brown sugar
300 ml/½ pint water
1 tablespoon cornflour
25 g/1 oz butter or margarine
2 tablespoons lemon juice
salt and pepper

American
4 ham steaks
1 tablespoon butter or
 margarine, melted
Sauce:
⅓ cup raisins
2 cloves
3 tablespoons brown sugar
1¼ cups water
1 tablespoon cornstarch
2 tablespoons butter or
 margarine
2 tablespoons lemon juice
salt and pepper

First make the sauce. Place the raisins, cloves, brown sugar, and all but 2 tablespoons of the water in a saucepan. Bring to the boil and simmer for 10 minutes.
 Meanwhile place the gammon (ham) steaks on the grill (broiler) rack and brush with the butter or margarine. Place under a preheated grill (broiler) and cook for 5 minutes on each side.
 Dissolve the cornflour (cornstarch) in the reserved water. Add to the saucepan with the butter or margarine, lemon juice and salt and pepper to taste. Simmer, stirring, until thickened.
 Serve the gammon (ham) steaks with the sauce.
Serves 4

Sausages with Horseradish Sauce

Metric/Imperial
500 g/1 lb pork sausages
4 tablespoons bottled French
  dressing
Sauce:
300 ml/½ pint mayonnaise
4 tablespoons double cream,
  whipped
1 tablespoon creamed
  horseradish
2 celery sticks, diced
2 dessert apples, cored and
  diced
1 dill pickle, diced

American
1 lb pork sausages
¼ cup bottled vinaigrette
  dressing
Sauce:
1¼ cups mayonnaise
¼ cup heavy cream, whipped
1 tablespoon prepared
  horseradish
2 celery stalks, diced
2 apples, cored and diced
1 dill pickle, diced

Grill (broil) or fry the sausages until they are browned on all sides and cooked through. Drain on kitchen paper towels and place in a shallow dish. Spoon over the dressing and chill for 2 hours.

To make the sauce, mix the mayonnaise with the cream and horseradish, then fold in the celery, apples and pickle. Chill.

Serve the sausages with the sauce.
Serves 4

Apple-Topped Gammon (Ham)

Metric/Imperial
25 g/1 oz butter or margarine
1 onion, chopped
2 large dessert apples, peeled,
  cored and chopped
1 tablespoon clear honey
3 tablespoons bottled brown
  sauce
salt and pepper
4 gammon steaks

American
2 tablespoons butter or
  margarine
1 onion, chopped
2 large apples, peeled, cored
  and chopped
1 tablespoon honey
3 tablespoons bottled steak
  sauce
salt and pepper
4 ham steaks

Melt the butter or margarine in a saucepan. Add the onion and apples and fry until the onion is softened. Stir in the honey, sauce and salt and pepper to taste.

Place each gammon (ham) steak on a piece of foil and pile the apple mixture on top. Wrap up the foil loosely and place the parcels on a baking sheet. Cook in a preheated moderate oven (180°C/350°F, Gas Mark 4) for 20 minutes. Serve hot.
Serves 4

Pork Chops with Onions

Metric/Imperial	American
6 pork chops	6 pork chops
salt and pepper	salt and pepper
25 g/1 oz butter or margarine	2 tablespoons butter or
1 tablespoon oil	margarine
1 kg/2 lb onions, thinly sliced	1 tablespoon oil
3 tablespoons cider vinegar	2 lb onions, thinly sliced
3 tablespoons dry white wine	3 tablespoons cider vinegar
1/4 teaspoon dried thyme	3 tablespoons dry white wine
	1/4 teaspoon dried thyme

Trim the fat from the pork chops and rub them on both sides with salt and pepper.

Melt the butter or margarine with the oil in a large frying pan (skillet). Add the onions and fry gently until softened and golden brown. Remove with a slotted spoon and keep warm.

Add the chops to the pan (skillet), with more butter or margarine and oil if necessary, and fry for about 20 minutes or until browned on both sides and cooked through. Transfer the chops to a warmed serving platter and keep hot.

Add the vinegar, wine and thyme to the pan (skillet) and bring to the boil, stirring to mix in any sediment from the bottom of the pan. Boil until the liquid has reduced by about half. Stir in the onions and season to taste with salt and pepper. Reheat thoroughly.

Spoon the onion mixture around the chops and serve hot.
Serves 6

Sausage Kebabs

Metric/Imperial	American
500 g/1 lb sausages, halved crossways	1 lb sausages, halved crosswise
1 × 500 g/1 lb 3 oz can potatoes, drained	1 × 1 lb 3 oz can potatoes, drained
225 g/8 oz small tomatoes	1/2 lb cherry tomatoes
150 ml/1/4 pint chicken stock	2/3 cup chicken stock or broth
2 tablespoons marmalade	2 tablespoons marmalade
1 teaspoon tomato purée	1 teaspoon tomato paste
1 teaspoon Worcestershire sauce	1 teaspoon Worcestershire sauce
1 tablespoon cornflour	1 tablespoon cornstarch
1 tablespoon water	1 tablespoon water

Thread the sausage pieces, potatoes and tomatoes onto four skewers.

Put the stock, marmalade, tomato purée (paste) and Worcestershire sauce into a saucepan and bring to the boil. Simmer for 5 minutes. Dissolve the cornflour (cornstarch) in the water and add to the pan. Simmer, stirring, until thickened.

Brush the sauce over the sausages and vegetables and grill (broil) for 10 minutes, turning frequently and brushing with the sauce. Serve hot.
Serves 4

Sausage and Noodle Casserole

Metric/Imperial
500 g/1 lb pork sausages
100 g/4 oz noodles
salt and pepper
50 g/2 oz butter or margarine
25 g/1 oz plain flour
1 × 400 g/14 oz can tomatoes,
   chopped with their juice
2 teaspoons dry mustard
1 tablespoon tomato purée

American
1 lb pork sausages
¼ lb noodles
salt and pepper
4 tablespoons butter or
   margarine
¼ cup all-purpose flour
1 × 16 oz can tomatoes, chopped
   with their juice
2 teaspoons dry mustard
1 tablespoon tomato paste

Arrange the sausages in an ovenproof dish and cook in a preheated moderately hot oven (200°C/400°F, Gas Mark 6) until browned.

Meanwhile cook the noodles in boiling salted water until just tender. Drain well. Add 25 g/1 oz (2 tablespoons) of the butter or margarine and toss to coat the noodles. Set aside.

Melt the remaining butter or margarine in a saucepan. Add the flour and cook, stirring, for 1 minute. Gradually stir in the tomatoes with their juice, the mustard, tomato purée (paste) and salt and pepper to taste. Bring to the boil, stirring, and simmer until thickened.

Remove the sausages from the dish. Pour off all the fat. Put half the noodles in the dish and arrange the sausages on top. Pour over the tomato sauce and surround with the remaining noodles. Return to the oven and cook for a further 10 minutes. Serve hot.
Serves 4

Devilled Porkburgers

Metric/Imperial
500 g/1 lb pork sausagemeat
1 onion, finely chopped
¼ teaspoon dried sage
salt and pepper
2 tablespoons plain flour
1 teaspoon dry mustard
1 teaspoon caster sugar
1 teaspoon curry powder
1 egg, beaten
50 g/2 oz salted peanuts,
   finely chopped
50 g/2 oz fresh breadcrumbs
5-6 tablespoons oil

American
1 lb pork sausagemeat
1 onion, finely chopped
¼ teaspoon dried sage
salt and pepper
2 tablespoons all-purpose flour
1 teaspoon dry mustard
1 teaspoon sugar
1 teaspoon curry powder
1 egg, beaten
½ cup finely chopped salted
   peanuts
1 cup soft bread crumbs
5-6 tablespoons oil

Mix together the sausagemeat, onion, sage and salt and pepper to taste. Shape into eight patties. Combine the flour, mustard, sugar and curry powder. Coat the patties with the seasoned flour, then dip in the beaten egg. Mix the peanuts with the breadcrumbs and use to coat the patties.

Heat the oil in a frying pan (skillet). Add the patties and fry for about 8 minutes on each side. Serve hot.
Serves 4

Ham and Egg Burgers

Metric/Imperial	American
225 g/8 oz cooked ham, diced	1 cup diced cooked ham
225 g/8 oz mashed potatoes	1 cup mashed potatoes
1 tablespoon chopped parsley	1 tablespoon chopped parsley
1 egg yolk	1 egg yolk
salt and pepper	salt and pepper
4 streaky bacon rashers, derinded	4 bacon slices
4 eggs	4 eggs

Mix together the ham, mashed potatoes, parsley, egg yolk and salt and pepper to taste. Shape into four patties and wrap a bacon rasher (slice) around each. Secure with wooden cocktail sticks, if necessary.

Arrange the burgers in a greased ovenproof dish and cook in a preheated moderately hot oven (190°C/375°F, Gas Mark 5) for 20 to 25 minutes.

Just before the burgers are ready, poach the eggs. Serve each burger topped with a poached egg.
Serves 4

Pasta Bows with Pork Sauce

Metric/Imperial	American
4 tablespoons oil	¼ cup oil
350 g/12 oz minced pork	¾ lb ground pork
2 garlic cloves, crushed	2 garlic cloves, crushed
1 tablespoon plain flour	1 tablespoon all-purpose flour
250 ml/8 fl oz beef stock	1 cup beef stock or broth
120 ml/4 fl oz white wine	½ cup white wine
2 tablespoons tomato purée	2 tablespoons tomato paste
½ teaspoon dried basil	½ teaspoon dried basil
½ teaspoon dried oregano	½ teaspoon dried oregano
salt and pepper	salt and pepper
350 g/12 oz mushrooms, sliced	¾ lb mushrooms, sliced
350 g/12 oz pasta bows	¾ lb pasta bows
grated Parmesan cheese to serve	grated Parmesan cheese to serve

Heat 2 tablespoons of the oil in a saucepan. Add the pork and fry until it is browned and crumbly. Add the garlic and cook for a further 2 minutes. Stir in the flour, then add the stock, wine, tomato purée (paste), herbs and salt and pepper to taste. Bring to the boil and simmer for 25 minutes.

Heat the remaining oil in a frying pan (skillet). Add the mushrooms and fry for 3 minutes or until tender. Stir into the pork sauce and cook for a further 5 minutes.

Meanwhile cook the pasta bows in boiling salted water until just tender. Drain well and return to the pan. Add the pork sauce and toss together. Serve hot with Parmesan cheese.
Serves 4

Pork with Apricots

Metric/Imperial
25 g/1 oz plain flour
salt and pepper
750 g/1½ lb pork fillet,
  cut into cubes
50 g/2 oz butter
1 tablespoon oil
1 × 400 g/14 oz can apricot
  halves
2 tablespoons Worcestershire
  sauce
2 tablespoons demerara sugar
2 teaspoons vinegar
2 teaspoons lemon juice
120 ml/4 fl oz water

American
¼ cup all-purpose flour
salt and pepper
1½ lb pork tenderloin, cut
  into cubes
4 tablespoons butter
1 tablespoon oil
1 × 16 oz can apricot halves
2 tablespoons Worcestershire
  sauce
2 tablespoons raw brown sugar
2 teaspoons vinegar
2 teaspoons lemon juice
½ cup water

Mix the flour with salt and pepper and use to coat the pork cubes. Melt the butter with the oil in a large frying pan (skillet). Add the pork cubes, a few at a time, and brown on all sides. Remove the pork from the pan.

Drain the apricots, reserving the syrup. Chop the apricots. Mix 120 ml/ 4 fl oz (½ cup) of the reserved syrup with the Worcestershire sauce, sugar, vinegar, lemon juice and water. Add to the frying pan (skillet) and bring to the boil, stirring to mix in any sediment from the bottom of the pan.

Return the pork cubes to the pan and stir in the apricots. Cover and simmer for 15 minutes or until the pork is cooked through and tender. Serve hot.
Serves 4

Sausages in Curry Sauce

Metric/Imperial
3 tablespoons oil
500 g/1 lb pork sausages
1 onion, chopped
1½ tablespoons curry powder
4 teaspoons gravy powder
600 ml/1 pint water
50 g/2 oz sultanas
1 tablespoon chutney
2 teaspoons tomato purée
salt and pepper

American
3 tablespoons oil
1 lb pork sausages
1 onion, chopped
1½ tablespoons curry powder
4 teaspoons gravy powder
2½ cups water
⅓ cup golden raisins
1 tablespoon chutney
2 teaspoons tomato paste
salt and pepper

Heat the oil in a frying pan (skillet). Add the sausages and brown on all sides. Remove from the pan.

Add the onion to the pan and fry until softened. Pour off all but about 1 tablespoon of the fat from the pan, then stir in the curry powder and cook for 2 minutes. Dissolve the gravy powder in a little of the water and add to the pan with the remaining water, the sultanas (raisins), chutney, tomato purée (paste) and salt and pepper to taste. Bring to the boil, stirring.

Cut the sausages into chunks and return to the pan. Simmer for 15 minutes, stirring occasionally. Serve hot.
Serves 4

Stir-Fried Pork with Bean Sprouts

Metric/Imperial
350 g/12 oz lean pork, shredded
2 tablespoons soy sauce
1 teaspoon dry sherry
2 teaspoons cornflour
3 tablespoons oil
2 spring onions, shredded
1 slice of fresh root ginger,
    peeled and shredded
1 teaspoon salt
225 g/8 oz bean sprouts
1 small leek, shredded

American
¾ lb lean pork, shredded
2 tablespoons soy sauce
1 teaspoon dry sherry
2 teaspoons cornstarch
3 tablespoons oil
2 scallions, shredded
1 slice of fresh ginger root,
    peeled and shredded
1 teaspoon salt
½ lb bean sprouts
1 small leek, shredded

Put the pork in a bowl with the soy sauce, sherry and cornflour (cornstarch) and mix well. Leave to marinate for about 20 minutes.

Heat 1 tablespoon of the oil in a wok or frying pan (skillet). Add the spring onions (scallions), ginger and pork and stir-fry until the pork changes colour. Remove the pork with a slotted spoon.

Heat the remaining oil in the wok or frying pan (skillet). Add the salt, then the bean sprouts and leek. Stir-fry for about 1 minute. Return the pork to the pan and stir-fry for a further 1 minute. Serve hot.
Serves 4

Apricot-Stuffed Gammon (Ham)

Metric/Imperial
1 × 400 g/14 oz can apricot halves
50 g/2 oz fresh breadcrumbs
3 tablespoons chopped parsley
salt and pepper
4 gammon steaks

American
1 × 16 oz can apricot halves
1 cup soft bread crumbs
3 tablespoons chopped parsley
salt and pepper
4 ham steaks

Drain the apricots, reserving the syrup. Chop the apricots and mix with the breadcrumbs, parsley and salt and pepper to taste. Divide the mixture between the gammon (ham) steaks and fold them over in half. Secure with wooden cocktail sticks and place in an ovenproof dish.

Pour 120 ml/4 fl oz (½ cup) of the reserved apricot syrup over the gammon (ham). Cover and cook in a preheated moderate oven (180°C/350°F, Gas Mark 4) for 20 minutes or until the gammon (ham) is tender. Serve hot.
Serves 4

Chinese-Style Porkburgers

Metric/Imperial
500 g/1 lb minced pork
50 g/2 oz fresh breadcrumbs
1 egg
salt and pepper
3 tablespoons oil
Sauce:
2 tablespoons cornflour
5 tablespoons vinegar
300 ml/½ pint water
1 tablespoon soy sauce
75 g/3 oz sugar
½ green pepper, cored, seeded
    and cut into strips
½ red pepper, cored, seeded
    and cut into strips
2 carrots, cut into strips
2 slices of canned pineapple,
    chopped

American
1 lb ground pork
1 cup soft bread crumbs
1 egg
salt and pepper
3 tablespoons oil
Sauce:
2 tablespoons cornstarch
5 tablespoons vinegar
1¼ cups water
1 tablespoon soy sauce
6 tablespoons sugar
½ green pepper, seeded
    and cut into strips
½ red pepper, seeded
    and cut into strips
2 carrots, cut into strips
2 slices of canned pineapple,
    chopped

Dissolve the cornflour (cornstarch) in the vinegar in a saucepan, then stir in the water, soy sauce and sugar. Bring to the boil, stirring to dissolve the sugar, and simmer until thickened. Add the vegetables and pineapple and simmer for 10 minutes.

Meanwhile mix together the pork, breadcrumbs, egg and salt and pepper to taste. Shape into eight patties. Heat the oil in a frying pan (skillet), add the patties and fry for about 5 minutes on each side.

Arrange the porkburgers on a warmed serving dish and pour over the sauce.
Serves 4

Quick Cassoulet

Metric/Imperial
2 tablespoons oil
1 large onion, sliced
1 garlic clove, crushed
500 g/1 lb chipolata sausages
100 g/4 oz streaky bacon,
  derinded and chopped
1 × 425 g/15 oz can red
  kidney beans, drained
150 ml/¼ pint beef stock
salt and pepper
8 thin slices of French bread
50 g/2 oz Cheddar cheese,
  grated

American
2 tablespoons oil
1 large onion, sliced
1 garlic clove, crushed
1 lb pork link sausages
¼ lb slab bacon, chopped
1 × 16 oz can red kidney beans,
  drained
⅔ cup beef stock or broth
salt and pepper
8 thin slices of French bread
½ cup grated Cheddar cheese

Heat the oil in a flameproof casserole. Add the onion and garlic and fry until softened. Add the sausages and bacon and fry until the sausages are browned on all sides. Stir in the beans, stock and salt and pepper to taste.

Cover the casserole and cook in a preheated moderate oven (180°C/350°F, Gas Mark 4) for 40 minutes.

Remove the lid. Arrange the bread slices over the sausage mixture to cover it and sprinkle the cheese on top. Return to the oven and cook, uncovered, for a further 10 to 15 minutes or until the cheese has melted and is golden brown. Serve hot.
Serves 4

Country Grill (Broil)

Metric/Imperial
4 slices of lamb's liver
4 lambs' kidneys, cored and
  split open lengthways
3 tablespoons oil
salt and pepper
4 tomatoes, halved
8 large mushrooms

American
4 slices of lamb's liver
4 lambs' kidneys, cored and
  split open lengthwise
3 tablespoons oil
salt and pepper
4 tomatoes, halved
8 large mushrooms

Place the liver in the centre of the grill (broiler) pan and surround with the kidneys. Brush with a little oil. Place under a preheated grill (broiler) and cook for about 3 minutes or until the liver and kidneys change colour.

Turn the liver and kidneys over and sprinkle with salt and pepper. Place the tomatoes, cut sides up, and mushrooms, caps up, around the liver and kidneys and brush with oil.

Return to the grill (broiler) and cook for a further 5 minutes. Serve hot.
Serves 4

Liver with Orange

Metric/Imperial
25 g/1 oz butter or margarine
1 onion, chopped
500 g/1 lb lamb's liver,
  thinly sliced
300 ml/½ pint beef stock
grated rind and juice of
  1 large orange
salt and pepper
1 orange, peeled and sliced

American
2 tablespoons butter or
  margarine
1 onion, chopped
1 lb lamb's liver, thinly sliced
1¼ cups beef stock or broth
grated rind and juice of
  1 large orange
salt and pepper
1 orange, peeled and sliced

Melt the butter or margarine in a frying pan (skillet). Add the onion and fry until softened. Add the liver slices, a few at a time, and brown on both sides. Remove the liver slices from the pan as they brown.

Add the stock, orange rind and juice and salt and pepper to taste to the pan and bring to the boil. Simmer for 5 minutes.

Return the liver slices to the pan and add the orange slices. Simmer for a further 2 to 5 minutes or until the liver is cooked to your taste. Serve hot.
Serves 4

Liver Paupiettes

Metric/Imperial
8 back bacon rashers, derinded
8 thin slices of calves' liver
juice of 1 lemon
salt and pepper
8 fresh thyme sprigs
50 g/2 oz butter or margarine
1 tablespoon plain flour
120 ml/4 fl oz Marsala
1 × 225 g/8 oz can tomatoes,
  drained and chopped
4 tablespoons beef stock

American
8 thin slices of Canadian bacon
8 thin slices of calves' liver
juice of 1 lemon
salt and pepper
8 fresh thyme sprigs
4 tablespoons butter or
  margarine
1 tablespoon all-purpose flour
½ cup Marsala
1 × 8 oz can tomatoes,
  drained and chopped
¼ cup beef stock or broth

Place a bacon rasher (slice) on each slice of liver. Sprinkle with the lemon juice and salt and pepper to taste and place a thyme sprig on top. Roll up and secure with string or wooden cocktail sticks.

Melt the butter or margarine in a frying pan (skillet). Add the liver rolls and fry until browned on all sides. Stir the flour into the fat in the pan, then stir in the Marsala, tomatoes and stock. Bring to the boil, cover and simmer for about 10 minutes or until the liver rolls are cooked through. Serve hot.
Serves 4

Liver with Herbs

Metric/Imperial
500 g/1 lb lamb's liver, sliced
25 g/1 oz butter or margarine,
  melted
1 tablespoon lemon juice
salt and pepper
2 teaspoons chopped parsley
2 teaspoons chopped fresh
  thyme
2 teaspoons chopped chives

American
1 lb lamb's liver, sliced
2 tablespoons butter or
  margarine, melted
1 tablespoon lemon juice
salt and pepper
2 teaspoons chopped parsley
2 teaspoons chopped fresh
  thyme
2 teaspoons chopped chives

Arrange the liver on the grill (broiler) rack and brush with some of the melted butter or margarine. Place under a preheated grill (broiler) and cook for 3 to 4 minutes on each side, brushing with the remaining butter or margarine when you turn the liver slices.

Arrange the liver on a warmed serving plate. Sprinkle over the lemon juice and salt and pepper to taste, then scatter over the herbs. Serve hot.
Serves 4

Italian-Style Liver

Metric/Imperial
2 tablespoons olive oil
1 onion, sliced
1 green pepper, cored,
  seeded and sliced
500 g/1 lb lamb's liver,
  cut into strips
2 tablespoons plain flour
1 × 400 g/14 oz can tomatoes
1 tablespoon Worcestershire
  sauce
½ teaspoon dried oregano
salt and pepper
100 g/4 oz pasta shells

American
2 tablespoons olive oil
1 onion, sliced
1 green pepper, seeded
  and sliced
1 lb lamb's liver, cut into
  strips
2 tablespoons all-purpose flour
1 × 16 oz can tomatoes
1 tablespoon Worcestershire
  sauce
½ teaspoon dried oregano
salt and pepper
¼ lb pasta shells

Heat the oil in a large frying pan (skillet). Add the onion and green pepper and fry until the onion is softened. Coat the liver strips with the flour and add to the pan. Fry until browned on all sides. Stir in the tomatoes with their juice, Worcestershire sauce, oregano and salt and pepper to taste. Cover and cook gently for 10 to 15 minutes.

Meanwhile cook the pasta shells in boiling salted water until just tender. Drain well, then add to the frying pan (skillet). Stir to mix with the liver and vegetables. Serve hot.
Serves 4

Liver and Bacon Hotpot

Metric/Imperial
1 tablespoon oil
4 streaky bacon rashers, derinded
  and chopped
100 g/4 oz button mushrooms
25 g/1 oz plain flour
salt and pepper
350 g/12 oz lamb's liver,
  sliced
300 ml/½ pint beef stock
225 g/8 oz tomatoes, skinned
  and chopped
2 tablespoons chutney

American
1 tablespoon oil
4 bacon slices, chopped
¼ lb button mushrooms
¼ cup all-purpose flour
salt and pepper
¾ lb lamb's liver, sliced
1¼ cups beef stock or broth
1 cup skinned and chopped
  tomatoes
2 tablespoons chutney

Heat the oil in a frying pan (skillet). Add the bacon and mushrooms and
fry for 5 minutes.
  Season the flour with salt and pepper and use to coat the liver slices.
Add to the pan and brown on both sides. Stir in the beef stock, chopped
tomatoes and chutney and bring to the boil. Cover and simmer for 20
minutes. Serve hot.
Serves 4

Tagliatelle with Herby Liver Sauce

Metric/Imperial
3 tablespoons oil
1 onion, chopped
1 garlic clove, crushed
350 g/12 oz chicken livers,
  chopped
1 tablespoon chopped parsley
1 tablespoon chopped fresh
  thyme
1 tablespoon chopped fresh
  marjoram
175 g/6 oz mushrooms, sliced
150 ml/¼ pint red wine
150 ml/¼ pint chicken stock
salt and pepper
500 g/1 lb tagliatelle

American
3 tablespoons oil
1 onion, chopped
1 garlic clove, crushed
¾ lb chicken livers, chopped
1 tablespoon chopped parsley
1 tablespoon chopped fresh
  thyme
1 tablespoon chopped fresh
  marjoram
1½ cups sliced mushrooms
⅔ cup red wine
⅔ cup chicken stock or broth
salt and pepper
1 lb tagliatelle

Heat the oil in a saucepan. Add the onion and garlic and fry until softened.
Add the chicken livers and fry until lightly browned. Stir in the herbs,
mushrooms, wine, stock and salt and pepper to taste and bring to the
boil. Cover and simmer for 15 minutes.
  Meanwhile cook the tagliatelle in boiling salted water until just tender.
Drain well and return to the pan. Add the liver sauce and toss well
together. Serve hot.
Serves 4

Stir-Fried Liver with Spinach

Metric/Imperial	American
350 g/12 oz pig's liver, thinly sliced	¾ lb pork liver, thinly sliced
2 tablespoons cornflour	2 tablespoons cornstarch
4 tablespoons oil	¼ cup oil
500 g/1 lb fresh spinach	1 lb fresh spinach
1 teaspoon salt	1 teaspoon salt
2 slices of fresh root ginger, peeled	2 slices of fresh ginger root, peeled
1 tablespoon soy sauce	1 tablespoon soy sauce
1 tablespoon dry sherry	1 tablespoon dry sherry
shredded spring onions to garnish	shredded scallions for garnish

Blanch the liver in boiling water for 30 seconds, then drain. Coat with the cornflour (cornstarch).

Heat 2 tablespoons of the oil in a wok or frying pan (skillet). Add the spinach and salt and stir-fry for 2 minutes or until the spinach is just tender. Arrange around the edge of a warmed serving dish and keep hot.

Heat the remaining oil in the wok or frying pan (skillet). Add the ginger, liver, soy sauce and sherry and stir-fry for 1 minute. Pour into the centre of the spinach ring. Garnish with spring onions (scallions) and serve hot.
Serves 4

Liver Stroganoff

Metric/Imperial	American
40 g/1½ oz butter or margarine	3 tablespoons butter or margarine
350 g/12 oz lamb's liver, cut into short narrow strips	¾ lb lamb's liver, cut into short narrow strips
1 onion, thinly sliced	1 onion, thinly sliced
1 green pepper, cored, seeded and thinly sliced	1 green pepper, seeded and thinly sliced
100 g/4 oz mushrooms, sliced	1 cup sliced mushrooms
1 tablespoon plain flour	1 tablespoon all-purpose flour
300 ml/½ pint beef stock	1¼ cups beef stock or broth
1 tablespoon tomato purée	1 tablespoon tomato paste
½ teaspoon sugar	½ teaspoon sugar
salt and pepper	salt and pepper
4 tablespoons single cream	¼ cup light cream

Melt the butter or margarine in a frying pan (skillet). Add the liver and fry until browned all over. Remove from pan with a slotted spoon.

Add the onion, green pepper and mushrooms to the pan and fry until the onion is softened. Stir in the flour, then stir in the stock, tomato purée (paste), sugar and salt and pepper to taste. Bring to the boil, stirring. Simmer for 10 minutes.

Return the liver to the pan and simmer for a further 5 minutes. Stir in the cream and serve hot.
Serves 4

Liver in Italian Sauce

Metric/Imperial	American
25 g/1 oz plain flour	¼ cup all-purpose flour
salt and pepper	salt and pepper
500 g/1 lb lamb's liver, thinly sliced	1 lb lamb's liver, thinly sliced
25 g/1 oz butter	2 tablespoons butter
1 tablespoon olive oil	1 tablespoon olive oil
2 onions, sliced	2 onions, sliced
150 ml/¼ pint beef stock	⅔ cup beef stock or broth
2 tablespoons tomato purée	2 tablespoons tomato paste
1 garlic clove, crushed	1 garlic clove, crushed
1 teaspoon dried basil	1 teaspoon dried basil
150 ml/¼ pint single cream	⅔ cup light cream

Mix the flour with salt and pepper and use to coat the liver slices. Melt the butter with the oil in a frying pan (skillet). Add the liver and fry for about 2 minutes on each side or until golden brown. Remove from the pan with a slotted spoon.

Add the onions to the pan and fry until golden. Stir in the stock, tomato purée (paste), garlic and basil. Bring to the boil. Return the liver to the pan, cover and simmer for 25 minutes.

Transfer the liver to a warm serving dish and keep hot.

Add the cream to the liquid in the pan and heat through gently. Taste and adjust the seasoning, then pour over the liver. Serve hot.
Serves 4

Devilled Kidneys

Metric/Imperial	American
50 g/2 oz butter or margarine	4 tablespoons butter or margarine
1 onion, chopped	1 onion, chopped
2 carrots, diced	2 carrots, diced
3 streaky bacon rashers, derinded and chopped	3 bacon slices, chopped
8 lambs' kidneys, skinned, halved and cored	8 lamb kidneys, skinned, halved and cored
3 tablespoons plain flour	3 tablespoons all-purpose flour
450 ml/¾ pint beef stock	2 cups beef stock or broth
1 tablespoon French mustard	1 tablespoon Dijon-style mustard
4 tablespoons tomato ketchup	¼ cup tomato ketchup
1 tablespoon Worcestershire sauce	1 tablespoon Worcestershire sauce
100 g/4 oz mushrooms, quartered	1 cup quartered mushrooms
salt and pepper	salt and pepper

Melt the butter or margarine in a saucepan. Add the onion, carrots and bacon and fry until golden brown. Add the kidneys and brown on all sides. Stir in the flour and cook for 2 minutes, then gradually stir in the stock. Add remaining ingredients with salt and pepper to taste and bring to the boil, stirring. Cover and simmer for 15 minutes until kidneys are tender.
Serves 4

Kidney and Mushroom Supper

Metric/Imperial
25 g/1 oz butter or margarine
1 onion, chopped
1 garlic clove, crushed
1 carrot, grated
100 g/4 oz button mushrooms
8 lambs' kidneys, cored and
  halved lengthways
2 tablespoons plain flour
2 teaspoons tomato purée
150 ml/¼ pint red wine
300 ml/½ pint beef stock
salt and pepper

American
2 tablespoons butter or
  margarine
1 onion, chopped
1 garlic clove, crushed
1 carrot, grated
¼ lb button mushrooms
8 lamb kidneys, cored and
  halved lengthwise
2 tablespoons all-purpose flour
2 teaspoons tomato paste
⅔ cup red wine
1¼ cups beef stock or broth
salt and pepper

Melt the butter or margarine in a frying pan (skillet). Add the onion, garlic and carrot and fry until the onion is softened. Add the mushrooms and kidneys and fry until the kidneys are browned all over. Using a slotted spoon, transfer the kidneys and vegetables to a casserole.

Stir the flour into the fat in the frying pan (skillet) and cook for 1 minute. Add the tomato purée (paste), wine, stock and salt and pepper to taste and bring to the boil, stirring well. Pour into the casserole.

Cover and cook the dish in a preheated moderate oven (180°C/350°F, Gas Mark 4) for 20 minutes. Serve hot.
Serves 4

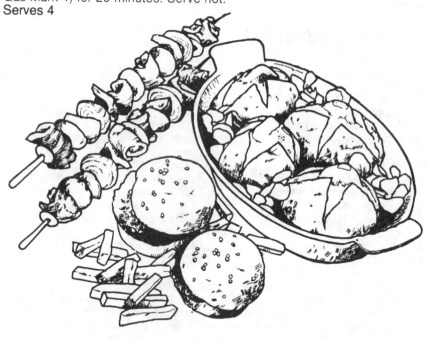

Kidneys with Mustard Sauce

Metric/Imperial
40 g/1½ oz butter or margarine
8 lambs' kidneys, skinned,
   halved and cored
1 onion, sliced
225 g/8 oz mushrooms, sliced
1 tablespoon French mustard
4 tablespoons milk
4 tablespoons single cream
¼ teaspoon grated nutmeg
salt and pepper

American
3 tablespoons butter or
   margarine
8 lamb kidneys, skinned,
   halved and cored
1 onion, sliced
½ lb mushrooms, sliced
1 tablespoon Dijon-style mustard
¼ cup milk
¼ cup light cream
¼ teaspoon grated nutmeg
salt and pepper

Melt the butter or margarine in a frying pan (skillet). Add the kidneys and cook until browned on all sides and tender. Remove from the pan.

Add the onion and mushrooms to the pan and fry until the onion is softened. Stir in the mustard, milk, cream, nutmeg and salt and pepper to taste. Return the kidneys to the pan and stir to mix with the sauce. Reheat gently and serve hot.
Serves 4

Spaghetti with Kidney and Liver

Metric/Imperial
2 tablespoons oil
1 onion, chopped
1 garlic clove, crushed
4 lambs' kidneys, skinned,
   cored and sliced
2 chicken livers, chopped
1 tablespoon plain flour
250 ml/8 fl oz chicken stock
100 g/4 oz mushrooms, sliced
1 × 225 g/8 oz can tomatoes,
   drained and chopped
1 tablespoon chopped parsley
150 ml/¼ pint red wine
salt and pepper
500 g/1 lb spaghetti

American
2 tablespoons oil
1 onion, chopped
1 garlic clove, crushed
4 lamb kidneys, skinned,
   cored and sliced
2 chicken livers, chopped
1 tablespoon all-purpose flour
1 cup chicken stock or broth
1 cup sliced mushrooms
1 × 8 oz can tomatoes, drained
   and chopped
1 tablespoon chopped parsley
⅔ cup red wine
salt and pepper
1 lb spaghetti

Heat the oil in a saucepan. Add the onion and garlic and fry until softened. Add the kidneys and livers and fry for a further 5 minutes. Stir in the flour and cook for 1 minute, then gradually stir in the stock. Bring to the boil, stirring. Add the mushrooms, tomatoes, parsley, wine and salt and pepper to taste and mix well. Cover and simmer for 20 minutes.

Meanwhile cook the spaghetti in boiling salted water until just tender. Drain well and spread out on a warmed serving dish. Pour over the kidney and liver sauce and serve hot.
Serves 4 to 6

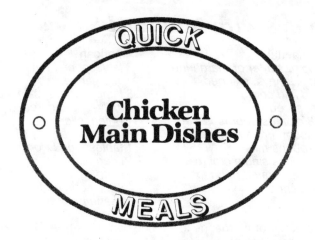

Quick Mandarin Barbecued Chicken

Metric/Imperial	American
25 g/1 oz butter or margarine	2 tablespoons butter or margarine
2 tablespoons oil	2 tablespoons oil
4 chicken quarters	1 × 3½-4 lb broiler/fryer, quartered
450 ml/¾ pint bottled or canned barbecue sauce	2 cups bottled barbecue sauce
1 × 300 g/11 oz can mandarin oranges	1 × 11 oz can mandarin oranges
2 tablespoons plain flour	2 tablespoons all-purpose flour
salt and pepper	salt and pepper

Melt the butter or margarine with the oil in a large frying pan (skillet). Add the chicken pieces and brown on all sides. Pour over the barbecue sauce and bring to the boil. Cover and simmer for 40 minutes or until the chicken is cooked through.

Transfer the chicken pieces to a warmed serving dish and keep hot.

Drain the mandarin oranges, reserving the syrup. Blend the flour with a little of the syrup, then add to the sauce in the pan, with the remaining syrup. Bring to the boil, stirring, and simmer until thickened. Stir in the mandarin orange segments and heat through. Add salt and pepper to taste.

Pour the sauce over the chicken and serve hot.

Serves 4

Devilled Chicken

Metric/Imperial
4 chicken quarters
50 g/2 oz butter or margarine,
  melted
salt and pepper
Sauce:.
75 g/3 oz butter or margarine
1 teaspoon made English
  mustard
½ teaspoon paprika
pinch of cayenne pepper
1 teaspoon vinegar
½ teaspoon salt

American
1 × 3 lb broiler/fryer, quartered
4 tablespoons butter or
  margarine, melted
salt and pepper
Sauce:
6 tablespoons butter or
  margarine
1 teaspoon prepared English
  mustard
½ teaspoon paprika
pinch of cayenne
1 teaspoon vinegar
½ teaspoon salt

Brush the chicken pieces with the melted butter or margarine and season with salt and pepper. Grill (broil) for about 20 minutes or until cooked through and golden brown on all sides. Baste with the melted butter or margarine occasionally.

Meanwhile make the sauce. Cream the butter or margarine with the remaining sauce ingredients until well combined. Spread the sauce over the chicken and continue grilling (broiling) until golden brown.
Serves 4

Stir-Fried Chicken with Noodles

Metric/Imperial
225 g/8 oz vermicelli noodles
chicken stock
4 tablespoons oil
6 spring onions, chopped
2 carrots, grated
50 g/2 oz button mushrooms,
  sliced
225 g/8 oz cooked chicken
  meat, diced
50 g/2 oz flaked almonds
2 tablespoons soy sauce
salt and pepper

American
½ lb vermicelli noodles
chicken stock or broth
¼ cup oil
6 scallions, chopped
2 carrots, grated
½ cup sliced mushrooms
1½ cups diced cooked chicken
  meat
½ cup slivered almonds
2 tablespoons soy sauce
salt and pepper

Cook the vermicelli in boiling chicken stock until tender.

Meanwhile heat the oil in a wok or large frying pan (skillet). Add the spring onions (scallions), carrots, mushrooms, chicken and almonds and stir-fry for 4 minutes.

Drain the vermicelli, then stir into the chicken mixture with the soy sauce and salt and pepper to taste. Stir-fry for a further 4 minutes. Serve hot.
Serves 4

Avocado Coronation Chicken

Metric/Imperial
500 g/1 lb long-grain rice
salt and pepper
1 tablespoon oil
1 onion, chopped
2 teaspoons curry powder
1 teaspoon tomato purée
150 ml/¼ pint dry red wine
150 ml/¼ pint chicken stock
1 bay leaf
1 tablespoon apricot jam,
   sieved
450 ml/¾ pint mayonnaise
100 g/4 oz frozen sweetcorn
   kernels, cooked
500 g/1 lb cooked chicken meat,
   diced
2 ripe avocados, peeled, stoned
   and sliced
juice of 1 lemon

American
2¼ cups rice
salt and pepper
1 tablespoon oil
1 onion, chopped
2 teaspoons curry powder
1 teaspoon tomato paste
⅔ cup dry red wine
⅔ cup chicken stock or broth
1 bay leaf
1 tablespoon apricot jam,
   strained
2 cups mayonnaise
¾ cup frozen whole kernel corn,
   cooked
2 cups diced cooked chicken meat
2 ripe avocados, peeled, seeded
   and sliced
juice of 1 lemon

Cook the rice in boiling salted water for about 20 minutes or until tender.

Meanwhile heat the oil in another saucepan. Add the onion and fry until softened. Stir in the curry powder and cook for a further 2 minutes. Add the tomato purée (paste), red wine, stock, bay leaf and salt and pepper to taste and bring to the boil, stirring well. Simmer for 10 minutes.

Remove the pan from the heat and cool. Discard the bay leaf, then stir in the jam and mayonnaise.

Drain the rice, if necessary, and cool.

Mix the rice with the corn and pile in a ring around the edge of a serving platter. Place the chicken in the centre and pour over the mayonnaise sauce. Coat the avocado slices with lemon juice to prevent discoloration, then arrange around the chicken. Chill lightly before serving.

Serves 6

Burgundy Chicken Sandwiches

Metric/Imperial	American
225 g/8 oz minced chicken	1 cup ground chicken
1 onion, finely chopped	1 onion, finely chopped
150 ml/¼ pint red wine	⅔ cup red wine
5 eggs	5 eggs
50 g/2 oz cornflakes, crushed	2 cups crushed cornflakes
salt and pepper	salt and pepper
3 tablespoons oil	3 tablespoons oil
25 g/1 oz butter or margarine	2 tablespoons butter or margarine
4 hamburger buns, split in half	4 hamburger buns, split in half

Mix together the chicken, onion, wine, one of the eggs, the cornflakes and salt and pepper to taste. Shape into four patties.

Heat the oil in a frying pan (skillet), add the patties and fry for 4 to 5 minutes on each side. Meanwhile, fry the remaining eggs in the butter or margarine.

Place a burger in each bun and top with the fried eggs.
Serves 4

Chicken Kebabs

Metric/Imperial	American
500 g/1 lb minced chicken	2 cups ground chicken
3 tablespoons fresh breadcrumbs	3 tablespoons soft bread crumbs
1 garlic clove, crushed	1 garlic clove, crushed
1 tablespoon chopped parsley	1 tablespoon chopped parsley
1 egg	1 egg
salt and pepper	salt and pepper
8 bacon rashers, derinded and cut into squares	8 bacon slices, cut into squares
2 pears, cored and cut into chunks	2 pears, cored and cut into chunks
4 courgettes, thickly sliced	4 zucchini, thickly sliced
1 tablespoon oil	1 tablespoon oil

Mix together the chicken, breadcrumbs, garlic, parsley, egg and salt and pepper to taste. Shape into 16 small sausages. Thread onto skewers alternating with the bacon squares, pear chunks and courgette (zucchini) slices. Brush with the oil.

Grill (broil) the kebabs, turning occasionally, for about 15 minutes. Serve hot.
Serves 4

Quick-Fried Chicken

Metric/Imperial	American
1 large chicken breast, skinned, boned and thinly sliced	1 large chicken breast, skinned, boned and thinly sliced
1-2 spring onions, chopped	1-2 scallions, chopped
1 slice of fresh root ginger, peeled and finely chopped	1 slice of fresh ginger root, peeled and finely chopped
1 tablespoon dry sherry	1 tablespoon dry sherry
2 teaspoons salt	2 teaspoons salt
1 egg, beaten	1 egg, beaten
2 teaspoons cornflour	2 teaspoons cornstarch
3 tablespoons oil	3 tablespoons oil
lettuce leaves	lettuce leaves
Sauce:	Sauce:
1 tablespoon tomato purée	1 tablespoon tomato paste
1 teaspoon caster sugar	1 teaspoon sugar
1 teaspoon sesame seed oil	1 teaspoon sesame seed oil
1 tablespoon water	1 tablespoon water

Place the chicken in a bowl with the spring onions (scallions), ginger, sherry and salt and mix well. Leave to marinate for about 20 minutes.

Stir the egg into the chicken mixture, then sprinkle over the cornflour (cornstarch) and toss to coat thoroughly.

Heat the oil in a wok or frying pan (skillet). Add the chicken mixture and fry until tender and golden on all sides. Remove from the pan with a slotted spoon and arrange on a bed of lettuce leaves on a serving platter. Keep warm.

Mix together the ingredients for the sauce. Add to the wok or frying pan (skillet) and bring to the boil, stirring. Pour the sauce over the chicken and serve hot.
Serves 2

Calcutta Chicken Burgers

Metric/Imperial	American
500 g/1 lb minced chicken	2 cups ground chicken
1 onion, grated	1 onion, grated
1 garlic clove, crushed	1 garlic clove, crushed
2 teaspoons grated fresh root ginger	2 teaspoons grated fresh ginger root
2 tablespoons lemon juice	2 tablespoons lemon juice
1 teaspoon ground coriander	1 teaspoon ground coriander
½ teaspoon ground cumin	½ teaspoon ground cumin
3 tablespoons plain yogurt	3 tablespoons plain yogurt
3 tablespoons fresh breadcrumbs	3 tablespoons soft bread crumbs
salt and pepper	salt and pepper

Mix together all the ingredients with salt and pepper to taste. Shape into eight patties. Grill (broil) the patties for 4 to 5 minutes on each side. Serve with pitta bread.
Serves 4

Dijon Chicken

Metric/Imperial
4 chicken quarters
75 g/3 oz butter or margarine,
   melted
1 tablespoon oil
3 tablespoons Dijon mustard
1 spring onion, finely chopped
¼ teaspoon dried thyme
pinch of cayenne pepper
salt and pepper

American
1 × 3½-4 lb broiler/fryer, cut up
6 tablespoons butter or
   margarine, melted
1 tablespoon oil
3 tablespoons Dijon mustard
1 scallion, finely chopped
¼ teaspoon dried thyme
pinch of cayenne
salt and pepper

Place the chicken pieces on the rack in the grill (broiler) pan, skin side up. Mix the butter or margarine with the oil and brush some of this mixture over the chicken. Place under a preheated grill (broiler) and cook for 10 minutes on each side, basting frequently with the butter mixture.

Combine the mustard, spring onion (scallion), thyme, cayenne and salt and pepper to taste. Stir in the remaining butter mixture, a few drops at a time.

Turn the chicken pieces skin side up again and brush with some of the mustard mixture. Continue grilling (broiling) for 10 minutes or until the chicken is golden brown and tender. Brush with the mustard mixture from time to time. Serve hot.
Serves 4

Simple Oven-Barbecued Chicken

Metric/Imperial
4 chicken quarters
75 g/3 oz butter or margarine
1 large onion, chopped
1 × 400 g/14 oz can tomatoes,
   drained and chopped
1 tablespoon brown sugar
4 tablespoons bottled brown
   sauce
salt and pepper

American
1 × 3 lb broiler/fryer,
   quartered
6 tablespoons butter or
   margarine
1 large onion, chopped
1 × 16 oz can tomatoes,
   drained and chopped
1 tablespoon brown sugar
¼ cup bottled steak sauce
salt and pepper

Arrange the chicken pieces in a roasting pan and dot with 50 g/2 oz (4 tablespoons) of the butter or margarine. Cook in a preheated moderately hot oven (200°C/400°F, Gas Mark 6) for 20 minutes.

Meanwhile melt the remaining butter or margarine in a saucepan. Add the onion and fry until softened. Stir in the remaining ingredients with salt and pepper to taste and simmer for 5 minutes.

Pour the sauce over the chicken and cook for a further 20 minutes or until the chicken is cooked through and tender. Baste with the sauce from time to time. Serve hot.
Serves 4

Indian Chicken Kebabs

Metric/Imperial
1 × 1.5 kg/3 lb chicken
150 ml/¼ pint plain yogurt
1 garlic clove, crushed
1 × 2.5 cm/1 inch piece fresh
   root ginger, peeled and
   finely chopped
1 teaspoon ground coriander
1 teaspoon garam masala
2 teaspoons paprika
1 teaspoon chilli powder
juice of 1 lemon

American
1 × 3 lb broiler/fryer
⅔ cup plain yogurt
1 garlic clove, crushed
1 × 1 inch piece fresh ginger
   root, peeled and finely
   chopped
1 teaspoon ground coriander
1 teaspoon garam masala
2 teaspoons paprika
1 teaspoon chili powder
juice of 1 lemon

Remove the skin from the chicken, then take the meat from the bones. Cut the meat into 2.5 cm/1 inch cubes. Mix together the remaining ingredients in a shallow dish. Add the chicken cubes and turn to coat. Cover and leave to marinate in the refrigerator overnight.

The next day, thread the chicken cubes onto skewers. Place under a preheated grill (broiler) and cook for about 10 minutes, turning occasionally, until the chicken is cooked through. Serve hot.
Serves 4 to 6

Chicken à la King

Metric/Imperial
25 g/1 oz butter or margarine
1 onion, finely chopped
100 g/4 oz mushrooms, sliced
2 tablespoons plain flour
450 ml/¾ pint milk
225 g/8 oz cooked chicken
   meat, diced
1 tablespoon chopped pimiento
1 tablespoon sherry
salt and pepper
buttered hot toast to serve

American
2 tablespoons butter or
   margarine
1 onion, finely chopped
1 cup sliced mushrooms
2 tablespoons all-purpose
   flour
2 cups milk
1 cup diced cooked chicken
   meat
1 tablespoon chopped pimiento
1 tablespoon sherry
salt and pepper
buttered hot toast to serve

Melt the butter or margarine in a saucepan. Add the onion and mushrooms and fry until the onion is softened. Stir in the flour and cook for 1 minute, then gradually stir in the milk. Bring to the boil, stirring, and simmer until thickened.

Add the chicken, pimiento, sherry and salt and pepper to taste and cook gently for 5 minutes or until the mixture is piping hot. Serve spooned over hot toast.
Serves 4

Indonesian Chicken Saté

Metric/Imperial	American
1 × 2 kg/4 lb chicken	1 × 4 lb broiler/fryer
2 tablespoons soy sauce	2 tablespoons soy sauce
2 shallots, thinly sliced	2 shallots, thinly sliced
1 garlic clove, crushed	1 garlic clove, crushed
pinch of chilli powder	pinch of chili powder
2 tablespoons lemon juice	2 tablespoons lemon juice

Remove the skin from the chicken, then take the meat from the carcass. Cut the meat into 2.5 cm/1 inch cubes.

Mix together the remaining ingredients in a shallow dish. Add the chicken cubes and turn to coat. Cover and leave to marinate for at least 1 hour.

Thread the chicken cubes onto skewers. Place under a preheated grill (broiler) and cook for 5 to 8 minutes, turning frequently and basting with the marinade. Serve hot.
Serves 4

Variation:

Pork saté: Use 750 g/1½ lb pork fillet, cut into cubes, instead of chicken. Make the marinade with 2 tablespoons soy sauce, 2 crushed garlic cloves, 2 chopped shallots, 1 tablespoon honey, 2 teaspoons five-spice powder and pepper to taste. Marinate for 2 to 3 hours. Thread the pork cubes onto skewers and grill (broil) gently for 15 minutes or until cooked through.

Chicken Fried with Garlic

Metric/Imperial	American
4 chicken breasts, skinned and boned	4 chicken breasts, skinned and boned
3 garlic cloves, crushed	3 garlic cloves, crushed
1 tablespoon freshly ground black pepper	1 tablespoon freshly ground black pepper
2 tablespoons soy sauce	2 tablespoons soy sauce
1 teaspoon caster sugar	1 teaspoon sugar
1 teaspoon salt	1 teaspoon salt
1 teaspoon sesame seed oil	1 teaspoon sesame seed oil
oil for frying	oil for frying

Make shallow cuts in the chicken breasts all over. Mix together the garlic, pepper, soy sauce, sugar, salt and sesame seed oil. Rub into the chicken, then leave to marinate for 2 hours.

Lightly oil a wok or frying pan (skillet) and heat it. Add the chicken breasts and fry for about 4 minutes on each side or until golden brown. Cut each breast in half and return to the pan to fry the newly cut edges until golden brown. Serve hot.
Serves 4

Sweet and Sour Chicken

Metric/Imperial	American
1 × 1.5 kg/3 lb chicken, cut into serving pieces	1 × 3 lb broiler/fryer, cut up
salt	salt
3 tablespoons soy sauce	3 tablespoons soy sauce
2 tablespoons oil	2 tablespoons oil
1 onion, chopped	1 onion, chopped
50 g/2 oz brown sugar	⅓ cup brown sugar
2 tablespoons vinegar	2 tablespoons vinegar
1 tablespoon cornflour	1 tablespoon cornstarch
1 tablespoon tomato purée	1 tablespoon tomato paste
1 tablespoon orange juice	1 tablespoon orange juice
150 ml/¼ pint water	⅔ cup water
100 g/4 oz green beans, sliced	½ cup sliced green beans
2 large carrots, thinly sliced	2 large carrots, thinly sliced

Rub the chicken pieces with salt and 1 tablespoon of the soy sauce. Heat the oil in a frying pan (skillet), add the chicken and brown on all sides. Remove from the pan.

Add the onion to the pan and fry until softened. Mix together the sugar, vinegar, cornflour (cornstarch), tomato purée (paste), orange juice, water and remaining soy sauce. Add to the pan and bring to the boil, stirring. Simmer until thickened.

Add the beans and carrots and return the chicken pieces to the pan. Simmer for a further 15 minutes, stirring occasionally. Serve with plain boiled rice.
Serves 4

Chicken and Vegetable Parcels

Metric/Imperial	American
2 onions, thinly sliced into rings	2 onions, thinly sliced into rings
2 celery sticks, chopped	2 celery stalks, chopped
2 large carrots, thinly sliced	2 large carrots, thinly sliced
4 chicken quarters	1 × 3 lb broiler/fryer, quartered
1 teaspoon dried tarragon	1 teaspoon dried tarragon
salt and pepper	salt and pepper
150 ml/¼ pint red wine	⅔ cup red wine

Divide the onions, celery and carrots between four sheets of foil. Place the chicken pieces on the vegetables and sprinkle with the tarragon and salt and pepper to taste. Add the wine. Wrap the foil loosely around the chicken, sealing the edges well, and place the parcels on a baking sheet.

Cook in a preheated moderately hot oven (190°C/375°F, Gas Mark 5) for 45 minutes, opening the parcels about 10 minutes before the end of the cooking time to allow the chicken to brown. Serve hot.
Serves 4

Chicken Korma

Metric/Imperial	American
2 tablespoons oil	2 tablespoons oil
2 onions, thinly sliced	2 onions, thinly sliced
2 green chillies (optional)	2 green chili peppers (optional)
1 tablespoon ground cumin	1 tablespoon ground cumin
1 teaspoon ground coriander	1 teaspoon ground coriander
½ teaspoon ground turmeric	½ teaspoon ground turmeric
½ teaspoon ground ginger	½ teaspoon ground ginger
½ teaspoon ground fenugreek	½ teaspoon ground fenugreek
1 tablespoon desiccated coconut	1 tablespoon shredded coconut
2 cardamom pods, crushed	2 cardamom pods, crushed
750 g/1½ lb chicken meat, cut into 2.5 cm/1 inch pieces	1½ lb chicken meat, cut into 1 inch pieces (about 4 cups)
300 ml/½ pint plain yogurt	1¼ cups plain yogurt
salt	salt

Heat the oil in a saucepan. Add the onions and whole chillies (chili peppers), if using, and fry until the onions are lightly browned. Stir in the cumin, coriander, turmeric, ginger, fenugreek and coconut and fry, stirring, until the spices darken.

Add the cardamom pods, chicken, about half the yogurt and salt to taste. Simmer, stirring occasionally, for 15 minutes or until the chicken is cooked. Add a little water if the mixture becomes too dry.

Stir in the remaining yogurt and heat through, then serve hot.
Serves 4

Chicken with Chinese Sauce

Metric/Imperial	American
50 g/2 oz butter or margarine	4 tablespoons butter or margarine
4 chicken portions	1 × 3 lb broiler/fryer, cut up
3 tablespoons cornflour	3 tablespoons cornstarch
4 tablespoons brown sugar	¼ cup firmly packed brown sugar
150 ml/¼ pint malt vinegar	⅔ cup malt vinegar
300 ml/½ pint chicken stock	1¼ cups chicken stock or broth
1 tablespoon soy sauce	1 tablespoon soy sauce
4 tablespoons tomato ketchup	¼ cup tomato ketchup
1 × 425 g/15 oz can pineapple chunks, drained	1 × 16 oz can pineapple chunks, drained
salt and pepper	salt and pepper

Melt the butter or margarine in a frying pan (skillet). Add the chicken and cook for 12 minutes on each side or until golden and cooked.

Meanwhile combine the cornflour (cornstarch), sugar, vinegar, stock, soy sauce and ketchup in a saucepan. Bring to the boil, stirring, and simmer until thickened. Stir in the pineapple and salt and pepper to taste and heat through. Serve the chicken with the sauce spooned over.
Serves 4

Chicken Patties in Mushroom Sauce

Metric/Imperial	American
750 g/1½ lb minced chicken	3 cups ground chicken
50 g/2 oz fresh breadcrumbs	1 cup soft bread crumbs
1 onion, grated	1 onion, grated
1 egg	1 egg
salt and pepper	salt and pepper
3 tablespoons oil	3 tablespoons oil
Sauce:	Sauce:
1 onion, sliced	1 onion, sliced
100 g/4 oz mushrooms, sliced	1 cup sliced mushrooms
1 tablespoon plain flour	1 tablespoon all-purpose flour
300 ml/½ pint chicken stock	1¼ cups chicken stock or broth
1 tablespoon tomato purée	1 tablespoon tomato paste

Mix together the chicken, half the breadcrumbs, the onion, egg and salt and pepper to taste. Shape into eight patties and coat with the remaining breadcrumbs.

Heat the oil in a frying pan (skillet), add the patties and fry for about 7 minutes on each side. Transfer to an ovenproof dish.

Add the onion to the pan and fry until softened. Add the mushrooms and fry for a further 2 minutes. Stir in the flour, then gradually stir in the stock and tomato purée (paste). Bring to the boil, stirring. Pour the sauce over the burgers.

Cook in a preheated moderate oven (180°C/350°F, Gas Mark 4) for 30 minutes.
Serves 4

Asparagus Chicken Pie

Metric/Imperial	American
1 × 50 g/2 oz packet dry asparagus soup mix	1 × 11½ oz can condensed asparagus soup
450 ml/¾ pint water	milk or water
350 g/12 oz cooked chicken meat, diced	2 cups diced cooked chicken meat
50 g/2 oz mushrooms, sliced	½ cup sliced mushrooms
salt and pepper	salt and pepper
225 g/8 oz frozen puff pastry, thawed	½ lb frozen puff pastry, thawed
beaten egg to glaze	beaten egg to glaze

Make up the asparagus soup with the water (or milk) according to the instructions on the packet (can). Bring to the boil, stirring. Add the chicken, mushrooms and salt and pepper to taste and mix well. Pour into a 1.2 litre/2 pint (5 cup) pie dish.

Roll out the dough and use to cover the dish. Decorate the top with leaves made from the dough trimmings. Brush with beaten egg.

Cook in a preheated hot oven (220°C/425°F, Gas Mark 7) for 25 to 30 minutes or until the pastry is risen and golden brown. Serve hot.
Serves 4

Korean Chicken

Metric/Imperial
1 × 1.5 kg/3 lb chicken,
  cut into serving pieces
1 green pepper, cored, seeded
  and thinly sliced
1 red pepper, cored, seeded
  and thinly sliced
2 carrots, thinly sliced
50 g/2 oz mushrooms, sliced
Sauce:
200 ml/⅓ pint soy sauce
450 ml/¾ pint water
4 spring onions, chopped
1 garlic clove, crushed
1 tablespoon caster sugar
1 tablespoon crushed fresh
  root ginger
2 teaspoons black pepper
½ teaspoon monosodium
  glutamate (optional)

American
1 × 3 lb broiler/fryer,
  cut up
1 green pepper, seeded
  and thinly sliced
1 red pepper, seeded
  and thinly sliced
2 carrots, thinly sliced
½ cup sliced mushrooms
Sauce:
1 cup soy sauce
2 cups water
4 scallions, chopped
1 garlic clove, crushed
1 tablespoon sugar
1 tablespoon crushed fresh
  ginger root
2 teaspoons black pepper
½ teaspoon msg (optional)

Cook the chicken in boiling water for 5 minutes.

Meanwhile place all the sauce ingredients in a saucepan and bring to the boil.

Drain the chicken and add to the sauce with peppers, carrots and mushrooms. Bring back to the boil, then simmer for 20 minutes or until the chicken is tender. Serve hot.

Serves 4

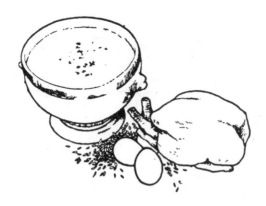

Marinated Chicken with Spicy Sauce

Metric/Imperial
½ teaspoon ground coriander
½ teaspoon chilli powder
½ teaspoon garam masala
pinch of salt
juice of 1 lemon
4 chicken breasts
oil for frying
Sauce:
300 ml/½ pint plain yogurt
½ teaspoon ground ginger
1 teaspoon curry powder
1 teaspoon cayenne pepper
1 garlic clove, crushed
1 tablespoon tomato purée
grated rind of 1 lemon
1 bay leaf

American
½ teaspoon ground coriander
½ teaspoon chili powder
½ teaspoon garam masala
pinch of salt
juice of 1 lemon
4 chicken breasts
oil for frying
Sauce:
1¼ cups plain yogurt
½ teaspoon ground ginger
1 teaspoon curry powder
1 teaspoon cayenne
1 garlic clove, crushed
1 tablespoon tomato paste
grated rind of 1 lemon
1 bay leaf

Mix together the coriander, chilli powder, garam masala, salt and lemon juice. Prick the chicken breasts all over with a fork, then rub with the spice mixture. Leave to marinate for 4 to 5 hours.

Heat a little oil in a frying pan (skillet). Add the chicken breasts and fry for 15 to 20 minutes or until golden brown on all sides and cooked through.

Meanwhile put all the sauce ingredients in a saucepan and heat through gently.

Arrange the chicken breasts on a warmed serving dish. Remove the bay leaf from the sauce and pour over the chicken. Serve hot.
Serves 4

Chicken Mornay Bake

Metric/Imperial	American
40 g/1½ oz butter or margarine	3 tablespoons butter or margarine
40 g/1½ oz plain flour	6 tablespoons all-purpose flour
600 ml/1 pint milk	2½ cups milk
175 g/6 oz Cheddar cheese, grated	1½ cups grated Cheddar cheese
salt and pepper	salt and pepper
350 g/12 oz cooked chicken meat, chopped	2 cups chopped cooked chicken
100 g/4 oz mushrooms, sliced	1 cup sliced mushrooms
50 g/2 oz fresh breadcrumbs	1 cup soft bread crumbs

Melt the butter or margarine in a saucepan. Stir in the flour and cook for 2 minutes, then gradually stir in the milk. Bring to the boil, stirring, and simmer until thickened. Add 100 g/4 oz (1 cup) of the cheese and stir until melted. Season to taste with salt and pepper.

Fold the chicken and mushrooms into the cheese sauce. Pour into a shallow ovenproof dish. Mix together the breadcrumbs and remaining cheese and scatter over the top.

Cook in a preheated hot oven (220°C/425°F, Gas Mark 7) for about 15 minutes or until piping hot and the top is golden brown. Serve hot.
Serves 4

Spaghetti with Creamy Chicken Sauce

Metric/Imperial	American
350 g/12 oz spaghetti	¾ lb spaghetti
salt and pepper	salt and pepper
75 g/3 oz butter or margarine	6 tablespoons butter or margarine
50 g/2 oz plain flour	½ cup all-purpose flour
450 ml/¾ pint chicken stock	2 cups chicken stock or broth
150 ml/¼ pint single cream	⅔ cup light cream
2 tablespoons sherry	2 tablespoons sherry
100 g/4 oz mushrooms, sliced	1 cup sliced mushrooms
350 g/12 oz cooked chicken meat, diced	1½ cups diced cooked chicken meat
grated Parmesan cheese to serve	grated Parmesan cheese to serve

Cook the spaghetti in boiling salted water until just tender.

Meanwhile melt 50 g/2 oz (4 tablespoons) of the butter or margarine in a saucepan. Stir in the flour and cook for 2 minutes, then gradually stir in the stock. Bring to the boil, stirring, and simmer until thickened. Add the cream, sherry and salt and pepper to taste and heat through.

Melt the remaining butter or margarine in a frying pan (skillet). Add the mushrooms and fry until tender. Drain the spaghetti and return to the pan. Add half the cream sauce and toss to coat. Keep hot.

Add the mushrooms and chicken to the remaining sauce and heat through, stirring well. Arrange the spaghetti on a warmed serving dish, spoon the chicken mixture on top and serve hot with Parmesan cheese.
Serves 4

Turkey Chow Mein

Metric/Imperial
500 g/1 lb cooked turkey meat,
  chopped
1 × 300 g/11 oz can condensed
  cream of chicken soup
3 tablespoons soy sauce
½ teaspoon ground ginger
salt and pepper
2 tablespoons oil
1 onion, sliced
2 celery sticks, sliced
1 green pepper, cored, seeded
  and thinly sliced
2 tablespoons cornflour
3 tablespoons water
350 g/12 oz bean sprouts
100 g/4 oz mushrooms, sliced

American
2 cups chopped cooked turkey
1 × 11 oz can condensed cream
  of chicken soup
3 tablespoons soy sauce
½ teaspoon ground ginger
salt and pepper
2 tablespoons oil
1 onion, sliced
2 celery stalks, sliced
1 green pepper, seeded
  and thinly sliced
2 tablespoons cornstarch
3 tablespoons water
¾ lb bean sprouts
1 cup sliced mushrooms

Mix together the turkey, soup, soy sauce, ginger and salt and pepper to taste.

Heat the oil in a frying pan (skillet). Add the onion, celery and green pepper and fry until softened. Stir in the turkey mixture and bring to the boil. Blend the cornflour (cornstarch) with the water and add to the pan with the bean sprouts and mushrooms. Simmer, stirring, for 10 minutes or until piping hot. Serve with rice.
Serves 4

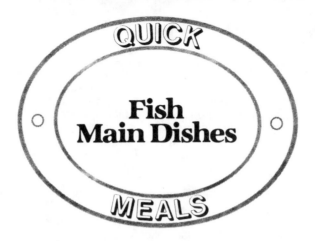

QUICK
Fish Main Dishes
MEALS

Mixed Fish Stew

Metric/Imperial
25 g/1 oz butter or margarine
1 onion, chopped
1 leek, chopped
1 celery stick, chopped
1 garlic clove, crushed
1 × 400 g/14 oz can tomatoes,
   drained and chopped
1 tablespoon chopped parsley
1 bay leaf
½ teaspoon dried thyme
juice of ½ lemon
salt and pepper
750 g/1½ lb mixed fish, eg
   cod, herring, whiting, etc.,
   skinned and boned if necessary
   and cut into chunks

American
2 tablespoons butter or margarine
1 onion, chopped
1 leek, chopped
1 celery stalk, chopped
1 garlic clove, crushed
1 × 16 oz can tomatoes,
   drained and chopped
1 tablespoon chopped parsley
1 bay leaf
½ teaspoon dried thyme
juice of ½ lemon
salt and pepper
1½ lb mixed fish, eg cod, herring,
   whiting, etc., skinned and boned
   if necessary and cut into
   chunks

Melt the butter or margarine in a saucepan. Add the onion, leek, celery
and garlic and fry until softened. Stir in the tomatoes, herbs, lemon juice
and salt and pepper to taste. Add the fish with enough water to cover.
Bring to the boil, then simmer for 10 minutes or until the fish will flake
easily when tested with a fork.
   Remove the bay leaf and serve hot.
Serves 4

Seafood with Leeks

Metric/Imperial
4 plaice fillets
salt and pepper
150 ml/¼ pint dry white wine
50 g/2 oz butter or margarine
225 g/8 oz leeks, thinly sliced
225 g/8 oz cooked shelled
  prawns
paprika

American
4 flounder fillets
salt and pepper
⅔ cup dry white wine
4 tablespoons butter or
  margarine
½ lb leeks, thinly sliced
½ lb cooked shelled shrimp
paprika

Sprinkle the fish fillets with salt and pepper and fold them in half. Arrange in a greased ovenproof dish and pour over the wine. Cover with foil and cook in a preheated moderately hot oven (200°C/400°F, Gas Mark 6) for 15 to 20 minutes or until the fish flakes easily when tested with a fork.

Meanwhile melt the butter or margarine in a frying pan (skillet). Add the leeks and fry, stirring frequently, until just tender. Stir in the prawns (shrimp) and salt and pepper to taste and heat through.

Place the fish fillets on a warmed serving platter. Pour the cooking liquid into the frying pan and mix with the leeks and prawns (shrimp). Pour this mixture over the fillets and sprinkle with paprika. Serve hot.
Serves 4

Fish Baked with Fennel

Metric/Imperial
4 cod steaks
2 tablespoons lemon juice
salt and pepper
15 g/½ oz butter or margarine
2 tomatoes, sliced
4 fennel sprigs

American
4 cod steaks
2 tablespoons lemon juice
salt and pepper
1 tablespoon butter or
  margarine
2 tomatoes, sliced
4 fennel sprigs

Place the cod steaks on four pieces of foil large enough to wrap around the fish. Sprinkle with the lemon juice and salt and pepper to taste, then dot with the butter or margarine. Place the tomato slices and fennel sprigs on top.

Wrap the foil around the fish and place the parcels on a baking sheet. Cook in a preheated moderate oven (180°C/350°F, Gas Mark 4) for 30 minutes or until the fish flakes easily when tested with a fork. Serve hot.
Serves 4

Hungarian Plaice (Flounder)

Metric/Imperial
4 plaice fillets
300 ml/½ pint milk
salt and pepper
40 g/1½ oz butter or margarine
50 g/2 oz mushrooms, sliced
1½ tablespoons plain flour
1 tablespoon paprika

American
4 flounder fillets
1¼ cups milk
salt and pepper
3 tablespoons butter or
  margarine
½ cup sliced mushrooms
1½ tablespoons all-purpose
  flour
1 tablespoon paprika

Place the fillets in an ovenproof dish and pour over the milk. Season to taste with salt and pepper. Cover and poach in a preheated moderate oven (160°C/325°F, Gas Mark 3) for 15 to 20 minutes or until the fish flakes easily when tested with a fork.

Meanwhile melt the butter or margarine in a saucepan. Add the mushrooms and fry until softened.

Transfer the fish fillets to a warmed serving dish and keep hot. Reserve the milk.

Add the flour and paprika to the mushrooms and stir well, then gradually stir in the milk. Bring to the boil, stirring, and simmer until thickened. Taste and adjust the seasoning. Pour the sauce over the fish and serve hot.
Serves 4

Fish Baked with Mushrooms

Metric/Imperial
1 × 400 g/14 oz can tomatoes
1 small green pepper, cored,
  seeded and diced
1 celery stick, diced
50 g/2 oz cucumber, diced
salt and pepper
500 g/1 lb mushrooms, sliced
1 teaspoon lemon juice
1 tablespoon grated onion
4 white fish steaks

American
1 × 16 oz can tomatoes
1 small green pepper,
  seeded and diced
1 celery stalk, diced
½ cup diced cucumber
salt and pepper
1 lb mushrooms, sliced
1 teaspoon lemon juice
1 tablespoon grated onion
4 white fish steaks

Put the tomatoes with their juice, the green pepper, celery, cucumber and salt and pepper to taste in a saucepan and simmer for about 10 minutes or until thickened.

Scatter the mushrooms over the bottom of a greased ovenproof dish and sprinkle with the lemon juice and onion. Place the fish steaks on top and pour over the tomato sauce.

Cook in a preheated moderate oven (180°C/350°F, Gas Mark 4) for 30 minutes or until the fish flakes easily when tested with a fork.
Serves 4

Halibut with Gorgonzola

Metric/Imperial
4 halibut or other white
  fish steaks
75 g/3 oz butter or margarine,
  softened
225 g/8 oz Gorgonzola cheese
4 tablespoons milk
salt and pepper

American
4 halibut or other white fish
  steaks
6 tablespoons butter or
  margarine, softened
½ lb Gorgonzola cheese
¼ cup milk
salt and pepper

Place the fish in the grill (broiler) pan and spread 25 g/1 oz
(2 tablespoons) of the butter or margarine over them. Grill (broil)
for 5 minutes.
 Meanwhile mash the cheese with the remaining butter or margarine,
the milk and salt and pepper to taste. Turn the fish steaks over and
spread the cheese mixture on top. Grill (broil) gently for a further 8 to 10
minutes or until the topping is melted and golden brown and the fish is
cooked through. Serve hot.
Serves 4

Fried Cod Napoli

Metric/Imperial
15 g/½ oz butter or margarine
2 tablespoons olive oil
1 onion, sliced
1 garlic clove, crushed
1 × 400 g/14 oz can tomatoes
2 tablespoons tomato purée
½ teaspoon dried basil
6 pickled gherkins, sliced
salt and pepper
50 g/2 oz plain flour
750 g/1½ lb cod fillet, cut
  into chunks
oil for deep frying
6-8 black olives

American
1 tablespoon butter or
  margarine
2 tablespoons olive oil
1 onion, sliced
1 garlic clove, crushed
1 × 16 oz can tomatoes
2 tablespoons tomato paste
½ teaspoon dried basil
6 pickled gherkins, sliced
salt and pepper
½ cup all-purpose flour
1½ lb cod fillet, cut into
  chunks
oil for deep frying
6-8 ripe olives

Melt the butter or margarine with the oil in a saucepan. Add the onion and
garlic and fry until softened. Stir in the tomatoes with their juice and
simmer for 10 minutes.
 Stir in the tomato purée (paste), basil, gherkins and salt and pepper to
taste. Leave to simmer very gently while you cook the fish.
 Mix the flour with salt and pepper and use to coat the fish chunks.
Deep fry for about 3 minutes or until crisp and golden. Drain on kitchen
paper towels and pile on a warmed serving dish.
 Pour the tomato sauce over the fish and scatter the olives on top.
Serves 4

Baked Halibut

Metric/Imperial	American
4 halibut fillets	4 halibut fillets
1 onion, sliced	1 onion, sliced
4 tablespoons chopped parsley	¼ cup chopped parsley
450 ml/¾ pint tomato juice	2 cups tomato juice
salt and pepper	salt and pepper

Place the fillets in a greased ovenproof dish. Scatter over the onion and sprinkle with the parsley. Pour over the tomato juice and season to taste with salt and pepper.

Cover and cook in a preheated moderately hot oven (200°C/400°F, Gas Mark 6) for 30 minutes or until the fish flakes easily when tested with a fork. Serve hot.
Serves 4

Piquant Fish with Courgettes (Zucchini)

Metric/Imperial	American
4 white fish fillets (about 225 g/8 oz each)	4 white fish fillets (about ½ lb each)
juice of 1 lemon	juice of 1 lemon
salt and pepper	salt and pepper
75 g/3 oz butter or margarine	6 tablespoons butter or margarine
1 small onion, thinly sliced	1 small onion, thinly sliced
4 courgettes, cut into sticks	4 zucchini, cut into sticks
1 × 50 g/2 oz can anchovy fillets, drained	1 × 2 oz can anchovy fillets, drained
1 tablespoon capers	1 tablespoon capers
lemon wedges to serve	lemon wedges to serve

Place the fish fillets on a sheet of foil large enough to enclose them and place on a baking sheet. Sprinkle with the lemon juice and salt and pepper to taste. Wrap the foil around the fish. Cook in a preheated moderately hot oven (200°C/400°F, Gas Mark 6) for about 20 minutes or until the fish flakes easily when tested with a fork.

Meanwhile melt the butter or margarine in a frying pan (skillet). Add the onion and fry until softened. Stir in the courgettes (zucchini) and cook gently for a further 5 minutes. Add the anchovies, capers and salt and pepper to taste and heat through gently.

Place the fish on a warmed serving platter and keep hot. Pour the liquid from the foil into the frying pan (skillet) and stir well. Pour the courgette (zucchini) mixture over the fish and serve with lemon wedges.
Serves 4

Spiced Fish Pilaf

Metric/Imperial	American
4 tablespoons oil	¼ cup oil
1 tablespoon ground coriander	1 tablespoon ground coriander
2 teaspoons ground cumin	2 teaspoons ground cumin
½ teaspoon ground turmeric	½ teaspoon ground turmeric
½ teaspoon ground fenugreek	½ teaspoon ground fenugreek
pinch of ground ginger	pinch of ground ginger
750 g/1½ lb white fish fillets, cut into 5 cm/2 inch pieces	1½ lb white fish fillets, cut into 2 inch pieces
salt	salt
2 large onions, chopped	2 large onions, chopped
500 g/1 lb long-grain rice	2⅔ cups rice
2 tablespoons desiccated coconut	2 tablespoons shredded coconut
juice of ½ lemon	juice of ½ lemon

Heat 2 tablespoons of the oil in a frying pan (skillet). Add the spices and fry, stirring, for 1 minute. Add the fish pieces and stir to coat with the spices. Pour over enough water to cover the fish and bring to the boil. Add salt to taste, then simmer until the fish flakes easily. Remove the fish pieces from the pan with a slotted spoon and keep hot. Reserve the spiced cooking liquid.

Heat the remaining oil in a saucepan. Add the onions and fry until lightly browned. Stir in the rice and coconut, then add the spiced cooking liquid from the frying pan and the lemon juice. Pour in enough water to make a 1 cm/½ inch layer of liquid over the rice. Bring to the boil, then cover and cook gently until the rice is tender and has absorbed all the liquid.

Fold the fish pieces into the rice mixture and reheat if necessary. Serve hot.
Serves 6

Fish Baked in Tomato Cream Sauce

Metric/Imperial	American
25 g/1 oz plain flour	¼ cup all-purpose flour
salt and pepper	salt and pepper
4 white fish fillets	4 white fish fillets
25 g/1 oz butter or margarine	2 tablespoons butter or margarine
1 small onion, chopped	1 small onion, chopped
2 tablespoons tomato ketchup	2 tablespoons tomato ketchup
300 ml/½ pint double cream	1¼ cups heavy cream
1 tablespoon chopped parsley	1 tablespoon chopped parsley

Mix the flour with salt and pepper and use to coat the fish. Arrange in a greased ovenproof dish.

Melt the butter or margarine in a saucepan. Add the onion and fry until softened. Stir in the tomato ketchup, cream, parsley and salt and pepper to taste. Pour the sauce over the fish.

Cover and cook in a preheated moderate oven (350°F/180°C, Gas Mark 4) for 30 minutes or until the fish flakes easily when tested with a fork.
Serves 4

Maryland Fish Bake

Metric/Imperial
25 g/1 oz butter or margarine
1 onion, chopped
75 g/3 oz fresh breadcrumbs
75 g/3 oz frozen sweetcorn
   kernels, thawed
salt and pepper
4 white fish steaks
4 streaky bacon rashers,
   derinded
1 × 275 g/10 oz can condensed
   mushroom soup
milk

American
2 tablespoons butter or margarine
1 onion, chopped
1½ cups soft bread crumbs
½ cup frozen whole kernel
   corn, thawed
salt and pepper
4 white fish steaks
4 bacon slices
1 × 10 oz can condensed
   mushroom soup
milk

Melt the butter or margarine in a frying pan (skillet), add the onion and fry until softened. Remove from the heat and stir in the breadcrumbs, corn and salt and pepper to taste.

Arrange the fish steaks in an ovenproof dish, in one layer, and spoon the corn mixture on top. Place a bacon rasher (slice) on top of each fish steak. Dilute the soup with ½ can of milk and pour around the fish.

Cover the dish and cook in a preheated moderate oven (180°C/350°F, Gas Mark 4) for 20 minutes. Uncover and continue baking for 10 to 15 minutes or until the top is crisp and browned and the fish flakes easily when tested with a fork.
Serves 4

Trawlerman's Treat

Metric/Imperial
100 g/4 oz self-raising flour
½ teaspoon salt
100 g/4 oz mashed potatoes
25 g/1 oz butter or margarine,
   melted
1 tablespoon milk
2 spring onions, shredded
50 g/2 oz mushrooms, sliced
2 large tomatoes, sliced
350 g/12 oz cod fillets,
   finely chopped
100 g/4 oz cheese, grated

American
1 cup self-rising flour
½ teaspoon salt
½ cup mashed potatoes
2 tablespoons butter or
   margarine, melted
3 tablespoons milk
2 scallions, shredded
½ cup sliced mushrooms
2 large tomatoes, sliced
¾ lb cod fillets, finely
   chopped
1 cup grated cheese

Sift the flour and salt into a bowl. Add the potatoes, butter or margarine and milk and mix to a stiff dough. Divide into four and shape into rounds. Grill (broil) until golden on both sides.

Place the spring onions (scallions) and mushrooms on the rounds and top with the tomato slices. Mix together the fish and cheese and spread over the tomatoes. Grill (broil) for a further 10 minutes or until the fish is cooked and the top is golden brown.
Serves 4

Baked Spiced Cod

Metric/Imperial	American
4 cod steaks	4 cod steaks
juice of ½ lemon	juice of ½ lemon
salt	salt
150 ml/¼ pint plain yogurt	⅔ cup plain yogurt
1 teaspoon garam masala	1 teaspoon garam masala
1 teaspoon ground cumin	1 teaspoon ground cumin
¼ teaspoon chilli powder	¼ teaspoon chili powder
2 garlic cloves, crushed	2 garlic cloves, crushed
2 teaspoons vinegar	2 teaspoons vinegar
lemon wedges to serve	lemon wedges to serve

Arrange the cod steaks in an ovenproof dish and sprinkle them with the lemon juice and salt. Mix together the yogurt, spices, garlic and vinegar and pour over the fish. Cover and leave to marinate in the refrigerator for about 4 hours.

Uncover and cook in a preheated moderately hot oven (190°C/375°F, Gas Mark 5) for 30 minutes or until the fish flakes easily when tested with a fork. Serve hot with lemon wedges.

Serves 4

Cod Kebabs

Metric/Imperial	American
500 g/1 lb cod fillet, skinned and cut into 2.5 cm/1 inch cubes	1 lb cod fillet, cut into 1 inch cubes
salt and pepper	salt and pepper
2 tablespoons lemon juice	2 tablespoons lemon juice
4 tablespoons oil	¼ cup oil
1 teaspoon chopped parsley	1 teaspoon chopped parsley
1 garlic clove, crushed	1 garlic clove, crushed
4 streaky bacon rashers, derinded and cut into squares	4 bacon slices, cut into squares
1 green pepper, cored, seeded and cut into squares	1 green pepper, seeded and cut into squares
4 small tomatoes	4 cherry tomatoes

Place the fish cubes in a shallow dish and season with salt and pepper. Mix together the lemon juice, oil, parsley and garlic and pour over the fish. Leave to marinate for 4 hours, turning occasionally.

Drain the fish, reserving the marinade. Thread the fish cubes onto skewers alternating with the bacon, green pepper squares and tomatoes.

Place under a preheated grill (broiler) and baste with the reserved marinade. Cook for 8 to 10 minutes or until the fish flakes easily when tested with a fork. Turn and baste with the marinade from time to time. Serve hot.

Serves 4

Cider Fish Curry

Metric/Imperial
225 g/8 oz white fish fillets
150 ml/¼ pint milk
150 ml/¼ pint water
50 g/2 oz butter or margarine
salt and pepper
1 onion, chopped
25 g/1 oz plain flour
2 tablespoons curry powder
450 ml/¾ pint cider
3 tablespoons sultanas
25 g/1 oz walnuts, chopped
1 dessert apple, cored and
   sliced
100 g/4 oz cooked shelled
   prawns

American
½ lb white fish fillets
⅔ cup milk
⅔ cup water
4 tablespoons butter or
   margarine
salt and pepper
1 onion, chopped
¼ cup all-purpose flour
2 tablespoons curry powder
2 cups hard or apple cider
3 tablespoons golden raisins
¼ cup chopped walnuts
1 apple, cored and sliced
¼ lb cooked shelled shrimp

Place the fish fillets in a frying pan (skillet) and add the milk, water, 25 g/ 1 oz (2 tablespoons) of the butter or margarine and salt and pepper to taste. Poach gently until the fish flakes easily. Drain the fish. Remove any skin and bones, then flake the fish.

Melt the remaining butter or margarine in a saucepan. Add the onion and fry until softened. Stir in the flour and curry powder and cook for 2 minutes, then gradually stir in the cider. Bring to the boil, stirring well. Add the sultanas (raisins), walnuts, apple, prawns (shrimp) and flaked fish and cook gently for 10 minutes.

Season to taste with salt and pepper, then serve hot with boiled rice.
Serves 4

Cod with Vegetables

Metric/Imperial
50 g/2 oz plain flour
salt and pepper
750 g/1½ lb cod fillet, skinned
 and cut into chunks
2 streaky bacon rashers, derinded
 and chopped
½ green pepper, cored, seeded
 and thinly sliced
4 tablespoons oil
3 tomatoes, quartered
50 g/2 oz Cheddar cheese,
 grated

American
½ cup all-purpose flour
salt and pepper
1½ lb cod fillet, cut into
 chunks
2 bacon slices, chopped
½ green pepper, seeded
 and thinly sliced
¼ cup oil
3 tomatoes, quartered
½ cup grated Cheddar cheese

Mix the flour with salt and pepper and use to coat the fish chunks. Fry the bacon and green pepper in a frying pan (skillet) until the bacon is browned. Add half the oil and half the fish. Fry until the fish chunks are browned on all sides and will flake easily. Remove from the pan with a slotted spoon.

Add the remaining oil and fish to the pan and fry. Stir in the tomatoes, then return the already fried fish to the pan to reheat. Season to taste with salt and pepper.

Spoon the mixture into a flameproof serving dish. Sprinkle the cheese on top. Place under a preheated grill (broiler) and cook until the cheese has melted and browned. Serve hot.
Serves 4

Baked Fish with Olives

Metric/Imperial
6 small whole fish (red mullet,
 whiting, etc.), cleaned and scaled
 if necessary
salt
150 ml/¼ pint olive oil
120 ml/4 fl oz white wine vinegar
75 g/3 oz green olives, stoned
 and chopped

American
6 small whole fish (gray mullet,
 snapper, whiting, etc.),
 cleaned and scaled if necessary
salt
⅔ cup olive oil
½ cup white wine vinegar
½ cup chopped pitted green
 olives

Sprinkle the fish inside and out with salt. Arrange in a flameproof dish. Drizzle over the oil and vinegar. Cook in a preheated moderate oven (180°C/350°F, Gas Mark 4) for 15 minutes or until the fish flakes easily when tested with a fork. Turn the fish over halfway through the cooking.

Remove the fish from the dish and place on a warmed serving platter. Keep hot.

Place the dish over heat on top of the stove. Stir in the olives and heat through. Spoon the olives and a little of the pan juices over the fish and serve hot.
Serves 6

Herrings with Tomato Sauce

Metric/Imperial	American
4 herrings, cleaned	4 herrings, cleaned
salt and pepper	salt and pepper
2 tablespoons oil	2 tablespoons oil
Sauce:	Sauce:
25 g/1 oz butter or margarine	2 tablespoons butter or
1 onion, chopped	margarine
1 × 400 g/14 oz can tomatoes	1 onion, chopped
½ teaspoon dried basil	1 × 16 oz can tomatoes
½ teaspoon dried thyme	½ teaspoon dried basil
1 bay leaf	½ teaspoon dried thyme
	1 bay leaf

Make two or three shallow cuts in both sides of each fish. Season with salt and pepper and brush with the oil. Place under a preheated grill (broiler) and cook for 5 minutes on each side.

Meanwhile make the sauce. Melt the butter or margarine in a saucepan. Add the onion and fry until softened. Stir in the tomatoes with their juice, the herbs and salt and pepper to taste. Simmer until thickened. Discard the bay leaf.

Serve the fish with the sauce.
Serves 4

Stuffed Mackerel

Metric/Imperial	American
100 g/4 oz cottage cheese	½ cup cottage cheese
grated rind and juice of	grated rind and juice of
1 lemon	1 lemon
100 g/4 oz fresh breadcrumbs	2 cups soft bread crumbs
1 teaspoon dried mixed herbs	1 teaspoon dried mixed herbs
salt and pepper	salt and pepper
1 egg, beaten	1 egg, beaten
4 × 225 g/8 oz mackerel,	4 × ½ lb mackerel, cleaned and
cleaned and backbones	backbones removed
removed	

Mix together the cottage cheese, lemon rind and juice, breadcrumbs, herbs and salt and pepper to taste. Bind with the egg. Stuff this mixture into the mackerel and wrap each individually in greased foil.

Cook in a preheated moderately hot oven (190°C/375°F, Gas Mark 5) for 30 minutes, or until the fish flakes easily when tested with a fork. Serve hot.
Serves 4

Herrings in Oatmeal

Metric/Imperial	American
4 herrings, cleaned and backbones removed	4 herrings, cleaned and backbones removed
lemon juice	lemon juice
salt and pepper	salt and pepper
100 g/4 oz oatmeal	2/3 cup oatmeal
40 g/1½ oz butter or margarine	3 tablespoons butter or margarine
2 tablespoons oil	2 tablespoons oil

Sprinkle the herrings with lemon juice and season to taste with salt and pepper. Coat with the oatmeal, pressing it on well.

Melt the butter or margarine with the oil in a frying pan (skillet). Add the herrings and fry for 4 to 5 minutes on each side or until the coating is golden and the fish flakes easily when tested with a fork. Serve hot.
Serves 4

Salt Grilled (Broiled) Fish

Metric/Imperial	American
1 × 750 g/1½ lb mackerel or red mullet, cleaned and scaled	1 × 1½ lb mackerel or red snapper, cleaned and scaled
salt	salt
lemon wedges to serve	lemon wedges to serve

Sprinkle the fish lightly inside and out with salt. Leave for 30 minutes.

Make three diagonal slashes on each side of the fish. Place under a preheated grill (broiler) and cook for about 5 minutes on each side or until the fish flakes easily when tested with a fork.

Serve hot with lemon wedges.
Serves 4

Mackerel with Orange

Metric/Imperial	American
2 oranges, peeled and chopped	2 oranges, peeled and chopped
½ onion, chopped	½ onion, chopped
50 g/2 oz fresh breadcrumbs	1 cup soft bread crumbs
1 tablespoon chopped parsley	1 tablespoon chopped parsley
grated rind and juice of ½ lemon	grated rind and juice of ½ lemon
salt and pepper	salt and pepper
4 mackerel, cleaned	4 mackerel, cleaned

Mix together the oranges, onion, breadcrumbs, parsley, lemon rind and juice and salt and pepper to taste. Fill the cavities in the fish with this stuffing and arrange in a greased ovenproof dish.

Cover and cook in a preheated moderate oven (160°C/325°F, Gas Mark 3) for 30 to 35 minutes or until the fish flakes easily when tested with a fork. Serve hot.
Serves 4

Mackerel with Mandarin Sauce

Metric/Imperial
4 mackerel, cleaned
juice of 1 lemon
salt and pepper
50 g/2 oz butter or margarine
1 onion, chopped
25 g/1 oz plain flour
1 × 350 g/12 oz can mandarin
oranges
2 tablespoons white wine
vinegar
75 g/3 oz Edam cheese, grated

American
4 mackerel, cleaned
juice of 1 lemon
salt and pepper
4 tablespoons butter or
margarine
1 onion, chopped
¼ cup all-purpose flour
1 × 12 oz can mandarin oranges
2 tablespoons white wine
vinegar
¾ cup grated Edam cheese

Arrange the mackerel in a large ovenproof dish. Sprinkle with the lemon juice and salt and pepper to taste and dot with 25 g/1 oz (2 tablespoons) of the butter or margarine. Cover and cook in a preheated moderately hot oven (190°C/375°F, Gas Mark 5) for 20 minutes.

Meanwhile melt the remaining butter or margarine in a saucepan. Add the onion and fry until softened. Stir in the flour and cook for 2 minutes. Drain the mandarin oranges, reserving the syrup. Add the vinegar to the syrup with enough water to make up to 150 ml/¼ pint (⅔ cup). Add to the saucepan and bring to the boil, stirring. Simmer until thickened. Add the mandarin oranges and salt and pepper to taste, then stir in the cheese until melted.

Pour the mandarin sauce over the fish and serve hot.
Serves 4

Kedgeree

Metric/Imperial
225 g/8 oz smoked haddock
50 g/2 oz butter or margarine
175 g/6 oz cooked rice
4 hard-boiled eggs, chopped
salt and pepper
1 egg, beaten
chopped parsley to garnish

American
½ lb finnan haddie (smoked
haddock)
4 tablespoons butter or
margarine
1 cup cooked rice
4 hard-cooked eggs, chopped
salt and pepper
1 egg, beaten
chopped parsley for garnish

Poach the fish gently in simmering water for about 10 minutes or until tender. Drain well and flake.

Melt the butter or margarine in a frying pan (skillet). Stir in the rice and fish and heat through gently. Fold in the hard-boiled eggs and salt and pepper to taste. Stir in the beaten egg and continue cooking gently until the mixture is creamy and piping hot. Serve sprinkled with parsley.
Serves 4

Smoked Haddock Casserole

Metric/Imperial
500 g/1 lb smoked haddock
25 g/1 oz butter or margarine
25 g/1 oz plain flour
300 ml/½ pint milk
salt and pepper
½ teaspoon dry mustard
75 g/3 oz mature Cheddar
  cheese, grated
2 eggs, separated
1 × 350 g/12 oz can sweetcorn
  kernels, drained
6 streaky bacon rashers
  derinded

American
1 lb finnan haddie (smoked
  haddock)
2 tablespoons butter or
  margarine
¼ cup all-purpose flour
1½ cups milk
salt and pepper
½ teaspoon dry mustard
¾ cup grated sharp Cheddar
  cheese
2 eggs, separated
1 × 12 oz can whole kernel corn,
  drained
6 bacon slices

Poach or steam the fish for about 10 minutes.
　　Meanwhile melt the butter or margarine in a saucepan. Stir in the flour
and cook for 1 minute, then gradually stir in the milk. Bring to the boil,
stirring, and simmer until thickened. Add salt and pepper to taste, the
mustard and cheese and stir until melted. Remove from the heat and cool
slightly, then beat in the egg yolks.
　　Drain and flake the fish. Beat the egg whites until stiff and fold into the
cheese sauce. Spoon half the sauce over the bottom of a greased
ovenproof dish. Scatter the haddock and corn over the top. Spoon over
the remaining sauce and arrange the bacon on top in a lattice.
　　Cook in a preheated moderately hot oven (200°C/400°F, Gas Mark 6)
for about 15 minutes or until the bacon is crisp and the haddock mixture is
puffed up and golden brown. Serve immediately.
Serves 4

Baked Haddock Cakes

Metric/Imperial
500 g/1 lb potatoes, grated
500 g/1 lb smoked haddock
  fillets, finely chopped
1 egg
1 teaspoon anchovy essence
juice of ½ lemon
salt and pepper
1 teaspoon oil

American
1 lb potatoes, grated
1 lb finnan haddie (smoked
  haddock fillets), finely
  chopped
1 egg
¼ teaspoon anchovy paste
juice of ½ lemon
salt and pepper
1 teaspoon oil

Squeeze the potatoes in a clean cloth to remove excess moisture. Mix
the potatoes with the fish, egg, anchovy essence (paste), lemon juice and
salt and pepper to taste. Shape into six patties.
　　Arrange the patties on a greased baking sheet and brush with the oil.
Cook in a preheated moderate oven (180°C/350°F, Gas Mark 4) for 30
minutes, turning the cakes over halfway through cooking. Serve hot.
Serves 4 to 6

Spaghetti Kedgeree

Metric/Imperial
500 g/1 lb smoked haddock
  fillets
350 g/12 oz spaghetti
salt and pepper
50 g/2 oz butter or margarine
2 tablespoons chopped parsley
3 eggs, beaten
juice of ½ lemon

American
1 lb finnan haddie (smoked
  haddock fillets)
¾ lb spaghetti
salt and pepper
4 tablespoons butter or
  margarine
2 tablespoons chopped parsley
3 eggs, beaten
juice of ½ lemon

Poach the fish in water to cover for about 15 minutes or until it flakes
easily. Drain well, then flake, removing any skin and bones. Keep warm.
    Cook the spaghetti in boiling salted water until just tender. Drain and
return to the pan. Add the flaked fish, butter or margarine, parsley and salt
and pepper to taste. Toss well together, then add the beaten eggs and
toss again. Serve hot, sprinkled with the lemon juice.
Serves 4

Crispy Tuna Bake

Metric/Imperial
25 g/1 oz butter or margarine
25 g/1 oz plain flour
300 ml/½ pint milk
50 g/2 oz Cheddar cheese
  grated
salt and pepper
1 × 200 g/7 oz can tuna fish,
  drained and flaked
1 × 326 g/11½ oz can sweetcorn
  kernels, drained
2 large tomatoes, thinly sliced
75 g/3 oz potato crisps, crushed

American
2 tablespoons butter or
  margarine
¼ cup all-purpose flour
1½ cups milk
½ cup grated Cheddar cheese
salt and pepper
1 × 7 oz can tuna fish,
  drained and flaked
1 × 11½ oz can whole kernel
  corn, drained
2 large tomatoes, thinly sliced
1 cup crushed potato chips

Melt the butter or margarine in a saucepan. Stir in the flour and cook for
2 minutes, then gradually stir in the milk. Bring to the boil, stirring, and
simmer until thickened. Stir in the cheese until melted and season to taste
with salt and pepper.
    Fold the tuna and corn into the cheese sauce. Pour into a greased
ovenproof dish. Arrange the tomato slices on top and sprinkle over the
crisps (chips).
    Cook in a preheated moderate oven (180°C/350°F, Gas Mark 4) for
about 20 minutes or until the top is brown and crisp. Serve hot.
Serves 4

Tuna and Rice Croquettes

Metric/Imperial
50 g/2 oz long-grain rice
salt and pepper
1 × 225 g/8 oz can pineapple
  chunks
1 × 200 g/7 oz can tuna fish,
  drained and flaked
1 teaspoon mayonnaise
1 teaspoon tomato purée
1 tablespoon chopped cucumber
1 egg
50 g/2 oz toasted breadcrumbs
oil for deep frying
Sauce:
2 tablespoons tomato ketchup
2 teaspoons vinegar
2 teaspoons sugar
1 tablespoon cornflour
1 tablespoon water

American
⅓ cup rice
salt and pepper
1 × 8 oz can pineapple chunks
1 × 7 oz can tuna fish, drained
  and flaked
1 teaspoon mayonnaise
1 teaspoon tomato paste
1 tablespoon chopped cucumber
1 egg
1 cup toasted bread crumbs
oil for deep frying
Sauce:
2 tablespoons tomato ketchup
2 teaspoons vinegar
2 teaspoons sugar
1 tablespoon cornstarch
1 tablespoon water

Cook the rice in boiling salted water for about 20 minutes or until tender. Drain, if necessary, and cool slightly.

Drain the pineapple, reserving the syrup for the sauce. Chop the pineapple. Mix the pineapple with the rice, tuna, mayonnaise, tomato purée (paste), cucumber, egg and salt and pepper to taste. Shape into 12 small patties or sausages and coat with the breadcrumbs.

Make up the pineapple syrup to 300 ml/½ pint (1¼ cups) with water and put into a saucepan with the ketchup, vinegar and sugar. Blend the cornflour (cornstarch) with the water and add to the pan. Bring to the boil, stirring, and simmer until thickened. Keep hot.

Deep fry the tuna and rice croquettes for 3 to 4 minutes or until golden brown. Drain on kitchen paper towels and serve hot with the sauce.
Serves 4 to 6

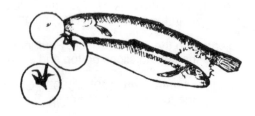

Spaghetti with Tuna Fish

Metric/Imperial
1 × 200 g/7 oz can tuna fish
1 garlic clove, chopped
3 tablespoons chopped parsley
2 tablespoons tomato purée
250 ml/8 fl oz chicken stock
salt and pepper
500 g/1 lb spaghetti

American
1 × 7 oz can tuna fish
1 garlic clove, chopped
3 tablespoons chopped parsley
2 tablespoons tomato paste
1 cup chicken stock or broth
salt and pepper
1 lb spaghetti

Drain the oil from the can of tuna into a frying pan (skillet). Add the garlic and fry for 1 minute, then add the tuna and flake it. Stir in the parsley, tomato purée (paste), stock and salt and pepper to taste. Bring to the boil and simmer for 15 minutes.
    Meanwhile cook the spaghetti in boiling salted water until just tender. Drain well and add to the frying pan. Toss to coat with the tuna sauce.
Serves 4

Fried Sardine and Cheese Pizza

Metric/Imperial
225 g/8 oz self-raising flour
1 teaspoon baking powder
1 teaspoon dry mustard
¼ teaspoon salt
pinch of cayenne pepper
50 g/2 oz butter or margarine
100 g/4 oz Cheddar cheese,
    grated
about 7 tablespoons milk
3 tablespoons oil
Topping:
6 tablespoons tomato purée
1 × 100 g/4 oz can sardines
    in oil, drained
2 spring onions, chopped
½ teaspoon dried thyme
50 g/2 oz Cheddar cheese, grated

American
2 cups self-rising flour
1 teaspoon baking powder
1 teaspoon dry mustard
¼ teaspoon salt
pinch of cayenne
4 tablespoons butter or
    margarine
1 cup grated Cheddar cheese
about ½ cup milk
3 tablespoons oil
Topping:
6 tablespoons tomato paste
1 × 4 oz can sardines in oil,
    drained
2 scallions, chopped
½ teaspoon dried thyme
½ cup grated Cheddar cheese

Sift the flour, baking powder, mustard, salt and cayenne into a bowl. Rub in the butter or margarine until the mixture resembles crumbs. Stir in the cheese, then bind to a soft dough with the milk.
    Roll out the dough to a round about 1 cm/½ inch thick. Heat the oil in a frying pan (skillet) large enough to hold the dough round. Fry the dough for about 5 minutes or until the underside is golden brown.
    Turn the dough base over and spread with the tomato purée (paste). Arrange the sardines on top like the spokes of a wheel. Sprinkle over the spring onions (scallions), thyme and cheese. Cover the pan and cook for a further 10 minutes or until the dough base is cooked through and the cheese on top has melted. Serve hot.
Serves 2 to 4

Spaghetti with Sardines

Metric/Imperial	American
3 tablespoons olive oil	3 tablespoons olive oil
1 onion, chopped	1 onion, chopped
1 garlic clove, crushed	1 garlic clove, crushed
1 × 400 g/14 oz can tomatoes, drained and chopped	1 × 16 oz can tomatoes, drained and chopped
1 × 100 g/4 oz can sardines in brine, drained	1 × 4 oz can sardines in brine, drained
25 g/1 oz pine nuts	¼ cup pine nuts
pinch of saffron powder	pinch of saffron powder
salt and pepper	salt and pepper
500 g/1 lb spaghetti	1 lb spaghetti

Heat the oil in a saucepan. Add the onion and garlic and fry until softened. Stir in the tomatoes, sardines, pine nuts, saffron and salt and pepper to taste. Cover and cook gently for 15 minutes, stirring occasionally.

Meanwhile cook the spaghetti in boiling salted water until just tender. Drain well and return to the pan. Add the sardine sauce and toss together. Serve hot.

Serves 4 to 6

Seafood Pasta

Metric/Imperial	American
2 tablespoons oil	2 tablespoons oil
1 onion, chopped	1 onion, chopped
1 garlic clove, crushed	1 garlic clove, crushed
1 × 200 g/7 oz can tuna fish, drained and flaked	1 × 7 oz can tuna fish, drained and flaked
100 g/4 oz cooked shelled prawns	¼ lb cooked shelled shrimp
250 ml/8 fl oz single cream	1 cup light cream
grated rind of ½ lemon	grated rind of ½ lemon
salt and pepper	salt and pepper
350 g/12 oz pasta shells	¾ lb pasta shells

Heat the oil in a saucepan. Add the onion and garlic and fry until softened. Stir in the tuna, prawns (shrimp), cream, lemon rind and salt and pepper to taste. Leave to heat through gently while you cook the pasta.

Cook the pasta shells in boiling salted water until just tender. Drain well and return to the pan. Add the sauce and toss together. Serve hot.

Serves 4

Tuna Shells

Metric/Imperial
225 g/8 oz pasta shells
salt and pepper
2 × 200 g/7 oz cans tuna
  fish, drained and flaked
1 × 5 cm/2 inch piece of
  cucumber, diced
2 tomatoes, skinned, seeded
  and chopped
6 tablespoons mayonnaise
grated rind and juice of
  ½ lemon
4 large outside leaves from
  a Webb's Wonder lettuce

American
½ lb pasta shells
salt and pepper
2 × 7 oz cans tuna fish,
  drained and flaked
1 × 2 inch piece of cucumber,
  diced (about ½ cup)
2 tomatoes, peeled, seeded
  and chopped
6 tablespoons mayonnaise
grated rind and juice of
  ½ lemon
4 large outside leaves from
  an iceberg lettuce

Cook the pasta shells in boiling salted water until just tender. Drain and cool.

Mix the pasta shells with the tuna fish, cucumber, tomatoes, mayonnaise, lemon rind and juice and salt and pepper to taste. Chill well.

Place the lettuce leaves, which should be curved like large shells, on individual serving plates and fill with the tuna mixture.
Serves 4

Pilchard Cakes

Metric/Imperial
1 × 225 g/8 oz can pilchards
  in tomato sauce, boned and
  flaked
225 g/8 oz mashed potatoes
1 tablespoon grated onion
1 teaspoon lemon juice
salt and pepper
1 egg, beaten
75 g/3 oz dry breadcrumbs
oil for deep frying

American
1 × 8 oz can pilchards or Pacific
  sardines in tomato sauce, boned
  and flaked
1 cup mashed potatoes
1 tablespoon grated onion
1 teaspoon lemon juice
salt and pepper
1 egg, beaten
1 cup dry bread crumbs
oil for deep frying

Mix together the pilchards and sauce, potatoes, onion, lemon juice and salt and pepper to taste. Shape into eight round flat cakes with floured hands. Dip in the beaten egg, then coat with the breadcrumbs.

Deep fry in oil heated to 180°C/350°F for 1 to 2 minutes or until crisp and golden brown. Drain on kitchen paper towels and serve hot.
Serves 4

Salmon Puffs

Metric/Imperial	American
1 × 200 g/7 oz can salmon, drained and flaked	1 × 7 oz can salmon, drained and flaked
225 g/8 oz mashed potatoes	1 cup mashed potatoes
1 tablespoon tomato ketchup	1 tablespoon tomato ketchup
pinch of cayenne pepper	pinch of cayenne
25 g/1 oz plain flour	¼ cup all-purpose flour
1 egg, beaten	1 egg, beaten
100 g/4 oz toasted breadcrumbs	1½ cups toasted breadcrumbs
oil for deep frying	oil for deep frying
Sauce:	Sauce:
2 tablespoons mayonnaise	2 tablespoons mayonnaise
1 tablespoon tomato chutney	1 tablespoon tomato chutney
2 tablespoons chopped chives	2 tablespoons chopped chives
1 canned pimiento, chopped	1 canned pimiento, chopped
½ small green pepper, cored, seeded and diced	½ small green pepper, seeded and diced
1 teaspoon paprika	1 teaspoon paprika

Mix together the sauce ingredients and place in a serving bowl. Chill.

Mash the salmon with the potatoes, then beat in the ketchup and cayenne. Shape into small balls or sausages. Coat in the flour, dip in the egg and coat in the toasted breadcrumbs.

Deep fry the puffs until golden. Drain on kitchen paper towels and serve hot or cold with the sauce.

Serves 8

Salmon Soufflé Omelette

Metric/Imperial	American
1 × 100 g/4 oz can salmon, drained	1 × 4 oz can salmon, drained
4 eggs, separated	4 eggs, separated
1 tablespoon water	1 tablespoon water
1 teaspoon lemon juice	1 teaspoon lemon juice
salt and pepper	salt and pepper
25 g/1 oz butter or margarine	2 tablespoons butter or margarine

Mash the salmon with the egg yolks, water, lemon juice and salt and pepper to taste. Beat the egg whites until stiff and fold into the salmon mixture.

Melt the butter or margarine in a frying pan (skillet). Add the salmon mixture and cook for about 5 minutes or until the underside of the omelette is lightly browned and set.

Place the pan under the grill (broiler) and continue cooking until the top of the omelette is set and puffed up. Fold the omelette over in half and cut into two portions. Serve immediately.

Serves 2

Stir-Fried Prawns (Shrimp) and Peas

Metric/Imperial
225 g/8 oz cooked shelled
  prawns
1 egg white
2 teaspoons cornflour
3 tablespoons oil
2 spring onions (white part
  only), finely chopped
1 slice of fresh root ginger,
  peeled and finely chopped
225 g/8 oz frozen peas,
  thawed
1 teaspoon salt
1 tablespoon dry sherry

American
½ lb cooked shelled shrimp
1 egg white
2 teaspoons cornstarch
3 tablespoons oil
2 scallions (white part only),
  finely chopped
1 slice of fresh ginger root,
  peeled and finely chopped
½ lb frozen peas, thawed
1 teaspoon salt
1 tablespoon dry sherry

Put the prawns (shrimp) in a bowl with the egg white and cornflour (cornstarch) and mix well. Leave to marinate in the refrigerator for about 20 minutes.

Heat the oil in a wok or frying pan (skillet). Add the prawns (shrimp) and stir-fry for about 1 minute. Remove from the pan with a slotted spoon.

Add the spring onions (scallions) and ginger and stir-fry for 1 minute. Add the peas and salt and stir-fry for a further 1 minute.

Return the prawns (shrimp) to the pan with the sherry and stir-fry for a final 1 minute. Serve hot.

Serves 4

Deep-Fried Prawns (Shrimp)

Metric/Imperial
500 g/1 lb unshelled Dublin
  Bay prawns
2 slices of fresh root ginger,
  peeled and finely chopped
1 teaspoon dry sherry
1½ teaspoons cornflour
oil for deep frying
1 teaspoon salt
1 teaspoon chilli sauce
  (optional)

American
1 lb unshelled jumbo shrimp
2 slices of fresh ginger root,
  peeled and finely chopped
1 teaspoon dry sherry
1½ teaspoons cornstarch
oil for deep frying
1 teaspoon salt
1 teaspoon chili sauce (optional)

Put the prawns (shrimp) in a bowl and add the ginger, sherry and cornflour (cornstarch). Stir well to mix, then leave to marinate in the refrigerator for about 20 minutes.

Deep fry the prawns (shrimp) in a wok or pan in oil heated to 180°C/350°F for about 1 minute. Drain on kitchen paper towels. Pour off the oil from the wok or pan, then return the prawns (shrimp) to it. Sprinkle over the salt and chilli sauce, if using, and mix well. Serve hot.

Serves 4

Noodles with Prawn (Shrimp) Sauce

Metric/Imperial
4 tablespoons olive oil
1 onion, chopped
2 garlic cloves, crushed
1 × 400 g/14 oz can tomatoes,
  drained and chopped
150 ml/¼ pint white wine
2 tablespoons chopped parsley
½ teaspoon dried basil
salt and pepper
225 g/8 oz cooked shelled
  prawns
500 g/1 lb egg noodles
15 g/½ oz butter or margarine

American
¼ cup olive oil
1 onion, chopped
2 garlic cloves, crushed
1 × 16 oz can tomatoes, drained
  and chopped
⅔ cup white wine
2 tablespoons chopped parsley
½ teaspoon dried basil
salt and pepper
½ lb cooked shelled shrimp
1 lb egg noodles
1 tablespoon butter or
  margarine

Heat the oil in a saucepan. Add the onion and garlic and fry until softened.
Stir in the tomatoes, wine, parsley, basil and salt and pepper to taste.
Bring to the boil and simmer for 5 minutes. Stir in the prawns (shrimp)
and simmer for a further 5 minutes.

Meanwhile cook the noodles in boiling salted water until just tender.
Drain well and return to the pan. Add the sauce and butter or margarine
and toss well together. Serve hot.
Serves 4 to 6

Grilled Spiced Scampi
(Broiled Spiced Shrimp)

Metric/Imperial
6 tablespoons water
1 teaspoon ground coriander
12 peppercorns
salt
500 g/1 lb scampi, shelled
50 g/2 oz butter or margarine
½ teaspoon ground cumin
1 teaspoon ground turmeric
2 teaspoons lemon or lime juice
lemon or lime wedges to serve

American
6 tablespoons water
1 teaspoon ground coriander
12 peppercorns
salt
1 lb jumbo shrimp, shelled
4 tablespoons butter or
  margarine
½ teaspoon ground cumin
1 teaspoon ground turmeric
2 teaspoons lemon or lime juice
lemon or lime wedges to serve

Put the water, ½ teaspoon of the coriander, the peppercorns and salt to
taste in a saucepan. Bring to the boil, then add the scampi (shrimp).
Simmer for 2 minutes or until they begin to turn pink. Drain the scampi
(shrimp).

Melt the butter or margarine in a shallow flameproof dish. Stir in the
spices including the remaining coriander, the lemon or lime juice and salt
to taste. Add the scampi (shrimp) and turn to coat with the spice mixture.
Place under a preheated grill (broiler) and cook for about 5 minutes,
turning once. Serve hot, with lemon or lime wedges.
Serves 6 to 8

Madras Dry Prawn (Shrimp) Curry

Metric/Imperial
50 g/2 oz butter or margarine
1 small onion, sliced
2 garlic cloves, sliced
1 teaspoon ground coriander
½ teaspoon ground turmeric
pinch of ground ginger
½ teaspoon ground cumin
½ teaspoon salt
500 g/1 lb cooked shelled
   prawns
1 tablespoon vinegar
pinch of chilli powder

American
4 tablespoons butter or
   margarine
1 small onion, sliced
2 garlic cloves, sliced
1 teaspoon ground coriander
½ teaspoon ground turmeric
pinch of ground ginger
½ teaspoon ground cumin
½ teaspoon salt
1 lb cooked shelled shrimp
1 tablespoon vinegar
pinch of chili powder

Melt the butter or margarine in a frying pan (skillet). Add the onion and garlic and fry until softened. Stir in the spices and salt and fry for 3 minutes, stirring constantly.

Add the prawns (shrimp) and turn to coat with the spice mixture. Stir the vinegar and fry for about 1 minute or until hot. Sprinkle over the chill powder and serve.
Serves 4

Tomato Prawn (Shrimp) Curry

Metric/Imperial
500 g/1 lb shelled prawns
salt
50 g/2 oz butter or margarine
3 large tomatoes, chopped
1 large onion, chopped
¼ teaspoon garlic powder
¼ teaspoon ground ginger
1 teaspoon chilli powder
2 teaspoons ground coriander
½ teaspoon ground turmeric
2 tablespoons desiccated
   coconut
150 ml/¼ pint water
2 teaspoons garam masala

American
1 lb shelled shrimp
salt
4 tablespoons butter or
   margarine
3 large tomatoes, chopped
1 large onion, chopped
¼ teaspoon garlic powder
¼ teaspoon ground ginger
1 teaspoon chili powder
2 teaspoons ground coriander
½ teaspoon ground turmeric
2 tablespoons shredded
   coconut
⅔ cup water
2 teaspoons garam masala

Sprinkle the prawns (shrimp) with salt. Melt the butter or margarine in a saucepan, add the prawns (shrimp) and fry for 2 minutes. Stir in the tomatoes, onion, garlic powder, ginger, chilli powder, coriander and turmeric and cook, stirring, for 5 minutes.

Add the coconut and water and bring to the boil. Stir in the garam masala and simmer for 5 minutes longer. Serve hot.
Serves 4

Prawn (Shrimp) Curry

Metric/Imperial
2 tablespoons oil
1 large onion, chopped
40 g/1½ oz desiccated coconut
½ teaspoon ground turmeric
1 teaspoon mustard seed
½ teaspoon chilli powder
½ teaspoon ground fenugreek
2 tablespoons plain yogurt
2 garlic cloves, crushed
300 ml/½ pint water
salt
500 g/1 lb cooked shelled
  prawns
juice of ½ lemon

American
2 tablespoons oil
1 large onion, chopped
½ cup shredded coconut
½ teaspoon ground turmeric
1 teaspoon mustard seed
½ teaspoon chili powder
½ teaspoon ground fenugreek
2 tablespoons plain yogurt
2 garlic cloves, crushed
1¼ cups water
salt
1 lb cooked shelled shrimp
juice of ½ lemon

Heat the oil in a saucepan. Add the onion and fry until golden. Stir in the coconut, spices, yogurt, garlic, water and salt to taste and bring to the boil. Simmer for 10 minutes, stirring occasionally.

Stir in the prawns (shrimp) and lemon juice and simmer for a further 10 minutes. Serve hot.
Serves 4

Crab Fritters

Metric/Imperial
100 g/4 oz plain flour
1 teaspoon curry powder
salt and pepper
200 ml/⅓ pint milk
2 eggs
225 g/8 oz fresh or canned
  crabmeat, flaked
50 g/2 oz cooked rice
oil for frying

American
1 cup all-purpose flour
1 teaspoon curry powder
salt and pepper
1 cup milk
2 eggs
½ lb fresh or canned
  crabmeat, flaked
⅓ cup cooked rice
oil for frying

Sift the flour and curry powder into a bowl. Add salt and pepper to taste. Add the milk and eggs and beat to make a smooth batter. Stir in the crabmeat and rice.

Pour enough oil into a frying pan (skillet) to make a 1 cm/½ inch layer and heat. Slide tablespoonfuls of the batter into the oil and cook until golden on each side. Drain on kitchen paper towels and serve hot.
Serves 4

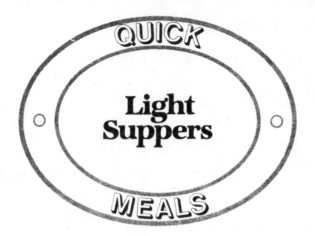

Spinach and Ham Bake

Metric/Imperial
1 × 225 g/8 oz packet frozen
   chopped spinach, thawed and
   well drained
juice of ½ lemon
salt and pepper
100 g/4 oz cooked ham, chopped
25 g/1 oz butter or margarine
175 g/6 oz mushrooms, sliced
2 eggs
2 tablespoons single cream
100 g/4 oz cheese, grated

American
1 × 8 oz package frozen chopped
   spinach, thawed and well
   drained
juice of ½ lemon
salt and pepper
½ cup chopped cooked ham
2 tablespoons butter or
   margarine
1½ cups sliced mushrooms
2 eggs
2 tablespoons light cream
1 cup grated cheese

Mix the spinach with the lemon juice and salt and pepper to taste. Fold in the ham. Spread the mixture over the bottom of a greased ovenproof dish.

Melt the butter or margarine in a frying pan (skillet). Add the mushrooms and fry until tender. Arrange the mushrooms over the spinach mixture.

Lightly beat the eggs with the cream and salt and pepper to taste. Stir in the cheese. Pour over the mushrooms.

Cook in a preheated moderately hot oven (200°C/400°F, Gas Mark 6) for 25 minutes. Serve hot.
Serves 4

Baked Corned Beef Hash

Metric/Imperial
25 g/1 oz butter or margarine
1 large onion, chopped
2-3 cooked carrots, grated
2 large cooked potatoes, grated
75 g/3 oz pickled beetroot,
  grated
1 × 350 g/12 oz can corned
  beef, chopped
1 tablespoon chopped parsley
2 tablespoons red wine
1 egg, beaten
salt and pepper
75 g/3 oz Cheddar cheese,
  grated

American
2 tablespoons butter or
  margarine
1 large onion, chopped
2-3 cooked carrots, grated
2 large cooked potatoes, grated
½ cup grated pickled beets
1 × 12 oz can corned beef,
  chopped
1 tablespoon chopped parsley
2 tablespoons red wine
1 egg, beaten
salt and pepper
¾ cup grated Cheddar cheese

Melt the butter or margarine in a frying pan (skillet). Add the onion and fry until softened. Tip the onion into a bowl and add the carrots, potatoes, beetroot (beets), corned beef, parsley, red wine, egg and salt and pepper to taste. Mix well.

Spoon the mixture into an ovenproof dish. Sprinkle the cheese on top. Cook in a preheated moderately hot oven (190°C/375°F, Gas Mark 5) for 30 minutes or until piping hot and the top is golden. Serve hot.
Serves 4

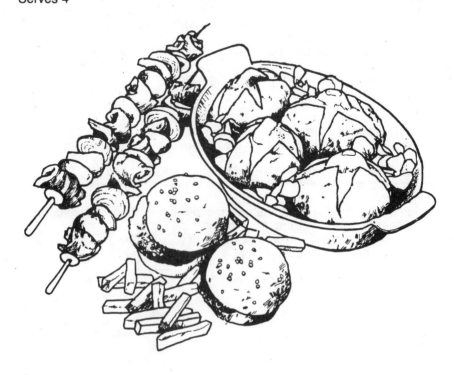

126

Mushroom Risotto

Metric/Imperial
75 g/3 oz butter or margarine
1 onion, sliced
225 g/8 oz brown rice
150 ml/¼ pint dry white wine
600 ml/1 pint boiling chicken
  stock
225 g/8 oz mushrooms, sliced
1½ teaspoons dried basil
salt and pepper
3 tablespoons grated Parmesan
  cheese

American
6 tablespoons butter or
  margarine
1 onion, sliced
1¼ cups brown rice
⅔ cup dry white wine
2½ cups boiling chicken stock
  or broth
½ lb mushrooms, sliced
1½ teaspoons dried basil
salt and pepper
3 tablespoons grated Parmesan
  cheese

Melt the butter or margarine in a saucepan. Add the onion and fry until golden. Stir in the rice and cook for a further 10 minutes, stirring frequently.

Add the wine and bring to the boil. Boil until well reduced. Stir in about one-third of the stock, the mushrooms, basil and salt and pepper to taste. Simmer, stirring occasionally, until the liquid has been absorbed. Continue adding the stock gradually as it is absorbed and cook until the rice is tender.

Spoon into a warmed serving dish and sprinkle the cheese on top. Serve hot.
Serves 4

Chicory (Endive) and Ham

Metric/Imperial
2 heads of chicory
4 slices of cooked ham
150 ml/¼ pint plain yogurt
4 tablespoons milk
1 egg yolk
salt and pepper
2 tablespoons grated Parmesan
  cheese

American
2 heads of Belgian endive
4 slices of cooked ham
⅔ cup plain yogurt
¼ cup milk
1 egg yolk
salt and pepper
2 tablespoons grated Parmesan
  cheese

Blanch the chicory (endive) in boiling water for 3 minutes. Drain well and cut each head in half lengthwise. Wrap a slice of ham around each half and arrange in a greased ovenproof dish.

Mix together the yogurt, milk, egg yolk and salt and pepper to taste. Pour over the ham and sprinkle the cheese on top. Cook in a preheated moderate oven (180°C/350°F, Gas Mark 4) for 25 minutes. Serve hot.
Serves 2 to 4

Tomato Tuna Pan Pizza

Metric/Imperial	American
225 g/8 oz self-raising flour	2 cups self-rising flour
salt and pepper	salt and pepper
100 g/4 oz shredded suet	½ cup shredded suet or shortening
1 teaspoon dried mixed herbs	1 teaspoon dried mixed herbs
150 ml/¼ pint water	¾ cup water
3 tablespoons oil	3 tablespoons oil
Topping:	Topping:
25 g/1 oz butter or	2 tablespoons butter or
margarine	margarine
1 onion, chopped	1 onion, chopped
1 × 225 g/8 oz can tomatoes,	1 × 8 oz can tomatoes, drained
drained and chopped	and chopped
½ × 340 g/11½ oz can condensed	½ × 11½ oz can condensed
tomato soup	tomato soup
1 × 200 g/7 oz can tuna fish,	1 × 7 oz can tuna fish,
drained and flaked	drained and flaked
juice of ½ lemon	juice of ½ lemon

Sift the flour into a bowl and season with salt and pepper. Rub in the suet. Stir in the herbs, then bind to a soft dough with the water.

Roll out the dough to a 25 cm/10 inch round. Heat the oil in a frying pan (skillet) large enough to hold the dough round. Fry the dough for about 5 minutes or until the underside is golden brown. Turn over the dough base and brown the other side.

Meanwhile melt the butter or margarine in a saucepan. Add the onion and fry until softened. Stir in the tomatoes, the undiluted soup and salt and pepper to taste. Simmer gently for 2 to 3 minutes.

Slide the pizza base out of the pan onto a warmed serving plate. Spread the tomato mixture on top. Scatter over the tuna fish and sprinkle with the lemon juice. Serve hot.
Serves 4

Spaghetti with Garlic and Chilli

Metric/Imperial	American
120 ml/4 fl oz olive oil	½ cup olive oil
4 garlic cloves, finely chopped	4 garlic cloves, finely chopped
1 red chilli, seeded and	1 red chili pepper, seeded
chopped	and chopped
500 g/1 lb spaghetti	1 lb spaghetti
salt and pepper	salt and pepper
2 tablespoons chopped parsley	2 tablespoons chopped parsley

Heat the oil in a large frying pan (skillet). Add the garlic and chilli (chili pepper) and fry for 1 to 2 minutes. Remove from the heat and keep hot.

Cook the spaghetti in boiling salted water until just tender. Drain well and add to the frying pan (skillet). Toss to coat with the oil mixture. Return to the heat and toss in the parsley and pepper to taste. Serve hot.
Serves 6

Artichoke and Tomato Pie

Metric/Imperial
225 g/8 oz frozen puff pastry,
  thawed
1 × 225 g/8 oz can artichoke
  hearts, drained and halved
1 × 400 g/14 oz can tomatoes,
  drained and chopped
25 g/1 oz Parmesan cheese,
  grated
1 garlic clove, crushed
2 tablespoons chopped parsley
1 tablespoon oil

American
½ lb frozen puff pastry,
  thawed
1 × 8 oz can artichoke hearts,
  drained and halved
1 × 16 oz can tomatoes, drained
  and chopped
¼ cup grated Parmesan cheese
1 garlic clove, crushed
2 tablespoons chopped parsley
1 tablespoon oil

Roll out the dough and use to line a 20 cm/8 inch flan or quiche pan. Arrange the artichoke hearts in the pastry case and spread over the tomatoes. Sprinkle with the cheese. Mix the garlic with the parsley and scatter on top. Drizzle over the oil.

Cook in a preheated hot oven (220°C/425°F, Gas Mark 7) for 20 to 25 minutes or until the pastry is golden brown. Serve hot.
Serves 2 to 4

Ham and Banana Layer

Metric/Imperial
50 g/2 oz butter or margarine
6 bananas, sliced
8 slices of cooked ham
25 g/1 oz plain flour
450 ml/¾ pint milk
salt and pepper
100 g/4 oz Cheddar cheese,
  grated

American
4 tablespoons butter or
  margarine
6 bananas, sliced
8 slices of cooked ham
¼ cup all-purpose flour
2 cups milk
salt and pepper
1 cup grated Cheddar cheese

Melt 25 g/1 oz (2 tablespoons) of the butter or margarine in a frying pan (skillet). Add the banana slices and fry gently until golden brown.

Arrange four ham slices on the bottom of a greased flameproof dish and cover with the banana slices. Place the remaining ham slices on top.

Melt the remaining butter or margarine in a saucepan. Stir in the flour and cook for 2 minutes, then gradually stir in the milk. Bring to the boil, stirring, and simmer until thickened. Add salt and pepper to taste, and stir in the cheese until melted.

Pour the cheese sauce over the ham. Place under a preheated grill (broiler) and cook until the top is lightly browned and bubbling. Serve hot.
Serves 4

Chakchouka

Metric/Imperial
2 tablespoons oil
2 onions, sliced
½ teaspoon chilli powder
2 red peppers, cored, seeded
  and sliced
2 green peppers, cored, seeded
  and sliced
6 tomatoes, chopped
salt and pepper
8 eggs

American
2 tablespoons oil
2 onions, sliced
½ teaspoon chili powder
2 red peppers, seeded
  and sliced
2 green peppers, seeded
  and sliced
6 tomatoes, chopped
salt and pepper
8 eggs

Heat the oil in a frying pan (skillet). Add the onions and fry until softened. Stir in the chilli powder and fry for 1 minute, then add the red and green peppers, tomatoes and salt and pepper to taste. Cover and cook for 10 minutes.

Divide the vegetable mixture between four shallow baking dishes and make two hollows in each. Break the eggs into the hollows and season with salt and pepper.

Cook in a preheated moderately hot oven (200°C/400°F, Gas Mark 6) for 8 to 10 minutes or until the eggs are set. Serve hot.
Serves 4

Spaghetti with Bacon and Tomato Sauce

Metric/Imperial
2 tablespoons oil
1 onion, chopped
225 g/8 oz back bacon, derinded
  and cut into strips
1 × 400 g/14 oz can tomatoes,
  drained and chopped
1 tablespoon chopped parsley
salt and pepper
500 g/1 lb spaghetti
50 g/2 oz pecorino cheese,
  grated

American
2 tablespoons oil
1 onion, chopped
½ lb Canadian bacon, cut into
  strips
1 × 16 oz can tomatoes, drained
  and chopped
1 tablespoon chopped parsley
salt and pepper
1 lb spaghetti
½ cup grated pecorino cheese

Heat the oil in a frying pan (skillet). Add the onion and bacon and fry until the onion is softened. Stir in the tomatoes, parsley and salt and pepper to taste. Leave to heat through while you cook the pasta.

Cook the spaghetti in boiling salted water until just tender. Drain well and return to the pan. Add the sauce and cheese and toss together. Serve hot.
Serves 4 to 6

Cottage Cheese Pudding

Metric/Imperial	American
300 ml/½ pint milk	1¼ cups milk
50 g/2 oz fresh breadcrumbs	1 cup soft bread crumbs
25 g/1 oz butter or margarine	2 tablespoons butter or
salt and pepper	margarine
350 g/12 oz cottage cheese,	salt and pepper
sieved	1½ cups cottage cheese,
1 tablespoon grated onion	strained
1 tablespoon chopped parsley	1 tablespoon grated onion
2 egg whites	1 tablespoon chopped parsley
	2 egg whites

Warm the milk in a saucepan, then remove from the heat and stir in the breadcrumbs, butter or margarine and salt and pepper to taste. Leave to cool for 15 minutes, then add the cottage cheese, onion and parsley and mix well.

Beat the egg whites until stiff and fold into the mixture. Spoon into a greased ovenproof dish and cook in a preheated moderately hot oven (200°C/400°F, Gas Mark 6) for about 25 minutes or until well risen and golden. Serve immediately.
Serves 2 to 3

Bread and Cheese Pudding

Metric/Imperial	American
75 g/3 oz butter or margarine	6 tablespoons butter or
1 large onion, chopped	margarine
6 slices of white bread, cut	1 large onion, chopped
about 1 cm/½ inch thick	6 slices of white bread, cut
1 tablespoon yeast extract	about ½ inch thick
100 g/4 oz Cheddar cheese,	1 tablespoon brewers' yeast
grated	1 cup grated Cheddar cheese
3 eggs	3 eggs
450 ml/¾ pint milk	2 cups milk
salt and pepper	salt and pepper

Melt 25 g/1 oz (2 tablespoons) of the butter or margarine in a frying pan (skillet). Add the onion and fry until softened.

Meanwhile spread the bread slices with the remaining butter or margarine. Spread over the yeast extract (brewers' yeast). Cut each slice of bread into four triangles and arrange half of them in the bottom of an ovenproof dish.

Spread half the onion over the bread and scatter over half the cheese. Repeat the layers.

Lightly beat the eggs with the milk and salt and pepper to taste. Pour into the ovenproof dish and leave to soak for 5 minutes.

Cook in a preheated moderate oven (180°C/350°F, Gas Mark 4) for about 50 minutes or until set and golden brown. Serve hot.
Serves 4

Beef and Rice Quiche

Metric/Imperial	American
225 g/8 oz long-grain rice	1 cup rice
salt and pepper	salt and pepper
2 eggs, beaten	2 eggs, beaten
225 g/8 oz Mozzarella cheese, grated	2 cups grated Mozzarella cheese
500 g/1 lb lean minced beef	1 lb lean ground beef
1 onion, chopped	1 onion, chopped
1 garlic clove, crushed	1 garlic clove, crushed
1 × 340 g/11½ oz can condensed tomato soup	1 × 11½ oz can condensed tomato soup
1 teaspoon dried oregano	1 teaspoon dried oregano
2 tomatoes, sliced	2 tomatoes, sliced
2 tablespoons grated Parmesan cheese	2 tablespoons grated Parmesan cheese

Cook the rice in simmering salted water until tender. Drain if necessary, then allow to cool slightly. Beat in the eggs and half the Mozzarella cheese. Press the mixture evenly over the bottom and up the sides of a greased 25 cm/10 inch flan or quiche pan. Cook in a preheated hot oven (230°C/450°F, Gas Mark 8) for 15 minutes.

Meanwhile fry the beef with the onion and garlic in a frying pan (skillet) until browned and crumbly. Drain off all excess fat from the pan, then stir in the tomato soup, oregano and salt and pepper to taste.

Pour the beef mixture into the rice crust. Arrange the tomato slices on top and scatter over the remaining Mozzarella cheese and the Parmesan cheese.

Return to the oven and cook for a further 10 to 12 minutes or until the cheeses have melted and the top is golden brown. Serve hot.

Serves 4 to 6

Buttered Tagliatelle

Metric/Imperial	American
500 g/1 lb tagliatelle	1 lb tagliatelle
salt and pepper	salt and pepper
100 g/4 oz butter or margarine, cut into pieces	½ cup butter or margarine, cut into pieces
75 g/3 oz Parmesan cheese, grated	¾ cup grated Parmesan cheese

Cook the tagliatelle in boiling salted water until just tender. Drain well, then return to the pan. Add the butter or margarine, cheese and salt and pepper to taste and toss until the fat has melted and the pasta is coated. Serve hot.

Serves 6

Egg and Onion Gratin

Metric/Imperial
50 g/2 oz butter or margarine
500 g/1 lb onions, sliced
salt and pepper
6 hard-boiled eggs, sliced
25 g/1 oz plain flour
300 ml/½ pint milk
1 teaspoon made mustard
100 g/4 oz Cheddar cheese,
  grated

American
4 tablespoons butter or
  margarine
1 lb onions, sliced
salt and pepper
6 hard-cooked eggs, sliced
¼ cup all-purpose flour
1½ cups milk
1 teaspoon prepared mustard
1 cup grated Cheddar cheese

Melt 25 g/1 oz (2 tablespoons) of the butter or margarine in a frying pan
(skillet). Add the onions and cook gently until softened. Spoon into a
flameproof serving dish and season to taste with salt and pepper. Arrange
the egg slices over the onions and keep warm.

Melt the remaining butter or margarine in a saucepan. Stir in the flour
and cook for 2 minutes, then gradually stir in the milk. Bring to the boil,
stirring, and simmer until thickened. Add the mustard and three-quarters
of the cheese and stir until melted. Season to taste with salt and pepper.

Pour the sauce over the egg slices and scatter the remaining cheese
on top. Place under a preheated grill (broiler) and cook until the top is
golden brown and bubbling. Serve hot.
Serves 4

Macaroni Cheese with Bacon

Metric/Imperial
225 g/8 oz short-cut macaroni
salt and pepper
350 g/12 oz streaky bacon
  rashers, derinded
1 tablespoon cornflour
450 ml/¾ pint milk
½ teaspoon dry mustard
100 g/4 oz Cheddar cheese,
  grated

American
½ lb elbow macaroni
salt and pepper
¾ lb bacon slices
1 tablespoon cornstarch
2 cups milk
½ teaspoon dry mustard
1 cup grated Cheddar cheese

Cook the macaroni in boiling salted water until just tender.

Meanwhile, grill (broil) or fry the bacon until it is crisp. Drain on kitchen
paper towels and crumble. Reserve.

Blend the cornflour(cornstarch) with the milk in a saucepan. Bring to the
boil, stirring, and simmer until thickened. Add the mustard and salt and
pepper to taste, and stir in the cheese until melted.

Drain the macaroni and stir into the cheese sauce. Pour into a warmed
serving dish and sprinkle the bacon on top. Serve hot.
Serves 4

Vegetable Cannelloni

Metric/Imperial
8 cannelloni tubes
salt and pepper
2 x 400 g/14 oz cans tomatoes
75 g/3 oz fresh breadcrumbs
75 g/3 oz Cheddar cheese,
    grated
1 tablespoon chopped parsley
1 teaspoon dried oregano

American
8 cannelloni tubes
salt and pepper
2 x 16 oz cans tomatoes
1½ cups soft bread crumbs
¾ cup grated Cheddar cheese
1 tablespoon chopped parsley
1 teaspoon dried oregano

Cook the cannelloni tubes in boiling salted water for 5 minutes.

Meanwhile drain one can of tomatoes and chop them. Mix with the breadcrumbs, cheese, parsley and salt and pepper to taste.

Drain the cannelloni tubes and dry on kitchen paper towels. Fill with the cheese mixture and arrange in a greased ovenproof dish. Chop the second can of tomatoes with its juice and pour over the cannelloni. Sprinkle the oregano on top.

Cook in a preheated moderate oven (180°C/350°F, Gas Mark 4) for 30 minutes. Serve hot.
Serves 4

Broad (Lima) Bean and Egg Casserole

Metric/Imperial
500 g/1 lb frozen broad beans
3 hard-boiled eggs, sliced
50 g/2 oz butter or margarine
40 g/1½ oz plain flour
450 ml/¾ pint milk
salt and pepper
50 g/2 oz Cheddar cheese,
    grated
4 tablespoons fresh bread-
    crumbs

American
1 lb frozen lima beans
3 hard-cooked eggs, sliced
4 tablespoons butter or
    margarine
6 tablespoons all-purpose
    flour
2 cups milk
salt and pepper
½ cup grated Cheddar cheese
¼ cup soft bread crumbs

Cook the beans according to the directions on the packet. Drain well.

Place half the beans in a greased ovenproof dish and cover with the egg slices. Top with the remaining beans.

Melt 40 g/1½ oz (3 tablespoons) of the butter or margarine in a saucepan. Stir in the flour and cook for 2 minutes, then gradually stir in the milk. Bring to the boil, stirring, and simmer until thickened. Season to taste with salt and pepper.

Pour the sauce over the beans. Mix together the cheese and breadcrumbs and scatter over the top. Dot with the remaining butter or margarine. Cook in a preheated hot oven (220°C/425°F, Gas Mark 7) for 15 minutes or until the top is golden brown. Serve hot.
Serves 4

Eggs Florentine

Metric/Imperial
1 × 300 g/10 oz packet
  frozen chopped spinach
8 eggs
40 g/1½ oz butter or margarine
500 g/1 lb tomatoes, skinned
  and sliced
pinch of grated nutmeg
salt and pepper
Sauce:
15 g/½ oz butter or margarine
15 g/½ oz plain flour
300 ml/½ pint milk
50 g/2 oz Cheddar cheese,
  grated
1 tablespoon grated
  Parmesan cheese

American
1 × 10 oz package frozen
  chopped spinach
8 eggs
3 tablespoons butter or
  margarine
1 lb tomatoes, peeled and
  sliced
pinch of grated nutmeg
salt and pepper
Sauce:
1 tablespoon butter or
  margarine
2 tablespoons all-purpose
  flour
1¼ cups milk
½ cup grated Cheddar cheese
1 tablespoon grated Parmesan
  cheese

Cook the spinach according to the instructions on the packet. Meanwhile poach or soft-boil the eggs.

Melt the butter or margarine in a frying pan (skillet). Add the tomato slices and fry for 2 minutes on each side. Transfer the tomato slices to an ovenproof dish.

Drain the spinach well, then tip it into the frying pan (skillet). Stir to mix with the butter. Add the nutmeg and salt and pepper to taste. Spread the spinach over the tomatoes in the ovenproof dish. Top with the eggs and keep hot.

Melt the butter or margarine for the sauce in a saucepan. Stir in the flour and cook for 1 minute, then gradually stir in the milk. Bring to the boil, stirring, and simmer until thickened. Stir in the Cheddar cheese and salt and pepper to taste.

Pour the cheese sauce over the eggs and sprinkle the Parmesan cheese on top. Grill (broil) until the top is golden brown. Serve hot.
Serves 4

Bubble and Squeak Supper

Metric/Imperial	American
500 g/1 lb potatoes, cooked and mashed	1 lb potatoes, cooked and mashed
225 g/8 oz cabbage, shredded and cooked	½ lb cabbage, shredded and cooked
salt and pepper	salt and pepper
75 g/3 oz butter or margarine	6 tablespoons butter or margarine
1 onion, chopped	1 onion, chopped
1 x 400 g/14 oz can baked beans in tomato sauce	1 x 16 oz can baked beans in tomato sauce
225 g/8 oz cooked ham, diced	1 cup diced cooked ham
1 tablespoon sweet pickle	1 tablespoon sweet pickle relish
1 teaspoon Worcestershire sauce	1 teaspoon Worcestershire sauce

Mix together the potatoes and cabbage and season to taste with salt and pepper. Melt 50 g/2 oz (4 tablespoons) of the butter or margarine in a large frying pan (skillet). Spread out the potato mixture in the pan and cook gently until the underside is golden brown. Turn over and brown the other side. This will take 15 to 20 minutes altogether.

Meanwhile melt the remaining butter or margarine in a saucepan. Add the onion and fry until softened. Stir in the remaining ingredients and heat through gently.

Slide the bubble and squeak base onto a warmed serving plate and top with the bean and ham mixture. Serve hot.

Serves 4

Noodles with Anchovy Sauce

Metric/Imperial	American
3 tablespoons oil	3 tablespoons oil
1 onion, chopped	1 onion, chopped
1 garlic clove, crushed	1 garlic clove, crushed
1 x 50 g/2 oz can anchovy fillets, drained and chopped	1 x 2 oz can anchovy fillets, drained and chopped
2 tablespoons chopped parsley	2 tablespoons chopped parsley
1 tablespoon chopped fresh fennel	1 tablespoon chopped fresh fennel
1 x 400 g/14 oz can tomatoes	1 x 16 oz can tomatoes
3 tablespoons sultanas	3 tablespoons golden raisins
salt and pepper	salt and pepper
500 g/1 lb egg noodles	1 lb egg noodles

Heat the oil in a saucepan. Add the onion and garlic and fry until softened. Stir in the anchovies, parsley, fennel, tomatoes with their juice, sultanas (raisins) and salt and pepper to taste. Simmer for 20 minutes, stirring occasionally.

Meanwhile, cook the noodles in boiling salted water until just tender. Drain well and return to the pan. Add the anchovy sauce and toss together. Serve hot.

Serves 6

Macaroni Cheese with Frankfurters

Metric/Imperial	American
225 g/8 oz short cut macaroni	½ lb elbow macaroni
salt and pepper	salt and pepper
8 frankfurter sausages	8 frankfurters
40 g/1½ oz butter or margarine	3 tablespoons butter or
40 g/1½ oz plain flour	margarine
450 ml/¾ pint milk	6 tablespoons all-purpose flour
1 teaspoon French mustard	2 cups milk
225 g/8 oz Cheddar cheese,	1 teaspoon Dijon-style mustard
grated	2 cups grated Cheddar cheese
1 × 200 g/7 oz can sweetcorn	1 × 7 oz can whole kernel corn,
kernels, drained	drained
2 spring onions, chopped	2 scallions, chopped

Cook the macaroni in boiling salted water until just tender. Cook the frankfurters in boiling water according to the instructions on the packet.

Meanwhile melt the butter or margarine in a saucepan. Stir in the flour and cook for 2 minutes, then gradually stir in the milk. Bring to the boil, stirring; and simmer until thickened. Add the mustard and salt and pepper to taste, then stir in 200 g/7 oz (1¾ cups) of the cheese until melted.

Drain the macaroni and return to the saucepan. Drain the frankfurters and cut into 2.5 cm/1 inch pieces. Add to the macaroni with the corn, spring onions (scallions) and cheese sauce. Fold together thoroughly.

Spoon the mixture into a flameproof serving dish and scatter the remaining cheese on top. Place under a preheated grill (broiler) and cook for 2 to 3 minutes or until the cheese has melted and the top is golden brown. Serve hot.
Serves 4

Bavarian Pizza

Metric/Imperial
100 g/4 oz self-raising flour
½ teaspoon baking powder
½ teaspoon dry mustard
½ teaspoon salt
25 g/1 oz butter or margarine
1 onion, grated
75 g/3 oz cheese, grated
½ teaspoon dried mixed herbs
1 egg, beaten
1 tablespoon milk
Topping:
¼ teaspoon dried oregano
4 tomatoes, skinned and sliced
50 g/2 oz cheese, grated
100 g/4 oz mushrooms, sliced
50 g/2 oz smoked German
  sausage, cut into thin strips

American
1 cup self-rising flour
½ teaspoon baking powder
½ teaspoon dry mustard
½ teaspoon salt
2 tablespoons butter or
  margarine
1 onion, grated
¾ cup grated cheese
½ teaspoon dried mixed herbs
1 egg, beaten
3 tablespoons milk
Topping:
¼ teaspoon dried oregano
4 tomatoes, peeled and sliced
½ cup grated cheese
1 cup sliced mushrooms
2 oz smoked German sausage,
  cut into thin strips

Sift the flour, baking powder, mustard and salt into a bowl. Rub in the butter or margarine, then add the onion, cheese, herbs, egg and milk and mix to a soft dough. Roll out to a 23 cm/9 inch round and place on a greased baking sheet.

Sprinkle the oregano over the dough round and cover with the remaining topping ingredients. Cook in a preheated moderately hot oven (200°C/400°F, Gas Mark 6) for 20 to 25 minutes. Serve hot.
Serves 2 to 4

Sausage Griddle Scone

Metric/Imperial
100 g/4 oz plain flour
pinch of salt
1 teaspoon baking powder
3 tablespoons oil
Topping:
100 g/4 oz liver sausage
225 g/8 oz tomatoes, sliced
100 g/4 oz German sausage,
  cut into strips
50 g/2 oz Cheddar cheese, grated
25 g/1 oz Parmesan cheese,
  grated

American
1 cup all-purpose flour
pinch of salt
1 teaspoon baking powder
3 tablespoons oil
Topping:
¼ lb liverwurst
½ lb tomatoes, sliced
¼ lb German sausage, cut into
  strips
½ cup grated Cheddar cheese
¼ cup grated Parmesan cheese

Sift the flour, salt and baking powder into a bowl. Work in enough water to make a fairly firm dough. Knead lightly; roll out to an 18 cm/7 inch round.

Heat the oil on a griddle or in a frying pan (skillet) large enough to hold the dough round. Fry the dough for 5 minutes or until the underside is golden brown. Turn the base over and spread the liver sausage (liverwurst) on top. Cover with the tomatoes, then the sausage strips. Sprinkle over the cheeses.

Cover the griddle or pan and continue cooking for 10 minutes or until the dough base is cooked through and the cheeses have melted. If you like, put the scone under a preheated grill (broiler) to brown the top.
Serves 2

Spaghetti Carbonara

Metric/Imperial
500 g/1 lb spaghetti
salt and pepper
1 tablespoon olive oil
175 g/6 oz back bacon, derinded
  and chopped
4 tablespoons single cream
2 eggs, beaten
50 g/2 oz Parmesan cheese,
  grated
pinch of cayenne pepper
40 g/1½ oz butter or
  margarine, cut into small
  pieces

American
1 lb spaghetti
salt and pepper
1 tablespoon olive oil
¾ cup chopped Canadian
  bacon
¼ cup light cream
2 eggs, beaten
½ cup grated Parmesan cheese
pinch of cayenne
3 tablespoons butter or
  margarine, cut into small
  pieces

Cook the spaghetti in boiling salted water until just tender.

Meanwhile, heat oil in a frying pan and fry the bacon until crisp.

Mix together the cream, eggs, cheese, cayenne and salt and pepper.

Drain the spaghetti and return to the pan. Add the butter or margarine and toss to coat, then add the bacon and egg mixture and toss well together. Serve immediately.
Serves 4

Syracuse Pasta

Metric/Imperial
4 tablespoons olive oil
1 large onion, sliced
2 garlic cloves, crushed
500 g/1 lb courgettes, chopped
1 green pepper, cored, seeded
 and chopped
1 × 400 g/14 oz can tomatoes,
 drained and chopped
100 g/4 oz black olives stoned
3 anchovy fillets, chopped
1 tablespoon chopped parsley
½ teaspoon dried marjoram
salt and pepper
500 g/1 lb tripoline (fluted
 wide noodles)
50 g/2 oz Parmesan cheese,
 grated

American
¼ cup olive oil
1 large onion, sliced
2 garlic cloves, crushed
1 lb zucchini, chopped
1 green pepper, seeded and
 chopped
1 × 16 oz can tomatoes, drained
 and chopped
¾ cup pitted ripe olives
3 anchovy fillets, chopped
1 tablespoon chopped parsley
½ teaspoon dried marjoram
salt and pepper
1 lb tripoline (fluted wide
 noodles)
½ cup grated Parmesan cheese

Heat the oil in a saucepan. Add the onion and garlic and fry until softened.
Add the courgettes (zucchini) and green pepper and fry for a further
5 minutes. Stir in the tomatoes, olives, anchovies, herbs and salt and
pepper to taste. Cover and leave to simmer while cooking the pasta.
  Cook the tripoline in boiling salted water until just tender. Drain well and
return to the pan. Add the sauce and cheese and toss together. Serve
hot.
Serves 4

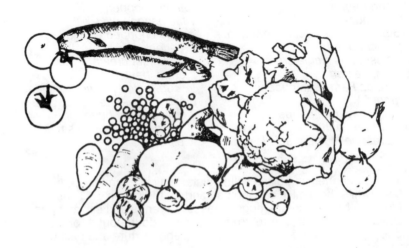

Chicken and Vegetable Savoury

Metric/Imperial
225 g/8 oz frozen sweetcorn
  kernels
4 tablespoons frozen peas
½ green pepper, cored, seeded
  and chopped
3 tablespoons oil
100 g/4 oz mushrooms, sliced
100 g/4 oz cooked chicken
  meat, diced
2 large tomatoes, chopped
5 eggs
1 chicken stock cube, crumbled
salt and pepper

American
½ lb frozen whole kernel corn
¼ cup frozen peas
½ green pepper, seeded
  and chopped
3 tablespoons oil
1 cup sliced mushrooms
½ cup diced cooked chicken
2 large tomatoes, chopped
5 eggs
1 chicken bouillon cube, crumbled
salt and pepper

Put the corn, peas and green pepper in a saucepan and cover with boiling water. Bring back to the boil, then cover and simmer for 5 minutes. Drain well and set aside.

Heat the oil in a large frying pan (skillet). Add the mushrooms and fry for 2 minutes. Stir in the chicken, tomatoes and cooked vegetables and cook, stirring occasionally, for 5 minutes.

Lightly beat the eggs with the stock (bouillon) cube and salt and pepper to taste. Pour into the pan and continue cooking, stirring occasionally, until the egg mixture has set. Cut into wedges to serve.
Serves 2 to 4

Spanish Omelette

Metric/Imperial
50 g/2 oz butter or margarine
175 g/6 oz potatoes, cooked
  and diced
4 tomatoes, skinned and
  chopped
100 g/4 oz mushrooms, sliced
175 g/6 oz frozen peas,
  thawed
6 eggs
salt and pepper

American
4 tablespoons butter or
  margarine
1 cup diced cooked potatoes
4 tomatoes, peeled and
  chopped
1 cup sliced mushrooms
1¼ cups frozen peas, thawed
6 eggs
salt and pepper

Melt the butter or margarine in a large frying pan (skillet). Add the potatoes and fry until golden brown. Stir in the tomatoes, mushrooms and peas and fry for a further 2 to 3 minutes.

Lightly beat the eggs with salt and pepper to taste and pour into the pan. Cover and cook gently until the eggs have just set.
Serves 3 to 4

Pasta Omelette

Metric/Imperial
100 g/4 oz short-cut macaroni
salt and pepper
40 g/1½ oz butter or margarine
1 onion, chopped
4 eggs
6 tablespoons milk
3 tomatoes, sliced
1 tablespoon Worcestershire
  sauce
75 g/3 oz mature Cheddar cheese,
  grated

American
¼ lb elbow macaroni
salt and pepper
3 tablespoons butter or
  margarine
1 onion, chopped
4 eggs
6 tablespoons milk
3 tomatoes, sliced
1 tablespoon Worcestershire
  sauce
¾ cup grated sharp Cheddar
  cheese

Cook the macaroni in boiling salted water until just tender. Drain well.
    Melt the butter or margarine in a frying pan (skillet). Add the onion and
fry until softened. Lightly beat the eggs with the milk and salt and pepper
to taste. Fold in the macaroni. Pour the mixture into the frying pan (skillet)
and stir to mix with the onion. Cook gently, stirring occasionally so that
the liquid egg mixture can run onto the pan. When the omelette has just
set, cover with the tomato slices. Sprinkle over the Worcestershire sauce
and scatter the cheese on top.
    Place the pan under a preheated grill (broiler) and cook until the
omelette 'rises' and the cheese is golden brown. Serve hot.
Serves 4

Italian Cheese Omelette

Metric/Imperial
225 g/8 oz tagliatelle
salt and pepper
6 eggs
25 g/1 oz Parmesan cheese,
  grated
2 tablespoons olive oil
175 g/6 oz Mozzarella cheese,
  thinly sliced

American
½ lb tagliatelle
salt and pepper
6 eggs
¼ cup grated Parmesan cheese
2 tablespoons olive oil
6 oz Mozzarella cheese, thinly
  sliced

Cook the tagliatelle in boiling salted water until just tender. Drain well,
then chop coarsely.
    Beat the eggs with the Parmesan cheese and salt and pepper to taste.
Stir in the tagliatelle. Heat the oil in a large frying pan (skillet). Pour in half
the egg mixture. Arrange the Mozzarella cheese slices on top and cover
with the remaining egg mixture.
    Fry until the underside of the omelette is golden brown, then slide out
of the pan onto a plate. Invert back into the pan and cook until the other
side is golden brown and the omelette is firm. Serve hot, cut into wedges.
Serves 3 to 4

Tuna and Pepper Omelette

Metric/Imperial
8 eggs
2 tablespoons water
salt and pepper
50 g/2 oz butter or margarine
tomato slices to garnish
Filling:
1 × 200 g/7 oz can tuna fish,
  drained and flaked
1 green pepper, cored, seeded
  and diced
100 g/4 oz frozen peas, thawed
2 tomatoes, finely chopped
4 tablespoons single cream
salt and pepper

American
8 eggs
2 tablespoons water
salt and pepper
4 tablespoons butter or
  margarine
tomato slices for garnish
Filling:
1 × 7 oz can tuna fish, drained
  and flaked
1 green pepper, seeded
  and diced
1 cup frozen peas, thawed
2 tomatoes, finely chopped
¼ cup light cream
salt and pepper

First make the filling. Put all the ingredients into a saucepan and heat through gently, stirring occasionally, while you make the omelettes.

Lightly beat the eggs with the water and salt and pepper to taste. Melt 15 g/½ oz (1 tablespoon) of the butter or margarine in a frying pan (skillet). Pour in one-quarter of the egg mixture and cook gently until the omelette is just set, lifting the set edges to let the uncooked egg run onto the pan. Place one-quarter of the tuna filling on one-half of the omelette and fold it over. Slide onto a warmed serving plate and keep hot while you cook the remaining three omelettes in the same way.

Serve hot, garnished with tomato slices.
Serves 4

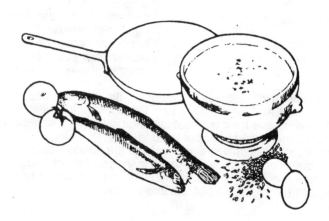

Hawaiian Omelette

Metric/Imperial
8 eggs
2 tablespoons water
salt and pepper
50 g/2 oz butter or margarine
Filling:
50 g/2 oz butter or margarine
175 g/6 oz mushrooms, chopped
100 g/4 oz cooked ham, diced
100 g/4 oz canned pineapple,
    chopped

American
8 eggs
2 tablespoons water
salt and pepper
4 tablespoons butter or
    margarine
Filling:
4 tablespoons butter or
    margarine
1½ cups chopped mushrooms
1 cup diced cooked ham
1 cup chopped canned pineapple

First make the filling. Melt the butter or margarine in a saucepan and stir in the mushrooms, ham and pineapple. Leave to heat through gently while you make the omelettes.

Lightly beat the eggs with the water and salt and pepper to taste. Melt 15 g/½ oz (1 tablespoon) of the butter or margarine in a frying pan (skillet). Pour in one-quarter of the egg mixture and cook gently until the omelette is just set, lifting the set edges to let the liquid egg run onto the pan.

Spoon one-quarter of the filling onto one-half of the omelette and fold it over. Slide onto a warmed serving plate and keep hot while you cook the remaining three omelettes in the same way. Serve hot.
Serves 4

Potato Omelette

Metric/Imperial
500 g/1 lb potatoes
salt and pepper
2 tablespoons milk
100 g/4 oz Cheddar cheese,
    grated
3 eggs, separated
1 tablespoon chopped parsley
25 g/1 oz butter or margarine

American
1 lb potatoes
salt and pepper
2 tablespoons milk
1 cup grated Cheddar cheese
3 eggs, separated
1 tablespoon chopped parsley
2 tablespoons butter or
    margarine

Cook the potatoes in boiling salted water for about 20 minutes or until tender. Drain well and return to the pan. Dry out over low heat, then mash until smooth. Remove from the heat and beat in the milk, cheese, egg yolks, parsley and salt and pepper to taste.

Beat the egg whites until stiff and fold into the potato mixture.

Melt the butter or margarine in a large frying pan (skillet). Add the potato mixture and cook for about 5 minutes on each side or until puffed up and golden brown. Serve hot, cut into wedges.
Serves 4

Finnan Haddie Soufflé Omelette

Metric/Imperial	American
350 g/12 oz smoked haddock fillets	¾ lb finnan haddie (smoked haddock fillets)
75 g/3 oz butter or margarine	6 tablespoons butter or margarine
1 tablespoon chopped parsley	1 tablespoon chopped parsley
8 eggs, separated	8 eggs, separated
salt and pepper	salt and pepper

Poach the haddock in water to cover for 3 to 5 minutes. Drain well, then remove any skin and bones and flake the fish. Melt 25 g/1 oz (2 tablespoons) of the butter or margarine in a saucepan. Stir in the flaked fish and parsley and keep warm.

Lightly beat the egg yolks with salt and pepper to taste. Beat the egg whites until stiff and fold into the yolks with the haddock mixture.

Melt 15 g/½ oz (1 tablespoon) of the remaining butter or margarine in a frying pan (skillet). Pour in one-quarter of the egg mixture and cook gently until the omelette is set and pale golden underneath. Place the pan under a preheated grill (broiler) and cook for 30 seconds to 1 minute to set and brown the top.

Fold the omelette in half and slide onto a warmed serving plate. Keep hot while you make the remaining three omelettes in the same way. Serve hot.
Serves 4

Smoked Salmon Omelette

Metric/Imperial	American
8 eggs	8 eggs
2 tablespoons water	2 tablespoons water
1 tablespoon chopped chives	1 tablespoon chopped chives
salt and pepper	salt and pepper
50 g/2 oz butter or margarine	4 tablespoons butter or margarine
100 g/4 oz smoked salmon, chopped	1 cup chopped smoked salmon

Lightly beat the eggs with the water, chives and salt and pepper to taste. Melt 15 g/½ oz (1 tablespoon) of the butter or margarine in a frying pan (skillet). Pour in one-quarter of the egg mixture and cook gently until the omelette is just set, lifting the set edges to let the uncooked egg run onto the pan.

Place one-quarter of the smoked salmon down the centre of the omelette and fold the two sides in to the centre. Slide onto a warmed serving plate and keep hot while you cook the remaining omelettes in the same way. Serve hot.
Serves 4

Variation:
Use flaked smoked mackerel or smoked trout fillets instead of the smoked salmon.

Chicken Liver Omelette

Metric/Imperial
8 eggs
1 tablespoon single cream
salt and pepper
25 g/1 oz butter or margarine
Filling:
1 tablespoon oil
100 g/4 oz chicken livers,
  cut into 1 cm/½ inch strips
1 small onion, chopped
1 garlic clove, crushed
1 tablespoon dry sherry
150 ml/¼ pint chicken stock
1 teaspoon tomato purée

American
8 eggs
1 tablespoon light cream
salt and pepper
2 tablespoons butter or
  margarine
Filling:
1 tablespoon oil
¼ lb chicken livers, cut into
  ½ inch strips
1 small onion, chopped
1 garlic clove, crushed
1 tablespoon dry sherry
⅔ cup chicken stock
1 teaspoon tomato paste

First make the filling. Heat the oil in a saucepan. Add the livers and fry, stirring, for 30 seconds. Add the onion and garlic and fry for a further 1 minute. Remove from the pan.

Add the sherry and stock to the pan and bring to the boil. Boil until reduced by about half, then stir in the tomato purée (paste) and salt and pepper to taste. Return the liver mixture to the pan and leave to heat through while you make the omelette.

Lightly beat the eggs with the cream and salt and pepper to taste. Melt the butter or margarine in a large frying pan (skillet), pour in the egg mixture and cook, stirring with a fork, until the mixture resembles lightly scrambled egg. Stop stirring and leave to cook until the omelette is set and golden brown underneath.

Slide the omelette onto a warmed serving plate and spread the liver filling over the top. Fold the omelette in half and serve hot.
Serves 3 to 4

Oriental Crab Omelette

Metric/Imperial	American
2 spring onions, shredded	2 scallions, shredded
4 eggs, beaten	4 eggs, beaten
salt	salt
3 tablespoons oil	3 tablespoons oil
2 slices of fresh root ginger, peeled and shredded	2 slices of fresh ginger root, peeled and shredded
175 g/6 oz fresh, frozen or canned crabmeat, flaked	6 oz fresh, frozen or canned crabmeat, flaked
1 tablespoon dry sherry	1 tablespoon dry sherry
1½ tablespoons soy sauce	1½ tablespoons soy sauce
2 teaspoons caster sugar	2 teaspoons sugar
shredded lettuce to garnish	shredded lettuce for garnish

Lightly beat the green part of the spring onions (scallions) with the eggs. Add salt to taste.

Heat the oil in a frying pan (skillet). Add the white part of the spring onions (scallions) and the ginger, then stir in the crabmeat and sherry. Stir-fry for a few seconds. Add the soy sauce and sugar and mix well.

Pour in the egg mixture and cook, stirring frequently, until the eggs are beginning to set. Stop stirring and cook until the omelette is firm. Serve hot, garnished with shredded lettuce.
Serves 2 to 4

Asparagus Omelette

Metric/Imperial	American
6 eggs	6 eggs
1 tablespoon water	1 tablespoon water
½ teaspoon dried mixed herbs	½ teaspoon dried mixed herbs
salt and pepper	salt and pepper
1 × 425 g/15 oz can asparagus spears, drained	1 × 16 oz can asparagus spears, drained
25 g/1 oz butter or margarine	2 tablespoons butter or margarine
4 tablespoons soured cream	¼ cup sour cream
2 tablespoons grated Parmesan cheese	2 tablespoons grated Parmesan cheese

Lightly beat the eggs with the water, herbs and salt and pepper to taste. Chop half the asparagus and stir into the egg mixture.

Melt the butter or margarine in a large frying pan (skillet). Pour in the egg mixture and cook until the omelette is just set, lifting the set edges to allow the liquid egg to run onto the pan. Spread the sour cream over the omelette and arrange the remaining asparagus spears on top like the spokes of a wheel. Sprinkle with the cheese.

Place the pan under a preheated grill (broiler) and cook for 1 to 2 minutes or until the top is golden brown. Serve hot.
Serves 4

Mushroom Croûton Omelette

Metric/Imperial
50 g/2 oz butter
4 slices of wholemeal bread,
    cut into 1 cm/½ inch dice
1 large onion, sliced
225 g/8 oz mushrooms, sliced
8 eggs
salt and pepper

American
4 tablespoons butter
4 slices of wholewheat bread,
    cut into ½ inch dice
1 large onion, sliced
½ lb mushrooms, sliced
8 eggs
salt and pepper

Melt 15 g/½ oz (1 tablespoon) of the butter in a frying pan (skillet). Add one-quarter of the bread dice and onion and fry until the bread is golden brown and the onion softened. Stir in one-quarter of the mushrooms and cook for a further 2 minutes.

Lightly beat two of the eggs with salt and pepper to taste. Pour into the pan and stir to mix with the mushroom mixture. Cover and cook until the omelette is set and golden brown underneath.

Fold in half, slide onto a warmed serving plate and keep hot while you make the remaining three omelettes in the same way. Serve hot.
Serves 4

Continental Meat Soufflé

Metric/Imperial
25 g/1 oz butter or margarine
25 g/1 oz plain flour
300 ml/½ pint milk
100 g/4 oz liver pâté
1 teaspoon dry mustard
salt and pepper
3 eggs, separated
50 g/2 oz garlic sausage,
    chopped
50 g/2 oz salami, chopped
100 g/4 oz mushrooms, sliced
2 tablespoons grated Parmesan
    cheese

American
2 tablespoons butter or
    margarine
¼ cup all-purpose flour
1½ cups milk
¼ lb liverwurst
1 teaspoon dry mustard
salt and pepper
3 eggs, separated
½ cup chopped garlic sausage
½ cup chopped salami
1 cup sliced mushrooms
2 tablespoons grated Parmesan
    cheese

Melt the butter or margarine in a saucepan. Stir in the flour and cook for 2 minutes, then gradually stir in the milk. Bring to the boil, stirring, and simmer until thickened. Remove from the heat and add the liver pâté (liverwurst), mustard and salt and pepper to taste. Stir until evenly combined. Cool slightly, then stir in the egg yolks.

Mix together the garlic sausage, salami and mushrooms.

Beat the egg whites until stiff and fold into the liver pâté (liverwurst) mixture. Make alternate layers of this and the meat mixture in a greased 1.2 litre/2 pint (5 cup) soufflé dish, ending with the liver pâté (liverwurst) mixture. Sprinkle the cheese on top.

Cook in a preheated moderate oven (180°C/350°F, Gas Mark 4) for 30 minutes or until well risen and golden. Serve immediately.
Serves 4

Blue Cheese Soufflé

Metric/Imperial
50 g/2 oz butter or margarine
25 g/1 oz plain flour
300 ml/½ pint milk
salt and pepper
100 g/4 oz blue cheese such
  as Stilton, grated
3 eggs, separated

American
4 tablespoons butter or
  margarine
¼ cup all-purpose flour
1½ cups milk
salt and pepper
1 cup grated blue cheese such as
  Stilton
3 eggs, separated

Melt the butter or margarine in a saucepan. Stir in the flour and cook for 2 minutes, then gradually stir in the milk. Bring to the boil, stirring, and simmer until thickened. Season to taste with salt and pepper. Stir in the cheese until melted.

Remove from the heat and cool slightly, then beat in the egg yolks. Beat the egg whites until stiff and fold into the mixture. Spoon into a greased 1.2 litre/2 pint (5 cup) soufflé dish and cook in a preheated moderately hot oven (190°C/375°F, Gas Mark 5) for 35 to 40 minutes or until well risen and golden brown. Serve immediately.
Serves 4

Variation:
Any cheese may be used in place of blue cheese. If you use a mild cheese such as Cheddar, add a pinch of grated nutmeg to the sauce base.

Orange Chicken Soufflé

Metric/Imperial
25 g/1 oz butter or margarine
25 g/1 oz plain flour
300 ml/½ pint chicken stock
grated rind of 1 orange
salt and pepper
3 egg yolks
175 g/6 oz cooked chicken
  meat, minced
4 egg whites

American
2 tablespoons butter or
  margarine
¼ cup all-purpose flour
1½ cups chicken stock or broth
grated rind of 1 orange
salt and pepper
3 egg yolks
1 cup ground cooked chicken
4 egg whites

Melt the butter or margarine in a saucepan. Stir in the flour and cook for 2 minutes, then gradually stir in the stock. Bring to the boil, stirring, and simmer until thickened. Stir in the orange rind and salt and pepper to taste.

Remove from the heat and cool slightly, then stir in the egg yolks followed by the chicken. Beat the egg whites until stiff and fold into the mixture.

Spoon into a greased 1.2 litre/2 pint (5 cup) soufflé dish and cook in a preheated moderately hot oven (190°C/375°F, Gas Mark 5) for 30 to 40 minutes or until well risen and golden brown. Serve immediately.
Serves 4

Savoury Tomato Pancakes (Crêpes)

Metric/Imperial	American
100 g/4 oz plain flour	1 cup all-purpose flour
pinch of salt	pinch of salt
1 egg	1 egg
300 ml/½ pint milk	1½ cups milk
oil for frying	oil for frying
Filling:	Filling:
25 g/1 oz butter or margarine	2 tablespoons butter or
1 onion, chopped	margarine
4 bacon rashers, derinded	1 onion, chopped
and diced	4 bacon slices, diced
1 x 400 g/14 oz can tomatoes	1 x 16 oz can tomatoes
salt and pepper	salt and pepper
75 g/3 oz Cheddar cheese, grated	¾ cup grated Cheddar cheese

Sift the flour and salt into a mixing bowl. Add the egg and half the milk and beat until smooth. Gradually beat in the remaining milk to make a thin batter.

Lightly oil an 18 cm/7 inch omelette or frying pan (skillet). Pour in just enough batter to cover the bottom of the pan, tilting the pan to spread out the batter evenly. Cook until the underside is golden, then toss or turn the pancake (crêpe) and cook the other side for 1 to 2 minutes. Slide onto a plate and keep hot while you cook the remaining pancakes (crêpes). This batter should make eight pancakes (crêpes).

To make the filling, melt the butter or margarine in another frying pan (skillet). Add the onion and bacon and fry until the onion is golden and the bacon is crisp. Stir in the tomatoes and salt and pepper to taste and simmer until thick.

Divide the tomato filling between the pancakes (crêpes) and roll them up. Arrange in a flameproof serving dish. Sprinkle the cheese on top and grill (broil) until the cheese has melted and is golden brown. Serve hot.
Serves 4

Variations:

Leek and Bacon Pancakes (Crêpes): Melt 40 g/1½ oz (3 tablespoons) butter or margarine in a frying pan (skillet), add 225 g/8 oz (1 cup) thinly sliced leeks and 4 diced bacon rashers (slices) and fry until golden brown. Stir in ½ teaspoon prepared English mustard and salt and pepper to taste. Divide this filling between the pancakes (crêpes), roll them up and serve hot, garnished with parsley sprigs.

Asparagus Pancakes (Crêpes): Make a white sauce with 25 g/1 oz (2 tablespoons) butter or margarine, 25 g/1 oz (¼ cup) flour, 150 ml/¼ pint (¾ cup) milk and salt and pepper to taste. Drain a 350 g/12 oz can of asparagus spears and divide between the pancakes (crêpes). Roll them up and arrange in a flameproof serving dish. Pour over the white sauce and sprinkle over 25 g/1 oz (¼ cup) grated Cheddar or Parmesan cheese. Grill (broil) gently to heat through the asparagus and until the top is golden brown.

Prawn Pancakes (Shrimp Crêpes): Make a white sauce with 50 g/2 oz (4 tablespoons) butter or margarine, 50 g/2 oz (½ cup) flour, 300 ml/½ pint (1½ cups) milk and salt and pepper to taste. Fold in 225 g/8 oz cooked shelled prawns (shrimp) and 1 tablespoon chopped parsley and heat through gently. Divide between the hot pancakes (crêpes), roll up and serve immediately.

Chinese Crab Rolls

Metric/Imperial	American
8 hot pancakes (see recipe left)	8 hot crêpes (see recipe left)
1 tablespoon plain flour	1 tablespoon all-purpose flour
1 tablespoon water	1 tablespoon water
oil for deep frying	oil for deep frying
Filling:	Filling:
2 tablespoons oil	2 tablespoons oil
1 egg, beaten	1 egg, beaten
1 spring onion, shredded	1 scallion, shredded
1 × 225 g/8 oz can crabmeat, drained and flaked	1 × 8 oz can crabmeat, drained and flaked
1 tablespoon dry sherry	1 tablespoon dry sherry
1 teaspoon soy sauce	1 teaspoon soy sauce
salt and pepper	salt and pepper
1 tablespoon cornflour	1 tablespoon cornstarch
3 tablespoons water	3 tablespoons water

To make the filling, heat the oil in a saucepan. Add the egg, spring onion (scallion) and crabmeat and stir-fry for about 1 minute. Stir in the sherry, soy sauce and salt and pepper to taste.

Dissolve the cornflour (cornstarch) in the water and add to the crab mixture. Cook, stirring, until thickened. Remove from the heat and cool slightly.

Divide the filling between the pancakes (crêpes). Fold in the sides, then roll up the pancakes (crêpes) to make neat parcels. Dissolve the flour in the water to make a paste and use to seal the ends of the parcels.

Deep fry the crab rolls until golden brown. Drain on kitchen paper towels and cut into diagonal pieces. Serve hot.
Serves 4

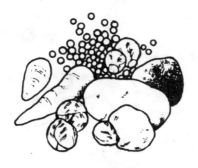

Kipper Soufflé

Metric/Imperial
8 slices of French bread, cut
  5 mm/¼ inch thick
75 g/3 oz butter or margarine
100 g/4 oz kipper fillets
150 ml/¼ pint milk
25 g/1 oz plain flour
3 eggs, separated
50 g/2 oz Leicester cheese,
  grated
salt and pepper

American
8 slices of French bread, cut
  ¼ inch thick
6 tablespoons butter or
  margarine
¼ lb kipper fillets
¾ cup milk
¼ cup all-purpose flour
3 eggs, separated
½ cup grated Brick cheese
salt and pepper

Spread the bread with 50 g/2 oz (4 tablespoons) of the butter or margarine. Use to line the sides of a 900 ml/1½ pint (1 quart) soufflé dish.
   Poach the kippers in the milk for 5 minutes, then drain, reserving the liquid. Add more milk, if necessary, to make the liquid up to 150 ml/ ¼ pint (¾ cup) again. Mash the kippers.
   Melt the remaining butter or margarine in a saucepan. Stir in the flour and cook for 2 minutes. Gradually stir in the liquid and bring to the boil, stirring. Simmer until thickened. Remove from the heat and cool slightly then mix in the kippers, egg yolks, cheese and salt and pepper to taste.
   Beat the egg whites until stiff and fold into the kipper mixture. Spoon into the soufflé dish. Cook in a preheated moderately hot oven (200°C/400°F, Gas Mark 6) for 30 to 35 minutes or until well risen and golden. Serve immediately.
Serves 4

Variations:
Smoked haddock soufflé: Use 175 g/6 oz smoked haddock fillets (finnan haddie) instead of the kippers and increase the milk to 250 ml/8 fl oz (1 cup). Add ¾ teaspoon each dry mustard and dried marjoram to the sauce base, and use 100 g/4 oz (1 cup) grated Cheddar cheese. If liked, omit the bread lining and cook in a preheated moderately hot oven (190°C/375°F, Gas Mark 5) for about 40 minutes.

Crab and Egg Layer

Metric/Imperial
25 g/1 oz butter or margarine
25 g/1 oz plain flour
300 ml/½ pint milk
1 × 225 g/8 oz can crabmeat,
    drained and flaked
1 tablespoon chopped parsley
squeeze of lemon juice
salt and pepper
8 hot pancakes (see recipe
    on page 150)
4 hard-boiled eggs, sliced
parsley sprigs to garnish

American
2 tablespoons butter or
    margarine
¼ cup all-purpose flour
1¼ cups milk
1 × 8 oz can crabmeat, drained
    and flaked
1 tablespoon chopped parsley
squeeze of lemon juice
salt and pepper
8 hot crêpes (see recipe
    on page 150)
4 hard-cooked eggs, sliced
parsley sprigs for garnish

Melt the butter or margarine in a saucepan. Stir in the flour and cook for 2 minutes, then gradually stir in the milk. Bring to the boil, stirring, and simmer until thickened. Add the crabmeat, parsley, lemon juice and salt and pepper to taste and heat through gently.

Place a pancake (crêpe) on a warmed serving plate and spread over some of the crab mixture. Top with a few egg slices, then place another pancake (crêpe) over the egg. Continue making layers in this way, ending with a pancake (crêpe). Garnish with parsley sprigs and serve immediately.
Serves 4

Special Corn Pancakes (Crêpes)

Metric/Imperial
15 g/½ oz butter or margarine
2 celery sticks, chopped
2 tablespoons plain flour
150 ml/¼ pint milk
1 × 350 g/12 oz can sweetcorn
    with peppers, drained
2 tomatoes, chopped
1 tablespoon chopped chives
salt and pepper
100 g/4 oz Cheddar cheese,
    grated
8 hot pancakes (see recipe
    on page 150)

American
1 tablespoon butter or
    margarine
2 celery stalks, chopped
2 tablespoons all-purpose flour
¾ cup milk
1 × 12 oz can whole kernel corn
    with peppers, drained
2 tomatoes, chopped
1 tablespoon chopped chives
salt and pepper
1 cup grated Cheddar cheese
8 hot crêpes (see recipe
    on page 150)

Melt the butter or margarine in a saucepan. Add the celery and fry for 5 minutes. Stir in the flour and cook for 1 minute, then gradually stir in the milk. Add the corn, tomatoes, chives and salt and pepper to taste and simmer, stirring, until thickened. Stir in the cheese until melted.

Divide the mixture between the pancakes (crêpes) and roll them up. Arrange on a warmed serving plate and serve hot.
Serves 4

Smoked Haddock Pancakes (Crêpes)

Metric/Imperial
350 g/12 oz smoked haddock
  fillets
1 red pepper, cored, seeded
  and diced
1 green pepper, cored, seeded
  and diced
25 g/1 oz butter or margarine
25 g/1 oz plain flour
150 ml/¼ pint milk
few drops of Tabasco sauce
pepper
8 hot pancakes (see recipe,
  page 150)

American
¾ lb finnan haddie (smoked
  haddock fillets)
1 red pepper, seeded and
  diced
1 green pepper, seeded
  and diced
2 tablespoons butter or
  margarine
¼ cup all-purpose flour
¾ cup milk
few drops of hot pepper sauce
pepper
8 hot crêpes (see recipe,
  page 150)

Poach the haddock in water to cover for 3 to 5 minutes. Drain, reserving
150 ml/¼ pint (¾ cup) of the poaching liquid. Remove any skin and
bones, then flake the fish. Mix the red and green peppers with the fish.

Melt the butter or margarine in a clean saucepan. Add the flour and
cook for 2 minutes, then gradually stir in the milk and reserved poaching
liquid. Bring to the boil, stirring, and simmer until thickened. Add the
Tabasco (hot pepper) sauce and pepper to taste. Add three-quarters of
the sauce to the fish mixture and stir well.

Divide the fish mixture between the pancakes (crêpes) and roll them
up. Arrange in a shallow ovenproof dish and pour over the remaining
sauce. Cook in a preheated moderately hot oven (200°C/400°F, Gas Mark
6) for 10 to 15 minutes to heat through, and serve hot.
Serves 4

Curried Chicken Pancakes (Crêpes)

Metric/Imperial
15 g/½ oz butter or margarine
1 small onion, chopped
350 g/12 oz cooked chicken
  meat, chopped
1 tablespoon mango chutney
2 teaspoons lemon juice
2 teaspoons curry powder
150 ml/¼ pint soured cream
salt and pepper
8 hot pancakes (see recipe
  on page 150)

American
1 tablespoon butter or
  margarine
1 small onion, chopped
2 cups chopped cooked chicken
1 tablespoon mango chutney
2 teaspoons lemon juice
2 teaspoons curry powder
⅔ cup sour cream
salt and pepper
8 hot crêpes (see recipe
  on page 150)

Melt the butter or margarine in a saucepan. Add the onion and fry until
softened. Stir in the chicken, chutney, lemon juice, curry powder, sour
cream and salt and pepper to taste and heat through gently.

Divide the mixture between the pancakes (crêpes) and roll them up.
Arrange on a warmed serving plate and serve hot.
Serves 4

Spinach Pancakes (Crêpes)

Metric/Imperial
100 g/4 oz frozen chopped
  spinach
100 g/4 oz plain flour
¼ teaspoon salt
1 egg, beaten
150 ml/¼ pint milk
oil for frying
Filling:
1 × 225 g/8 oz packet cream
  cheese
2 tablespoons milk
4 tablespoons chopped chives

American
¼ lb frozen chopped spinach
1 cup all-purpose flour
¼ teaspoon salt
1 egg, beaten
¾ cup milk
oil for frying
Filling:
1 × 8 oz package cream cheese
2 tablespoons milk
¼ cup chopped chives

First make the filling. Beat the cream cheese with the milk until softened, then beat in the chives.

Cook the spinach according to the directions on the packet. Drain well, pressing out all excess moisture. Purée the spinach in a blender or food processor.

Sift the flour and salt into a bowl and add the egg and milk. Beat until smooth, then stir in the spinach purée.

Lightly oil an 18 cm/7 inch pancake (crêpe) or frying pan (skillet). Pour in just enough batter to cover the bottom of the pan, tilting the pan to spread out the batter evenly. Cook until the underside is golden, then toss or turn the pancake (crêpe) and cook the other side for 1 to 2 minutes. Slide onto a plate and keep hot while you cook the remaining pancakes (crêpes). This batter should make eight pancakes (crêpes).

Divide the filling between the pancakes (crêpes) and roll them up. Serve hot.
Serves 4

Bacon and Sour Cream Pancakes (Crêpes)

Metric/Imperial
*8 hot pancakes (see recipe
  on page 150)*
*100 g/4 oz Cheddar cheese,
  grated*
Filling:
225 g/8 oz bacon, chopped
300 ml/½ pint soured cream
1 garlic clove, crushed
2 tablespoons chopped chives
salt and pepper

American
*8 hot crêpes (see recipe
  on page 150)*
1 cup grated Cheddar cheese
Filling:
½ lb bacon, chopped
1 ¼ cups sour cream
1 garlic clove, crushed
2 tablespoons chopped chives
salt and pepper

To make the filling, fry the bacon until it is crisp. Drain on kitchen paper towels, then mix with the sour cream, garlic, chives and salt and pepper.
   Divide the filling between the pancakes (crêpes) and roll them up. Arrange in an ovenproof dish and sprinkle over the cheese. Cover with foil and cook in a preheated moderately hot oven (190°C/375°F, Gas Mark 5) for 10 minutes.
   Uncover and cook for a further 10 minutes to lightly brown the top. Serve hot, with honeydew melon wedges if liked.
Serves 4

Crispy Corned Beef Pancakes (Crêpes)

Metric/Imperial
*8 hot pancakes (see recipe
  on page 150)*
*1 × 300 g/10½ oz can
  condensed cream of tomato
  soup, undiluted*
*1 × 50 g/2 oz packet crisps,
  crushed*
Filling:
25 g/1 oz butter or margarine
1 onion, chopped
*1 × 225 g/8 oz can corned
  beef, chopped*
salt and pepper

American
*8 hot crêpes (see recipe
  on page 150)*
*1 × 10½ oz can condensed
  cream of tomato soup,
  undiluted*
1 cup crushed potato chips
Filling:
*2 tablespoons butter or
  margarine*
1 onion, chopped
*1 × 8 oz can corned beef,
  chopped*
salt and pepper

First make the filling. Melt the butter or margarine in a frying pan (skillet), add the onion and fry until softened. Stir in the corned beef and salt and pepper to taste and fry for a further 2 minutes.
   Divide the filling between the pancakes (crêpes) and roll them up. Arrange in one layer in an ovenproof dish. Pour over the tomato soup and sprinkle the crisps (chips) on top.
   Cook in a preheated moderately hot oven (190°C/375°F, Gas Mark 5) for 20 minutes. Serve hot.
Serves 4

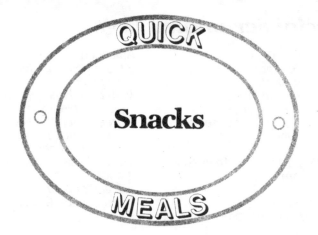

QUICK

Snacks

MEALS

Avocado and Bacon Toasts

Metric/Imperial
75 g/3 oz butter or margarine
100 g/4 oz back bacon, derinded
and cut into strips
4 French bread rolls, halved
lengthways
2 ripe avocados, peeled, stoned
and sliced
lemon juice
French mustard
175 g/6 oz Cheddar cheese,
grated
50 g/2 oz Parmesan cheese,
grated

American
6 tablespoons butter or
margarine
¼ lb Canadian bacon, cut
into strips
4 French bread rolls, halved
lengthwise
2 ripe avocados, peeled, seeded
and sliced
lemon juice
Dijon-style mustard
1½ cups grated Cheddar cheese
½ cup grated Parmesan cheese

Melt 25 g/1 oz (2 tablespoons) of the butter or margarine in a frying pan (skillet). Add the bacon strips and fry until crisp.

Meanwhile toast the cut sides of the rolls under the grill (broiler). Spread with the remaining butter or margarine. Toss the avocado slices in lemon juice to prevent discoloration, then arrange on the rolls. Spread the avocado with mustard and sprinkle over the cheeses. Grill (broil) until the cheeses have melted and the tops are golden brown.

Drain the bacon strips on kitchen paper towels and arrange on top of the cheese. Serve hot.
Serves 4

Special Scrambled Eggs

Metric/Imperial
25 g/1 oz butter or margarine
225 g/8 oz skinless pork
   sausages, cut into
   1 cm/½ inch pieces
1 green pepper, cored, seeded
   and chopped
1 onion, chopped
1 × 275 g/10 oz can cream-style
   sweetcorn
4 eggs
salt and pepper
50 g/2 oz Cheddar cheese,
   grated

American
2 tablespoons butter or
   margarine
½ lb pork sausages, cut into
   ½ inch pieces
1 green pepper, seeded
   and chopped
1 onion, chopped
1 × 10 oz can cream-style corn
4 eggs
salt and pepper
½ cup grated Cheddar cheese

Melt the butter or margarine in a frying pan (skillet). Add the sausage pieces, green pepper and onion and fry until the sausage pieces are browned on all sides. Stir in the corn.
   Lightly beat the eggs with salt and pepper to taste and pour into the pan. Cook gently, stirring frequently, until the eggs are scrambled. Spoon the mixture into a flameproof serving dish and sprinkle the cheese on top. Grill (broil) until the cheese has melted and is golden brown. Serve hot.
Serves 4

Scrambled Eggs with Chillis

Metric/Imperial
8 eggs
1 teaspoon salt
4 tomatoes, chopped
50 g/2 oz butter or margarine
1 onion, sliced
2 green chillis, seeded and
   chopped
1 teaspoon ground turmeric
1 teaspoon ground coriander

American
8 eggs
1 teaspoon salt
4 tomatoes, chopped
4 tablespoons butter or
   margarine
1 onion, sliced
2 green chili peppers, seeded
   and chopped
1 teaspoon ground turmeric
1 teaspoon ground coriander

Lightly beat the eggs with the salt. Mix in the tomatoes.
   Melt the butter or margarine in a frying pan (skillet). Add the onion and fry until softened. Stir in the chillis (chili peppers) and spices and fry for 2 minutes, stirring constantly.
   Add the egg mixture and cook gently, stirring occasionally, until the eggs are lightly scrambled. Serve hot.
Serves 4

Quick Egg Foo Yung

Metric/Imperial	American
6 eggs	6 eggs
salt and pepper	salt and pepper
2 spring onions, shredded	2 scallions, shredded
225 g/8 oz peeled prawns	½ lb cooked shelled shrimp
2 tablespoons oil	2 tablespoons oil
soy sauce to serve	soy sauce to serve

Lightly beat the eggs with salt and pepper to taste, then mix in the spring onions (scallions) and prawns (shrimp).

Heat the oil in a large frying pan (skillet) and pour in the egg mixture. Cook, turning over once, until golden brown on both sides. Slide onto a warmed serving plate, drizzle over a little soy sauce and serve hot.
Serves 2 to 4

Mushroom Scramble

Metric/Imperial	American
50 g/2 oz butter or margarine	4 tablespoons butter or margarine
225 g/8 oz mushrooms, chopped	½ lb mushrooms, chopped
10 eggs	10 eggs
4 tablespoons milk	¼ cup milk
salt and pepper	salt and pepper

Melt 25 g/1 oz (2 tablespoons) of the butter or margarine in a saucepan. Add the mushrooms and fry for 3 minutes. Remove from the heat and keep hot.

Lightly beat the eggs with the milk and salt and pepper to taste. Melt the remaining butter or margarine in a frying pan (skillet). Pour in the egg mixture and cook gently, stirring. When the eggs start to set, stir in the mushrooms. Continue cooking until eggs are lightly scrambled. Serve hot.
Serves 6

Crispy Meat Fingers

Metric/Imperial	American
1 large can chopped pork and ham, cut into 8 fingers	1 large can chopped pork and ham, cut into 8 fingers
1 egg, beaten	1 egg, beaten
100 g/4 oz oatmeal	1 cup oatmeal
oil for frying	oil for frying

Dip the pork and ham fingers in the beaten egg, then coat with the oatmeal, pressing it on well.

Pour enough oil into a frying pan (skillet) to make a 1 cm/½ inch layer and heat. Add the meat fingers and fry until golden and crisp all over. Drain on kitchen paper towels and serve hot with cranberry sauce.
Serves 4

Baked Eggs Rarebit

Metric/Imperial
4 slices of bread
50 g/2 oz butter or margarine
100 g/4 oz mushrooms, sliced
8 eggs
salt and pepper
100 g/4 oz cheese, grated
3 tablespoons beer or cider
½ teaspoon made English
mustard

American
4 slices of bread
4 tablespoons butter or
margarine
1 cup sliced mushrooms
8 eggs
salt and pepper
1 cup grated cheese
3 tablespoons beer or apple
cider
½ teaspoon prepared English
mustard

Toast the bread and spread with half the butter or margarine. Cut each
slice of toast into four triangles and arrange over the bottom of an
ovenproof dish. Scatter the mushrooms on top. Break the eggs on top
of the mushrooms and season to taste with salt and pepper.

Melt the remaining butter or margarine in a saucepan. Stir in the
cheese, beer or cider and mustard and cook gently until the cheese has
melted. Pour this mixture over the eggs.

Cook in a preheated hot oven (220°C/425°F, Gas Mark 7) for
20 minutes. Serve hot.
Serves 4

Fried Ham Sandwiches

Metric/Imperial
8 large slices of white
bread, crusts removed
50 g/2 oz butter or margarine
2 teaspoons made mustard
4 slices of cooked ham
4 slices of Cheddar cheese
2 eggs
6 tablespoons milk
salt and pepper
oil for shallow frying

American
8 large slices of white
bread, crusts removed
4 tablespoons butter or
margarine
2 teaspoons prepared mustard
4 slices of cooked ham
4 slices of American cheese
2 eggs
6 tablespoons milk
salt and pepper
oil for shallow frying

Spread the slices of bread with the butter or margarine, then spread four
slices with the mustard and top with a slice of ham and cheese. Place the
other bread slices on top, buttered sides down. Cut each sandwich in half
diagonally.

Lightly beat the eggs with the milk and salt and pepper to taste in a
shallow dish. Dip the sandwiches in the mixture to coat all over.

Pour enough oil into a large frying pan (skillet) to make a 1 cm/½ inch
layer. Heat the oil, then fry the sandwiches until they are golden brown on
both sides. Drain on kitchen paper towels and serve hot.
Serves 4

Savoury Mushrooms

Metric/Imperial
50 g/2 oz butter or margarine
500 g/1 lb mushrooms, sliced
25 g/1 oz flaked almonds
1 tablespoon soy sauce
2 drops of Angostura bitters
salt and pepper
4 slices of bread
2 tablespoons double cream
1 tablespoon chopped parsley

American
4 tablespoons butter or
  margarine
1 lb mushrooms, sliced
¼ cup sliced almonds
1 tablespoon soy sauce
2 drops of Angostura bitters
salt and pepper
4 slices of bread
2 tablespoons heavy cream
1 tablespoon chopped parsley

Melt half the butter or margarine in a frying pan (skillet). Add the mushrooms, almonds, soy sauce, bitters and salt and pepper to taste. Cook for about 3 minutes, stirring frequently.

Meanwhile, toast the bread and spread with the remaining butter or margarine.

Remove the frying pan (skillet) from the heat and stir in the cream and parsley. Pile the mushrooms on the toast and serve hot.
Serves 4

Cheese and Mushroom Fondue

Metric/Imperial
1 garlic clove, halved
150 ml/¼ pint dry cider
1 teaspoon lemon juice
500 g/1 lb Gouda cheese,
  grated
1 tablespoon cornflour
1½ tablespoons gin, brandy
  or sherry
100 g/4 oz mushrooms, chopped
pinch of grated nutmeg
pepper
1 loaf of French bread, cut
  into cubes

American
1 garlic clove, halved
⅔ cup hard cider
1 teaspoon lemon juice
4 cups grated Gouda cheese
1 tablespoon cornstarch
1½ tablespoons gin, brandy or
  sherry
1 cup chopped mushrooms
pinch of grated nutmeg
pepper
1 loaf of French bread, cut
  into cubes

Rub the inside of an earthenware fondue pot or flameproof casserole with the garlic clove, then discard the garlic. Put the cider and lemon juice into the pot and bring to the boil. Gradually stir in the cheese until melted and smooth.

Dissolve the cornflour (cornstarch) in the gin, brandy or sherry and add to the pot. Cook, stirring, until thickened. Add the mushrooms, nutmeg and pepper to taste and stir well to mix.

Serve the fondue over a spirit (alcohol) burner, with the bread cubes and long forks for dipping.
Serves 6 to 8

Sausage and Bacon Burgers

Metric/Imperial
25 g/1 oz butter or margarine
1 onion, finely chopped
500 g/1 lb sausagemeat
4 streaky bacon rashers,
    derinded and chopped
2 teaspoons gravy powder
1 teaspoon dried mixed herbs
salt and pepper
plain flour for coating
oil for frying

American
2 tablespoons butter or
    margarine
1 onion, finely chopped
1 lb sausagemeat
4 bacon slices, chopped
2 teaspoons gravy powder
1 teaspoon dried mixed herbs
salt and pepper
all-purpose flour for coating
oil for frying

Melt the butter or margarine in a frying pan (skillet). Add the onion and fry until softened. Pour the onion into a bowl and add the sausagemeat, bacon, gravy powder, herbs and salt and pepper to taste. Mix together well. Shape into four burgers and chill until firm.

Coat the burgers with flour. Pour enough oil into a frying pan to make a 1 cm/½ inch layer and heat. Add the burgers and fry for about 4 minutes on each side or until cooked through and golden brown. Serve hot.
Serves 4

Egg Pizza

Metric/Imperial
1 small onion, grated
3 tablespoons tomato purée
1 teaspoon dried oregano
salt and pepper
4 soft rolls, split in
    half
8 hard-boiled eggs, halved
8 black olives, halved and
    stoned
225 g/8 oz cheese, grated
2 eggs, beaten
½ teaspoon made mustard

American
1 small onion, grated
3 tablespoons tomato paste
1 teaspoon dried oregano
salt and pepper
4 hamburger buns, split in
    half
8 hard-cooked eggs, halved
8 pitted ripe olives, halved
2 cups grated cheese
2 eggs, beaten
½ teaspoon prepared mustard

Mix together the onion, tomato purée (paste), oregano and salt and pepper to taste. Spread over the cut surfaces of the rolls (buns). Top each with two egg halves, cut sides down, and two olive halves.

Combine the cheese, beaten eggs and mustard. Spread over the eggs and arrange on a baking sheet. Cook in a preheated hot oven (220°C/425°F, Gas Mark 7) for 10 to 15 minutes or until the topping is risen and browned. Serve hot.
Serves 4

Open Sausage Sandwiches

Metric/Imperial
8 chipolata sausages
4 slices of bread
25 g/1 oz butter or margarine
4-8 tomato slices
100 g/4 oz Cheddar cheese,
  grated
1 teaspoon made mustard
1 teaspoon Worcestershire
  sauce
1 tablespoon tomato ketchup

American
8 pork link sausages
4 slices of bread
2 tablespoons butter or
  margarine
4-8 tomato slices
1 cup grated Cheddar cheese
1 teaspoon prepared mustard
1 teaspoon Worcestershire
  sauce
1 tablespoon tomato ketchup

Grill (broil) the sausages. Toast the bread and spread with the butter or margarine. Top each slice of toast with tomato slices, then add the sausages. Mix together the remaining ingredients and spoon on top of the sausages. Grill (broil) for a further 2 to 3 minutes or until the cheese topping is melted and golden brown. Serve hot.
Serves 4

Mackerel Rolls

Metric/Imperial
350 g/12 oz smoked mackerel
  fillets, flaked
75 g/3 oz fresh breadcrumbs
2 celery sticks, diced
grated rind of ½ lemon
1 egg, beaten
salt and pepper
4 finger rolls, split open
butter or margarine
mayonnaise
radish slices

American
¾ lb smoked mackerel fillets,
  flaked
1½ cups soft bread crumbs
2 celery stalks, diced
grated rind of ½ lemon
1 egg, beaten
salt and pepper
4 hot dog buns, split open
butter or margarine
mayonnaise
radish slices

Mix together the mackerel, breadcrumbs, celery, lemon rind, egg and salt and pepper to taste. Shape into four sausages, the same length as the rolls (buns), and flatten them slightly. Grill (broil) until golden on both sides.

Spread the cut surfaces of the rolls (buns) with butter or margarine and then with mayonnaise. Place a mackerel 'sausage' in each roll (bun) and top with radish slices. Serve hot.
Serves 4

Toasted Turkey Sandwiches

Metric/Imperial
225 g/8 oz cooked turkey meat,
  diced
2 tablespoons mayonnaise
1 celery stick, finely chopped
100 g/4 oz cheese, grated
1 × 200 g/7 oz can sweetcorn
  kernels, drained
8 slices of wholemeal bread
melted butter

American
1 cup diced cooked turkey
2 tablespoons mayonnaise
1 celery stalk, finely chopped
1 cup grated cheese
1 × 7 oz can whole kernel
  corn, drained
8 slices of wholewheat bread
melted butter

Mix together the turkey, mayonnaise, celery, cheese and corn. Use to make four sandwiches with the wholemeal (wholewheat) bread. Arrange on the grill (broiler) pan and brush with melted butter. Grill (broil) until the bread is browned, then turn over and brush with more melted butter. Continue grilling (broiling) until the other sides of the sandwiches are browned. Serve hot.
Serves 4
Variations:
Cooked chicken meat or canned tuna fish may be substituted for the turkey.

Barbecue Buns

Metric/Imperial
100 g/4 oz minced beef
½ onion, chopped
50 g/2 oz canned sweetcorn
  kernels, drained
4 tablespoons canned or
  bottled barbecue sauce
¼ teaspoon chilli powder
1 tablespoon water
4 frankfurter sausages
4 finger rolls, split in half

American
¼ lb ground beef
½ onion, chopped
⅓ cup drained canned whole
  kernel corn
¼ cup bottled barbecue sauce
¼ teaspoon chili powder
1 tablespoon water
4 frankfurters
4 hot dog buns, split in
  half

Fry the beef with the onion in a dry frying pan (skillet) until the beef is browned and crumbly. Drain off all excess fat from the pan, then stir in the corn, barbecue sauce, chilli powder and water. Cover and simmer for 15 minutes.

Meanwhile cook the frankfurters in hot water according to the instructions on the packet. Drain the frankfurters and cut each in half crossways. Place two halves in each roll (bun) and spoon over the barbecue meat sauce. Serve hot.
Serves 4

Cottage Toasties

Metric/Imperial
4 slices of bread, toasted
butter or margarine
4 tomatoes, sliced
50 g/2 oz button mushrooms,
  sliced
225 g/8 oz cottage cheese
25 g/1 oz dried milk
  powder
4 spring onions, chopped
salt and pepper

American
4 slices of bread, toasted
butter or margarine
4 tomatoes, sliced
½ cup sliced mushrooms
1 cup cottage cheese
⅓ cup dried milk powder
4 scallions, chopped
salt and pepper

Spread the toast with butter or margarine. Arrange the tomatoes and mushrooms on the toast. Mix together the cottage cheese, milk powder, spring onions (scallions) and salt and pepper to taste and pile on top of the toast. Grill (broil) until golden brown. Serve hot.
Serves 4

Sardine Bread Pizza

Metric/Imperial
4 slices of bread
25 g/1 oz butter or margarine
1 × 100 g/4 oz can sardines,
  drained and mashed
4 large thin tomato slices
8 anchovy fillets
4 black olives

American
4 slices of bread
2 tablespoons butter or margarine
1 × 4 oz can sardines, drained
  and mashed
4 large thin tomato slices
8 anchovy fillets
4 ripe olives

Toast the bread under the grill (broiler). Spread the toast with butter or margarine, then spread the sardines on top. Continue grilling (broiling) until the sardines are hot.

Place a tomato slice on each slice of toast and top with two crossed anchovy fillets. Return to the grill (broiler) and cook for a further 3 to 4 minutes. Garnish each 'pizza' with an olive and serve hot.
Serves 4

Cheese Sizzlers

Metric/Imperial	American
4 soft white rolls, split in half	4 hamburger buns, split in half
100 g/4 oz liver sausage or ham spread	¼ lb liverwurst or deviled ham spread
40 g/1½ oz butter or margarine	3 tablespoons butter or margarine
1 onion, finely chopped	1 onion, finely chopped
4 tablespoons tomato ketchup	¼ cup tomato ketchup
pinch of dried thyme	pinch of dried thyme
225 g/8 oz Gouda cheese, grated	2 cups grated Gouda cheese

Toast the cut surfaces of the rolls (buns) under the grill (broiler). Spread with the liver sausage (liverwurst) or ham spread.

Melt the butter or margarine in a frying pan (skillet). Add the onion and fry until softened. Stir in the ketchup and thyme. Spread over the liver sausage (liverwurst) or ham. Top with the cheese.

Grill (broil) until the cheese has melted and is lightly browned. Serve hot.

Serves 4

Fish Deckers

Metric/Imperial	American
4 small white fish fillets	4 small white fish fillets
25 g/1 oz butter or margarine, melted	2 tablespoons butter or margarine, melted
salt and pepper	salt and pepper
4 back bacon rashers, derinded	4 slices of Canadian bacon
4 thin slices of Cheddar cheese	4 thin slices of Cheddar cheese
4 large bread rolls	4 large hamburger buns
4 thick tomato slices	4 thick tomato slices

Place the fillets on the grill (broiler) rack and brush with the butter or margarine. Sprinkle with salt and pepper. Place the bacon on the rack. Grill (broil) for 3 to 4 minutes or until the fish is cooked through and the bacon is crisp. Remove the bacon from the pan and keep hot.

Place a slice of cheese on each fish fillet and grill (broil) until the cheese has melted.

Slice each roll (bun) into three layers. Place the cheese-topped fish in the bottom slit and the bacon and tomato in the top slit. Serve hot.

Serves 4

Frankfurter Rolls

Metric/Imperial	American
6 slices of white bread	6 slices of white bread
butter or margarine	butter or margarine
6 slices of processed cheese	6 slices of American cheese
6 frankfurter sausages	6 frankfurters
6 large mushrooms	6 large mushrooms

Spread both sides of the bread with butter or margarine. Place a slice of cheese on each slice of bread and top with a frankfurter, placed diagonally across the bread. Wrap the bread around the frankfurter and secure with a wooden cocktail stick. Put a mushroom on the end of each stick and brush the mushroom with a little melted butter or margarine.

Arrange the frankfurter rolls on a baking sheet. Cook in a preheated hot oven (220°C/425°F, Gas Mark 7) for 10 minutes or until the frankfurters are heated through and the bread is golden brown. Serve hot, with mustard and relishes.
Serves 4 to 6

Walnut and Cheese Patties

Metric/Imperial	American
175 g/6 oz walnuts, coarsely ground	1½ cups coarsely ground walnuts
50 g/2 oz fresh breadcrumbs	1 cup soft bread crumbs
100 g/4 oz Cheddar cheese, grated	1 cup grated Cheddar cheese
1 onion, grated	1 onion, grated
salt and pepper	salt and pepper
1 egg, beaten	1 egg, beaten
1 tablespoon tomato purée	1 tablespoon tomato paste
oil for frying	oil for frying

Mix together 100 g/4 oz (1 cup) of the walnuts, the breadcrumbs, cheese, onion and salt and pepper to taste. Add the egg and tomato purée (paste) to bind the ingredients. Divide the mixture into four and shape into patties about 1 cm/½ inch thick. Coat with the remaining walnuts.

Heat a little oil in a frying pan (skillet). Add the patties and fry for about 5 minutes or until golden brown on both sides. Serve hot or cold.
Serves 4

Eggs in Bacon Nests

Metric/Imperial
40 g/1½ oz butter or margarine
25 g/1 oz fresh breadcrumbs
4 streaky bacon rashers, derinded
50 g/2 oz Cheddar cheese,
  grated
4 eggs
salt and pepper

American
3 tablespoons butter or
  margarine
½ cup soft bread crumbs
4 bacon slices
½ cup grated Cheddar cheese
4 eggs
salt and pepper

Melt 25 g/1 oz (2 tablespoons) of the butter or margarine in a frying pan (skillet). Add the breadcrumbs and fry until golden brown. Drain on kitchen paper towels.

Partially cook the bacon in the same frying pan (skillet). Mix together the breadcrumbs and cheese and divide between four greased ramekin dishes. Line the sides of the dishes with the bacon. Break an egg into each dish and season with salt and pepper. Dot with the remaining butter or margarine.

Cook in a preheated moderately hot oven (200°C/400°F, Gas Mark 6) for about 8 minutes or until the eggs are just set. Serve hot.
Serves 4

Apple Sausage Burgers

Metric/Imperial
2 dessert apples, peeled, cored
  and grated
225 g/8 oz pork sausagemeat
25 g/1 oz fresh breadcrumbs
1 egg, beaten
salt and pepper
4 streaky bacon rashers, derinded

American
2 apples, peeled, cored and
  grated
½ lb pork sausagemeat
½ cup soft bread crumbs
1 egg, beaten
salt and pepper
4 bacon slices

Mix together the apples, sausagemeat, breadcrumbs, egg and salt and pepper to taste. Shape into four burgers.

Fry the bacon in a frying pan (skillet) until crisp. Drain on kitchen paper towels and roll up. Keep hot.

Add the burgers to the pan (skillet) and fry for about 3 minutes on each side or until cooked through and golden brown. Drain on kitchen paper towels.

Top each burger with a bacon roll and serve hot.
Serves 4

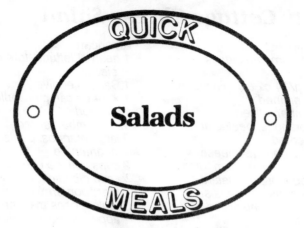

Watermelon Creole

Metric/Imperial	American
1 watermelon, halved	½ watermelon
225 g/8 oz cooked shelled prawns	½ lb cooked shelled shrimp
1 small green pepper, cored, seeded and diced	1 small green pepper, seeded and diced
300 ml/½ pint mayonnaise	1¼ cups mayonnaise
2 teaspoons tomato purée	2 teaspoons tomato paste
1 teaspoon curry powder	1 teaspoon curry powder

Scoop out the watermelon flesh with a melon baller or cut into cubes, discarding all the seeds. Put the watermelon balls or cubes into a bowl and add the prawns (shrimp) and green pepper.

Mix together the mayonnaise, tomato purée (paste) and curry powder. Pour this dressing over the watermelon mixture and fold together gently.
Serves 4

Piquant Chicken Salad

Metric/Imperial	American
350 g/12 oz cooked chicken meat, chopped	1½ cups chopped cooked chicken
1 Spanish onion, chopped	1 Bermuda onion, chopped
2 hard-boiled eggs, chopped	2 hard-cooked eggs, chopped
500 g/1 lb potatoes, cooked and chopped	1 lb potatoes, cooked and chopped
2 dill pickles, thinly sliced	2 dill pickles, thinly sliced
1 tablespoon capers	1 tablespoon capers
6 stuffed green olives, sliced	6 pimiento-stuffed olives, sliced
150 ml/¼ pint mayonnaise	¾ cup mayonnaise

Put the chicken, onion, eggs, potatoes, pickles, capers and olives in a bowl and gently fold in the mayonnaise. Serve chilled.
Serves 4 to 6

Fruity Cottage Cheese Salad

Metric/Imperial
1 lettuce, torn into pieces
1 chicory
1 × 400 g/14 oz can pineapple
  rings, drained
½ cucumber, sliced
2 large oranges, peeled and
  segmented
500 g/1 lb cottage cheese
100 g/4 oz cooked ham, diced
1 teaspoon made mustard
3 tablespoons mayonnaise
1 apple, cored and sliced
lemon juice

American
1 head of lettuce, torn into
  pieces
1 Belgian endive
1 × 14 oz can pineapple rings,
  drained
½ cucumber, sliced
2 large oranges, peeled and
  segmented
2 cups cottage cheese
½ cup diced cooked ham
1 teaspoon prepared mustard
3 tablespoons mayonnaise
1 apple, cored and sliced
lemon juice

Arrange a bed of lettuce and chicory (endive) on a serving platter. Place the pineapple rings, cucumber slices and orange segments around the edge. Mix together the cottage cheese, ham, mustard and mayonnaise and pile in the centre.

Dip the apple slices in the lemon juice to prevent discoloration and use to garnish the salad.
Serves 4 to 6

Summer Chicken Salad

Metric/Imperial
350 g/12 oz cooked chicken
  meat, diced
100 g/4 oz green grapes,
  halved and pipped
2 red dessert apples, cored
  and diced
½ cucumber, diced
4 tablespoons mayonnaise
1 tablespoon Worcestershire
  sauce
salt and pepper

American
1½ cups diced cooked chicken
¼ lb seedless grapes, halved
2 red-skinned apples, cored and
  diced
½ cucumber, diced
¼ cup mayonnaise
1 tablespoon Worcestershire
  sauce
salt and pepper

Put the chicken, grapes, apples and cucumber in a salad bowl. Mix together the mayonnaise, Worcestershire sauce and salt and pepper to taste, then pour this dressing over the salad ingredients. Toss together well. Serve lightly chilled.
Serves 4

Toasted Cheese Salad

Metric/Imperial
4 thick slices of white bread
75 g/3 oz Cheddar cheese,
  grated
1 lettuce, torn into pieces
4 spring onions, chopped
3 celery sticks, chopped
6 radishes, sliced
175 g/6 oz cooked ham, diced
50 g/2 oz salami, cut into
  strips
4-6 tablespoons bottled
  French dressing

American
4 thick slices of white bread
¾ cup grated Cheddar cheese
1 head of lettuce, torn into
  pieces
4 scallions, chopped
3 celery stalks, chopped
6 radishes, sliced
¾ cup diced cooked ham
2 oz salami, cut into strips
4-6 tablespoons bottled Italian
  dressing

Toast the bread lightly on both sides under the grill (broiler). Sprinkle the cheese over the toast and grill (broil) until melted and lightly browned. Cut the slices into 1 cm/½ inch cubes and cool.

Put the lettuce, spring onions (scallions), celery, radishes, ham and salami in a salad bowl. Add the dressing and toss well. Scatter over the toasted cheese bread cubes and serve.
Serves 4

Spiced Egg Salad

Metric/Imperial
8 hard-boiled eggs, quartered
3 green peppers, cored, seeded
  and sliced
1 red pepper, cored, seeded
  and sliced
4 mushrooms, sliced
6 black olives, stoned
1 tablespoon chopped walnuts
Dressing:
6 tablespoons oil
2 tablespoons wine vinegar
1 garlic clove, crushed
1 teaspoon paprika
½ teaspoon caster sugar
salt and pepper

American
8 hard-cooked eggs, quartered
3 green peppers, seeded
  and sliced
1 red pepper, seeded
  and sliced
4 mushrooms, sliced
6 pitted ripe olives
1 tablespoon chopped walnuts
Dressing:
6 tablespoons oil
2 tablespoons wine vinegar
1 garlic clove, crushed
1 teaspoon paprika
½ teaspoon sugar
salt and pepper

Arrange the eggs, green and red peppers, mushrooms and olives in a salad bowl. Sprinkle the walnuts on top.

Combine the dressing ingredients, with salt and pepper to taste, in a screwtop jar. Shake well to mix. Pour the dressing over the salad. Chill for 30 minutes before serving.
Serves 4

Tongue and Rice Salad

Metric/Imperial
100 g/4 oz long-grain rice
salt and pepper
½ small red pepper, cored,
    seeded and diced
½ small green pepper, cored,
    seeded and diced
25 g/1 oz raisins
5 tablespoons mayonnaise
1 teaspoon curry powder
1 teaspoon French mustard
225 g/8 oz cooked tongue,
    sliced
2 tablespoons mango chutney

American
½ cup rice
salt and pepper
½ small red pepper, seeded
    and diced
½ small green pepper, seeded
    and diced
3 tablespoons raisins
5 tablespoons mayonnaise
1 teaspoon curry powder
1 teaspoon Dijon-style mustard
½ lb cooked tongue, sliced
2 tablespoons mango chutney

Cook the rice in boiling salted water for about 20 minutes or until tender. Drain well and cool.

Add the red and green peppers and raisins to the rice. Combine the mayonnaise, curry powder, mustard and salt and pepper to taste, then fold this dressing into the rice mixture. Spread out on a serving platter. Arrange the tongue slices on top and spoon over the chutney.
Serves 4

German Salad

Metric/Imperial
6 frankfurter sausages,
    cooked and chopped
175 g/6 oz cooked chicken
    meat, chopped
750 g/1½ lb potatoes, cooked
    and diced
150 ml/¼ pint mayonnaise
6 spring onions, chopped
salt and pepper
cayenne pepper

American
6 frankfurters, cooked and
    chopped
1 cup chopped cooked chicken
1½ lb potatoes, cooked and
    diced
¾ cup mayonnaise
6 scallions, chopped
salt and pepper
cayenne

Put the frankfurters, chicken and potatoes in a bowl and fold in the mayonnaise, spring onions (scallions) and salt and pepper to taste. Chill before serving, sprinkled with cayenne.
Serves 6

Bean and Mushroom Salad

Metric/Imperial
225 g/8 oz frozen broad beans
225 g/8 oz button mushrooms
4 spring onions, chopped
150 ml/¼ pint plain yogurt
salt and pepper

American
½ lb frozen lima beans
½ lb button mushrooms
4 scallions, chopped
⅔ cup plain yogurt
salt and pepper

Cook the beans according to the instructions on the packet. Drain and cool.

Mix the beans with the mushrooms, spring onions (scallions), yogurt and salt and pepper to taste. Chill before serving.
Serves 4

Italian Salad

Metric/Imperial
2 slices of white bread,
  cut about 1 cm/½ inch thick,
  crusts removed
50 g/2 oz butter or margarine
1 garlic clove, halved
1 lettuce, torn into pieces
1 small onion, thinly sliced
  into rings
25 g/1 oz Parmesan cheese,
  grated
50 g/2 oz mushrooms, sliced
175 g/6 oz cooked ham, diced
1 × 50 g/2 oz can anchovy
  fillets, drained
Dressing:
4 tablespoons olive oil
1 tablespoon lemon juice
2 tablespoons Worcestershire
  sauce
salt and pepper

American
2 slices of white bread, cut
  about ½ inch thick, crusts
  removed
4 tablespoons butter or
  margarine
1 garlic clove, halved
1 head of lettuce, torn into
  pieces
1 small onion, thinly sliced
  into rings
¼ cup grated Parmesan cheese
½ cup sliced mushrooms
¾ cup diced cooked ham
1 × 2 oz can anchovy fillets,
  drained
Dressing:
¼ cup olive oil
1 tablespoon lemon juice
2 tablespoons Worcestershire
  sauce
salt and pepper

Cut the bread into 1 cm/½ inch cubes. Melt the butter or margarine in a frying pan (skillet), add the bread cubes and fry until golden brown on all sides. Drain the croûtons on kitchen paper towels and cool.

Rub the inside of a salad bowl with the cut surfaces of the garlic, then discard the garlic. Put the lettuce, onion, cheese, mushrooms, ham and anchovies in the bowl and mix together.

Combine the dressing ingredients with salt and pepper to taste. Pour the dressing over the salad, add the croûtons and toss well. Serve immediately.
Serves 4 to 6

Ham and Asparagus Salad

Metric/Imperial
225 g/8 oz cooked ham, diced
1 × 200 g/7 oz can asparagus
   spears, drained and chopped
1 lettuce, torn into pieces
2 spring onions, chopped
6 stuffed green olives, halved
Dressing:
6 tablespoons oil
4 tablespoons wine vinegar
½ teaspoon dried mixed herbs
salt and pepper

American
1 cup diced cooked ham
1 × 8 oz can asparagus spears,
   drained and chopped
1 head of lettuce, torn into
   pieces
2 scallions, chopped
6 pimiento-stuffed olives, halved
Dressing:
6 tablespoons oil
¼ cup wine vinegar
½ teaspoon dried mixed herbs
salt and pepper

Put the ham, asparagus, lettuce, spring onions (scallions) and olives in a salad bowl.

Put the dressing ingredients, with salt and pepper to taste, in a screw-topped jar and shake well. Pour the dressing over the salad and toss together. Serve immediately.

Serves 4

Curried Seafood Salad

Metric/Imperial
1 small cauliflower, broken
   into florets
salt
250 ml/8 fl oz mayonnaise
½ teaspoon garam masala
½ teaspoon paprika
1 green chilli, seeded and
   finely chopped (optional)
3 spring onions, chopped
500 g/1 lb cooked shelled
   prawns
lettuce leaves
chopped fresh mint to garnish

American
1 small cauliflower, broken
   into florets
salt
1 cup mayonnaise
½ teaspoon garam masala
½ teaspoon paprika
1 green chili pepper, seeded
   and finely chopped (optional)
3 scallions, chopped
1 lb cooked shelled shrimp
lettuce leaves
chopped fresh mint for garnish

Cook the cauliflower in boiling salted water until just tender but still crisp. Drain well and cool.

Mix the mayonnaise with the garam masala, paprika, chilli (chili pepper) if using and spring onions (scallions). Fold in the cauliflower and prawns (shrimp). Chill lightly.

Serve the salad on a bed of lettuce leaves, sprinkled with mint.

Serves 4

Chicken Melon Salad

Metric/Imperial
1 honeydew or ogen melon,
   halved and seeded
500 g/1 lb cooked chicken meat,
   diced
1 green pepper, cored, seeded
   and chopped
100 g/4 oz walnuts, chopped
6 tablespoons mayonnaise

American
1 honeydew or cantaloup melon,
   halved and seeded
2 cups diced cooked chicken
1 green pepper, seeded
   and chopped
1 cup chopped walnuts
6 tablespoons mayonnaise

Scoop out the melon flesh with a melon baller or cut into cubes. Mix with the remaining ingredients in a salad bowl. Chill before serving.
Serves 4 to 6

Variation:
Minted Chicken Salad: Omit the green pepper and walnuts. Mix the mayonnaise with 1 tablespoon lemon juice, 1 tablespoon chopped chives and 2 tablespoons chopped fresh mint. Fold in the chicken and melon and serve on a bed of lettuce leaves.

Chicken and Macaroni Salad

Metric/Imperial
225 g/8 oz short-cut macaroni
salt and pepper
225 g/8 oz cooked chicken
   meat, diced
1 celery stick, diced
1 × 200 g/7 oz can sweetcorn
   kernels, drained
1 × 375 g/13 oz can pineapple
   chunks, drained
1 tablespoon flaked almonds
1 green pepper, cored, seeded
   and chopped
1 tablespoon mayonnaise
2 tablespoons lemon juice

American
½ lb elbow macaroni
salt and pepper
1 cup diced cooked chicken
1 celery stalk, diced
1 × 7 oz can whole kernel corn,
   drained
1 × 13 oz can pineapple chunks,
   drained
1 tablespoon sliced almonds
1 green pepper, seeded
   and chopped
1 tablespoon mayonnaise
2 tablespoons lemon juice

Cook the macaroni in boiling salted water until just tender. Drain and cool.
   Mix the macaroni with the chicken, celery, corn, pineapple, almonds and green pepper in the salad bowl. Combine the mayonnaise, lemon juice and salt and pepper to taste and fold into the salad. Serve chilled.
Serves 4

Black and White Salad

Metric/Imperial
350 g/12 oz potatoes, cooked
   and diced
225 g/8 oz tomatoes, skinned
   and chopped
3 spring onions, chopped
50 g/2 oz black olives, stoned
4 tablespoons mayonnaise
2 tablespoons milk
salt and pepper

American
1½ cups diced cooked potatoes
1 cup peeled chopped tomatoes
3 scallions, chopped
⅓ cup pitted ripe olives
¼ cup mayonnaise
2 tablespoons milk
salt and pepper

Put the potatoes, tomatoes, spring onions (scallions) and olives in a bowl
and fold together. Combine the mayonnaise, milk and salt and pepper to
taste, then fold this dressing into the salad ingredients. Chill before
serving.
Serves 4

Mushroom Salad

Metric/Imperial
225 g/8 oz mushrooms, sliced
3 tablespoons olive oil
juice of 1 lemon
1 garlic clove, crushed
1 teaspoon caster sugar
few drops of Tabasco sauce
salt and pepper
225 g/8 oz cooked shelled
   prawns
150 ml/¼ pint double cream

American
½ lb mushrooms, sliced
3 tablespoons olive oil
juice of 1 lemon
1 garlic clove, crushed
1 teaspoon sugar
few drops of hot pepper sauce
salt and pepper
½ lb cooked shelled shrimp
⅔ cup heavy cream

Put the mushrooms into a bowl and sprinkle over the oil. Leave to soak
for 1 hour.
   Add the lemon juice, garlic, sugar, Tabasco (hot pepper) sauce and salt
and pepper to taste and mix well. Fold in the prawns (shrimp) and cream
and serve.
Serves 4

Waldorf Salad

Metric/Imperial
2 red dessert apples, cored
   and chopped
2 large celery sticks, chopped
50 g/2 oz walnuts, chopped
6 tablespoons mayonnaise

American
2 red-skinned apples, cored and
   chopped
2 large celery stalks, chopped
½ cup chopped walnuts
6 tablespoons mayonnaise

Mix together all the ingredients, then chill well before serving.
Serves 4

Provençale Pasta Salad

Metric/Imperial
175 g/6 oz pasta rings
salt and pepper
120 ml/4 fl oz bottled French
  dressing
6 tomatoes, chopped
100 g/4 oz French beans,
  cooked and cooled
12 black olives, stoned
1 × 200 g/7 oz can tuna fish,
  drained and flaked
shredded lettuce
1 × 50 g/2 oz can anchovy
  fillets, drained

American
6 oz (1½ cups) pasta rings
salt and pepper
½ cup bottled Italian
  dressing
6 tomatoes, chopped
¼ lb green beans, cooked
  and cooled
12 pitted ripe olives
1 × 7 oz can tuna fish,
  drained and flaked
shredded lettuce
1 × 2 oz can anchovy fillets,
  drained

Cook the pasta rings in boiling salted water until just tender. Drain, toss with 2 tablespoons of the dressing and cool.

Mix together the tomatoes, beans, olives, tuna fish, pasta rings and salt and pepper to taste. Add the remaining dressing and fold together gently.

Make a bed of shredded lettuce on a serving platter. Pile the salad on top and garnish with the anchovy fillets.
Serves 6

Holstein Salad

Metric/Imperial
500 g/1 lb small new potatoes
2 dessert apples, cored and
  diced
2 celery sticks, chopped
1 pear, cored and diced
225 g/8 oz cherries, halved
  and stoned
100 g/4 oz cottage cheese
225 g/8 oz Cheddar cheese,
  diced
150 ml/¼ pint soured cream
mint sprigs to garnish
  (optional)

American
1 lb small new potatoes
2 apples, cored and diced
2 celery stalks, chopped
1 pear, cored and diced
½ lb cherries, halved and pitted
½ cup cottage cheese
½ lb Cheddar cheese, diced
⅔ cup sour cream
mint sprigs for garnish
  (optional)

Cook the potatoes in boiling water until they are tender. Drain and cool, then cut in half.

Mix the potatoes with the remaining ingredients and put into a salad bowl. Garnish with mint sprigs, if liked.
Serves 4

Ham and Melon Salad

Metric/Imperial
225 g/8 oz cooked ham, cut
   into strips
1 tablespoon finely chopped
   onion
4 celery sticks, chopped
1 tablespoon chopped parsley
½ honeydew melon, peeled,
   seeded and cut into balls
   or cubes
watercress to garnish
Dressing:
2 tablespoons mayonnaise
2 tablespoons single cream
1 teaspoon creamed horseradish
1 teaspoon lemon juice
salt and pepper

American
½ lb cooked ham, cut into
   strips
1 tablespoon finely chopped
   onion
4 celery stalks, chopped
1 tablespoon chopped parsley
½ honeydew melon, peeled,
   seeded and cut into balls
   or cubes
watercress for garnish
Dressing:
2 tablespoons mayonnaise
2 tablespoons light cream
1 teaspoon prepared horseradish
1 teaspoon lemon juice
salt and pepper

Mix together the ham, onion, celery, parsley and melon. Combine the dressing ingredients, with salt and pepper to taste. Pour the dressing over the salad and fold together gently. Spoon into a serving dish and garnish with watercress.
Serves 4

Chef's Salad

Metric/Imperial
225 g/8 oz cold cooked pork,
   rare beef or ham, cut into
   strips
100 g/4 oz mushrooms, sliced
2 celery sticks, chopped
100 g/4 oz spinach, torn into
   pieces
1 lettuce, torn into pieces
6 tablespoons bottled French
   dressing
2 hard-boiled eggs, quartered
75 g/3 oz Gruyère cheese, cut
   into strips

American
½ lb cold cooked pork, rare
   beef or ham, cut into
   strips
1 cup sliced mushrooms
2 celery stalks, chopped
¼ lb spinach, torn into
   pieces
1 head of lettuce, torn into
   pieces
6 tablespoons bottled Italian
   dressing
2 hard-cooked eggs, quartered
3 oz Gruyère cheese, cut
   into strips

Place the meat, mushrooms, celery, spinach and lettuce in a salad bowl. Pour over the dressing and toss well. Arrange the eggs and cheese on top and serve.
Serves 4 to 6

Avocado Slaw

Metric/Imperial
350 g/12 oz white cabbage,
  shredded
1 small onion, grated
4 carrots, grated
50 g/2 oz walnuts, chopped
4 tomatoes, chopped
1 large avocado, peeled, stoned
  and diced
4 tablespoons bottled French
  dressing

American
¾ lb white cabbage, shredded
1 small onion, grated
4 carrots, grated
½ cup chopped walnuts
4 tomatoes, chopped
1 large avocado, peeled, seeded
  and diced
¼ cup bottled Italian dressing

Put the cabbage, onion, carrots, walnuts and tomatoes in a salad bowl.
Toss the avocado in the dressing to prevent discoloration, then add to the
salad and fold together gently. Serve lightly chilled.
Serves 6

Autumn Slaw

Metric/Imperial
225 g/8 oz red cabbage, shredded
2 dessert apples, cored and
  sliced
4 celery sticks, chopped
Dressing:
150 ml/¼ pint oil
3 tablespoons cider vinegar
2 teaspoons French mustard
1 tablespoon caster sugar
salt and pepper

American
½ lb red cabbage, shredded
2 apples, cored and sliced
4 celery stalks, chopped
Dressing:
⅔ cup oil
3 tablespoons cider vinegar
2 teaspoons Dijon-style mustard
1 tablespoon sugar
salt and pepper

Put the cabbage, apples and celery in a bowl.
   Combine the dressing ingredients, with salt and pepper to taste, in a
screwtop jar and shake well. Pour the dressing over the salad and toss.
Cover and chill overnight.
Serves 4 to 6

Fruit and Vegetable Salad

Metric/Imperial
2 satsumas or clementines,
  peeled and segmented
2 dessert apples, peeled, cored
  and chopped
4 large celery sticks, chopped
25 g/1 oz walnuts, chopped
150 ml/¼ pint plain yogurt
salt and pepper

American
2 tangerines, peeled and
  segmented
2 apples, peeled, cored and
  chopped
4 large celery stalks, chopped
¼ cup chopped walnuts
⅔ cup plain yogurt
salt and pepper

Mix together all the ingredients, with salt and pepper to taste. Chill lightly.
Serves 4 to 6

Curried Spaghetti and Mushroom Salad

Metric/Imperial
350 g/12 oz spaghetti, broken
  into short lengths
salt and pepper
4 spring onions, chopped
2 celery sticks, chopped
175 g/6 oz mushrooms, sliced
1 tablespoon chopped parsley
lettuce leaves
Dressing:
6 tablespoons oil
2 tablespoons wine vinegar
2 teaspoons curry powder
2 tablespoons tomato purée
1 teaspoon brown sugar

American
¾ lb spaghetti, broken into
  short lengths
salt and pepper
4 scallions, chopped
2 celery stalks, chopped
1½ cups sliced mushrooms
1 tablespoon chopped parsley
lettuce leaves
Dressing:
6 tablespoons oil
2 tablespoons wine vinegar
2 teaspoons curry powder
2 tablespoons tomato paste
1 teaspoon brown sugar

Cook the spaghetti in boiling salted water until just tender. Drain and cool.
  Mix together the dressing ingredients with salt and pepper to taste. Add
to the spaghetti and toss well to coat. Add the spring onions (scallions),
celery, mushrooms and parsley and mix well.
  Line a serving dish with lettuce leaves and pile the salad on top.
Serves 6 to 8

Crunchy Bean Salad

Metric/Imperial
1 × 425 g/15 oz can red kidney
  beans, drained and rinsed
4 celery sticks, chopped
4 tomatoes, chopped
12 black olives, halved and
  stoned
1 teaspoon chopped chives
1 teaspoon chopped fresh mint
Dressing:
4 tablespoons olive oil
1 tablespoon cider vinegar
salt and pepper

American
1 × 15 oz can red kidney beans,
  drained and rinsed
4 celery stalks, chopped
4 tomatoes, chopped
12 pitted ripe olives, halved
1 teaspoon chopped chives
1 teaspoon chopped fresh mint
Dressing:
¼ cup olive oil
1 tablespoon cider vinegar
salt and pepper

Mix together the beans, celery, tomatoes and olives in a salad bowl.
Combine the dressing ingredients with salt and pepper to taste and pour
into the bowl. Toss well, then chill.
  Sprinkle over the chives and mint and toss again before serving.
Serves 4

Herring and Apple Salad

Metric/Imperial	American
100 g/4 oz pasta shells	1 cup pasta shells
salt and pepper	salt and pepper
2 tablespoons bottled French dressing	2 tablespoons bottled Italian dressing
2 red dessert apples, cored and thinly sliced	2 red-skinned apples, cored and thinly sliced
2 tablespoons raisins	2 tablespoons raisins
150 ml/¼ pint soured cream	⅔ cup sour cream
grated rind and juice of ½ lemon	grated rind and juice of ½ lemon
1 tablespoon chopped parsley	1 tablespoon chopped parsley
4 rollmops, chopped	4 rollmop herrings, chopped

Cook the pasta shells in boiling salted water until just tender. Drain and cool slightly, then toss with the dressing. Fold in the apples and raisins. Cool completely.

Mix together the sour cream, lemon rind and juice, parsley and salt and pepper to taste.

Spread out the pasta mixture in a serving dish and arrange the rollmops on top. Spoon over the sour cream dressing and serve.

Serves 4

Chicken-Stuffed Tomatoes

Metric/Imperial	American
50 g/2 oz miniature pasta	½ cup miniature pasta
salt and pepper	salt and pepper
8 large tomatoes	8 large tomatoes
4 spring onions, chopped	4 scallions, chopped
100 g/4 oz cooked chicken meat, diced	¾ cup diced cooked chicken
2 canned pimientos, diced	2 canned pimientos, diced
3 tablespoons mayonnaise	3 tablespoons mayonnaise
1 teaspoon curry powder	1 teaspoon curry powder
2 tablespoons double cream	2 tablespoons heavy cream

Cook the pasta in boiling salted water until just tender. Drain and cool.

Cut the tops off the tomatoes and scoop out the seeds. Turn the tomatoes upside-down on kitchen paper towels to drain.

Mix together the spring onions (scallions), chicken, pimientos, mayonnaise, curry powder, cream and pasta. Season to taste with salt and pepper.

Fill the tomatoes with the chicken mixture and replace the tops.

Serves 4

Rainbow Salad

Metric/Imperial
175 g/6 oz pasta shells
salt and pepper
1 green pepper, cored, seeded
  and chopped
4 spring onions, chopped
100 g/4 oz cooked sweetcorn
  kernels
4 tomatoes, chopped
100 g/4 oz salami, chopped
4 tablespoons mayonnaise
2 tablespoons single cream
watercress to garnish

American
6 oz (1½ cups) pasta shells
salt and pepper
1 green pepper, seeded
  and chopped
4 scallions, chopped
¾ cup cooked whole kernel corn
4 tomatoes, chopped
¼ lb salami, chopped
¼ cup mayonnaise
2 tablespoons light cream
watercress for garnish

Cook the pasta shells in boiling salted water until just tender. Drain well and cool.

Mix together the pasta shells, green pepper, spring onions (scallions), corn, tomatoes and salami and spoon into a serving dish. Combine the mayonnaise, cream and salt and pepper to taste and pour over the salad. Toss well together, then garnish with watercress and serve.
Serves 4 to 6

Date and Apple Salad

Metric/Imperial
100 g/4 oz dates, stoned and
  chopped
2 red dessert apples, cored
  and diced
3 celery sticks, chopped
50 g/2 oz walnuts, chopped
8 Chinese cabbage leaves,
  shredded
Dressing:
150 ml/¼ pint plain yogurt
1 tablespoon honey
juice of ½ lemon
salt and pepper

American
¾ cup chopped pitted dates
2 red-skinned apples, cored
  and diced
3 celery stalks, chopped
½ cup chopped walnuts
8 Chinese cabbage (bok choy)
  leaves, shredded
Dressing:
⅔ cup plain yogurt
1 tablespoon honey
juice of ½ lemon
salt and pepper

Mix together the dates, apples, celery and walnuts. Combine the dressing ingredients with salt and pepper to taste and fold into the date mixture.

Line a small salad bowl with the shredded Chinese cabbage (bok choy) leaves and pile the date mixture on top.
Serves 4

Celeriac Rémoulade

Metric/Imperial	American
1 celeriac, cut into julienne strips	1 head celeriac (celery root), cut into julienne strips
1 tablespoon white vinegar	1 tablespoon white vinegar
salt	salt
6 tablespoons mayonnaise	6 tablespoons mayonnaise
1 tablespoon Dijon mustard	1 tablespoon Dijon-style mustard
1½ tablespoons lemon juice	1½ tablespoons lemon juice

Put the celeriac in a bowl, cover with water and add the vinegar and salt. Leave to soak for 15 minutes.

Drain the celeriac, then blanch in boiling water for 15 seconds. Drain and rinse under cold water. Cool. Mix together the mayonnaise, mustard and lemon juice. Fold in the celeriac. Chill well before serving.
Serves 4

Orange and Beetroot (Beet) Salad

Metric/Imperial	American
lettuce leaves	lettuce leaves
4 oranges, peeled and sliced	4 oranges, peeled and sliced
3-4 pickled beetroot, sliced	3-4 pickled beets, sliced
120 ml/4 fl oz olive oil	½ cup olive oil
3 tablespoons wine vinegar	3 tablespoons wine vinegar
1 tablespoon caster sugar	1 tablespoon sugar
salt and pepper	salt and pepper

Arrange a bed of lettuce leaves on four individual salad plates. Place the orange and beetroot (beet) slices on top.

Combine the remaining ingredients with salt and pepper to taste in a screwtop jar and shake well. Pour the dressing over the salad.
Serves 4

Rice Salad

Metric/Imperial	American
100 g/4 oz long-grain rice	½ cup rice
salt and pepper	salt and pepper
25 g/1 oz raisins	3 tablespoons raisins
25 g/1 oz salted peanuts	¼ cup salted peanuts
4 tomatoes, chopped	4 tomatoes, chopped
½ green pepper, cored, seeded and diced	½ green pepper, seeded and diced
1 × 200 g/7 oz can sweetcorn kernels, drained	1 × 7 oz can whole kernel corn, drained
3 tablespoons bottled French dressing	3 tablespoons bottled Italian dressing

Cook the rice in boiling salted water for about 20 minutes or until tender. Drain and cool. Add the remaining ingredients to the rice and fold together well. Chill before serving.
Serves 4 to 6

Nutty Cauliflower Salad

Metric/Imperial
1 cauliflower, broken into
   florets
salt
50 g/2 oz hazelnuts, chopped
50 g/2 oz blue cheese, diced
1 bunch of watercress
Dressing:
3 tablespoons oil
1 tablespoon wine vinegar
¼ teaspoon sugar
¼ teaspoon dry mustard
salt and pepper

American
1 cauliflower, broken into
   florets
salt
½ cup chopped hazelnuts
½ cup diced blue cheese
1 bunch of watercress
Dressing:
3 tablespoons oil
1 tablespoon wine vinegar
¼ teaspoon sugar
¼ teaspoon dry mustard
salt and pepper

Cook the cauliflower in boiling salted water until just tender but still crisp. Drain well and cool.

Mix the cauliflower, nuts, cheese and watercress in a salad bowl. Combine the dressing ingredients in a screwtop jar with salt and pepper to taste and shake well. Pour the dressing over the salad ingredients and toss gently. Serve lightly chilled.
Serves 4

Spinach and Walnut Salad

Metric/Imperial
100 g/4 oz spinach, torn into
   pieces
25 g/1 oz walnuts, chopped
2 shallots, finely chopped
2 tablespoons walnut or olive
   oil
2 teaspoons white wine vinegar
salt and pepper

American
¼ lb spinach, torn into
   pieces
¼ cup chopped walnuts
2 shallots, finely chopped
2 tablespoons walnut or olive
   oil
2 teaspoons white wine vinegar
salt and pepper

Place the spinach, walnuts and shallots in a salad bowl.

Combine the remaining ingredients with salt and pepper to taste. Pour this dressing over the salad and toss well.
Serves 4

Sunshine Salad

Metric/Imperial
1 curly endive
1 onion, thinly sliced into
  rings
1 × 113 g/4 oz can pimientos,
  drained and sliced
2 oranges, peeled and thinly
  sliced
16 green olives, stoned
Dressing:
4 tablespoons olive oil
1 tablespoon wine vinegar
1 garlic clove, crushed
pinch of caster sugar
pinch of dried tarragon
salt and pepper

American
1 head chicory
1 onion, thinly sliced into
  rings
1 × 4 oz can pimientos, drained
  and sliced
2 oranges, peeled and thinly
  sliced
16 green olives, pitted
Dressing:
¼ cup olive oil
1 tablespoon wine vinegar
1 garlic clove, crushed
pinch of sugar
pinch of dried tarragon
salt and pepper

Put the endive (chicory), onion, pimientos, oranges and olives in a salad bowl.
    Combine all the dressing ingredients with salt and pepper to taste in a screwtop jar. Shake well, then pour the dressing over the salad. Toss gently and serve.
Serves 4

Cheesy Coleslaw

Metric/Imperial
350 g/12 oz white cabbage,
  shredded
1 large carrot, grated
2 tablespoons sultanas
4 tablespoons chopped stoned
  dates
75 g/3 oz Gouda cheese, diced
Dressing:
3 tablespoons oil
1 tablespoon lemon juice
1 tablespoon clear honey
salt and pepper

American
3 cups shredded cabbage
1 large carrot, grated
2 tablespoons golden raisins
¼ cup chopped pitted dates
3 oz Gouda cheese, diced
  (about ¾ cup)
Dressing:
3 tablespoons oil
1 tablespoon lemon juice
1 tablespoon honey
salt and pepper

Place the cabbage, carrot, sultanas (raisins) and dates in a salad bowl.
    Combine the dressing ingredients with salt and pepper to taste and pour over the salad. Toss well. Fold in the cheese and serve.
Serves 4 to 6

Spaghetti Salad

Metric/Imperial
1 × 425 g/15 oz can spaghetti
   in tomato sauce
6 tablespoons bottled French
   dressing
3 celery sticks, chopped
1 green pepper, cored, seeded
   and chopped
1 onion, finely chopped
½ lettuce, torn into pieces
25 g/1 oz unsalted peanuts,
   chopped
salt and pepper
croûtons to garnish

American
1 × 15 oz can spaghetti in
   tomato sauce
6 tablespoons bottled Italian
   dressing
3 celery stalks, chopped
1 green pepper, seeded
   and chopped
1 onion, finely chopped
½ head of lettuce, torn into
   pieces
¼ cup chopped unsalted peanuts
salt and pepper
croûtons for garnish

Put the spaghetti into a saucepan with half the dressing and heat, stirring occasionally, until the dressing has been absorbed by the pasta. Remove from the heat and cool.

Put the celery, green pepper, onion, lettuce and peanuts in a salad bowl and add the spaghetti, remaining dressing and salt and pepper to taste. Toss well together and serve garnished with croûtons.
Serves 4 to 6

Kidney Bean Salad

Metric/Imperial
1 onion, thinly sliced
salt and pepper
1 × 425 g/15 oz can red kidney
   beans, drained
chopped parsley to garnish
Dressing:
3 tablespoons olive oil
1 tablespoon wine vinegar
1 garlic clove, crushed
pinch of dry mustard
½ teaspoon dried basil

American
1 onion, thinly sliced
salt and pepper
1 × 16 oz can red kidney beans,
   drained
chopped parsley for garnish
Dressing:
3 tablespoons olive oil
1 tablespoon wine vinegar
1 garlic clove, crushed
pinch of dry mustard
½ teaspoon dried basil

Sprinkle the onion with salt and leave for 30 minutes.

Meanwhile combine all the dressing ingredients with salt and pepper to taste in a screwtop jar. Shake well.

Rinse the onion and pat dry with kitchen paper towels. Place the onion in a salad bowl and add the kidney beans. Pour over the dressing and toss well. Sprinkle with parsley before serving.
Serves 4

Exotic Cucumber Salad

Metric/Imperial	American
2 medium cucumbers, peeled, seeded and cut into 7.5 cm/3 inch strips	2 medium cucumbers, peeled, seeded and cut into 3 inch strips
3 tablespoons vinegar	3 tablespoons vinegar
1 teaspoon salt	1 teaspoon salt
6 tablespoons oil	6 tablespoons oil
2 onions, sliced	2 onions, sliced
1 garlic clove, sliced	1 garlic clove, sliced
pinch of ground turmeric	pinch of ground turmeric
1 teaspoon sugar	1 teaspoon sugar

Put the cucumber in a saucepan and add water to cover and 2 tablespoons of the vinegar. Bring to the boil and simmer for about 4 minutes or until the cucumber becomes transparent. Drain, sprinkle with ½ teaspoon of the salt and cool.

Heat the oil in a frying pan (skillet). Add the onions and garlic and fry until golden and crisp. Remove from the pan with a slotted spoon and drain on kitchen paper towels.

Stir the turmeric, sugar and remaining salt into the oil in the pan, then cool. Stir in the remaining vinegar, then fold in the cucumber to coat well with the dressing. Drain the cucumber and place in a serving dish. Sprinkle over the onions and garlic and serve cold or chilled.
Serves 4

Oriental Pasta Salad

Metric/Imperial	American
225 g/8 oz pasta shapes	½ lb pasta shapes
salt and pepper	salt and pepper
1 × 225 g/8 oz can pineapple chunks	1 × 8 oz can pineapple chunks
175 g/6 oz bean sprouts	3 cups bean sprouts
2 carrots, grated	2 carrots, grated
½ cucumber, chopped	½ cucumber, chopped
Dressing:	Dressing:
6 tablespoons oil	6 tablespoons oil
2 tablespoons orange juice	2 tablespoons orange juice
1 tablespoon soy sauce	1 tablespoon soy sauce
pinch of ground ginger	pinch of ground ginger

Cook the pasta in boiling salted water until just tender.

Meanwhile drain the pineapple, reserving the syrup. Chop the pineapple and set aside. Mix 2 tablespoons of the pineapple syrup with the remaining dressing ingredients.

Drain the pasta and tip into a salad bowl. Add the dressing and toss well. Leave to cool.

Add the bean sprouts, carrots, cucumber and chopped pineapple to the pasta and fold together. Serve lightly chilled.
Serves 6

Country Salad

Metric/Imperial
225 g/8 oz pasta rings
salt and pepper
1 tablespoon olive oil
4 tomatoes, chopped ·
1 green pepper, cored, seeded
  and chopped
50 g/2 oz stuffed olives,
  sliced
175 g/6 oz button mushrooms,
  sliced
6 tablespoons bottled French
  dressing
1 tablespoon tomato ketchup

American
½ lb pasta rings
salt and pepper
1 tablespoon olive oil
4 tomatoes, chopped
1 green pepper, seeded
  and chopped
⅓ cup sliced pimiento-stuffed
  olives
1½ cups sliced mushrooms
6 tablespoons bottled Italian
  dressing
1 tablespoon tomato ketchup

Cook the pasta rings in boiling salted water until just tender. Drain well, toss with the oil to coat and cool.

Combine the tomatoes, green pepper, olives and mushrooms. Add the pasta rings. Mix together the dressing, ketchup and salt and pepper to taste. Add to the salad and mix well together. Serve lightly chilled.
Serves 4 to 6

Courgette (Zucchini) Salad

Metric/Imperial
175 g/6 oz pasta shells
salt and pepper
4 courgettes, thinly sliced
6 tablespoons bottled French
  dressing
2 tomatoes, chopped
8 black olives, stoned
2 spring onions, chopped
1 tablespoon chopped parsley

American
6 oz (1½ cups) pasta shells
salt and pepper
4 zucchini, thinly sliced
6 tablespoons bottled Italian
  dressing
2 tomatoes, chopped
8 pitted ripe olives
2 scallions, chopped
1 tablespoon chopped parsley

Cook the pasta shells in boiling salted water until just tender.

Meanwhile cook the courgettes (zucchini) in boiling water until just tender but still crisp. Drain well and cool.

Drain the pasta shells and mix with 2 tablespoons of the dressing; cool.

Mix together the pasta shells, courgettes (zucchini), tomatoes, olives, spring onions (scallions), parsley and remaining dressing. Serve the salad lightly chilled.
Serves 4

Macaroni and Mushroom Salad

Metric/Imperial
225 g/8 oz button mushrooms,
  sliced
4 tablespoons lemon juice
2 tablespoons wine vinegar
1 garlic clove, crushed
salt and pepper
500 g/1 lb short cut macaroni
1 red pepper, cored, seeded
  and chopped
150 ml/¼ pint mayonnaise
150 ml/¼ pint plain yogurt

American
½ lb mushrooms, sliced
¼ cup lemon juice
2 tablespoons wine vinegar
1 garlic clove, crushed
salt and pepper
1 lb elbow macaroni
1 red pepper, seeded
  and chopped
⅔ cup mayonnaise
⅔ cup plain yogurt

Combine the mushrooms, lemon juice, vinegar, garlic and salt and pepper
to taste. Leave to marinate for 30 minutes.
   Meanwhile cook the macaroni in boiling salted water until just tender.
Drain well and cool.
   Add the macaroni to the mushrooms with the red pepper, mayonnaise,
yogurt and salt and pepper to taste. Fold together well. Serve the salad
lightly chilled.
Serves 6

Italian Avocado Salad

Metric/Imperial
175 g/6 oz pasta shells
salt
2 celery sticks, diced
1 green pepper, cored, seeded
  and diced
100 g/4 oz mushrooms, sliced
1 tablespoon chopped walnuts
4 tablespoons bottled French
  dressing
1 ripe avocado, peeled, stoned
  and chopped
lemon juice
lettuce leaves

American
6 oz (1½ cups) pasta shells
salt
2 celery sticks, diced
1 green pepper, seeded
  and diced
1 cup sliced mushrooms
1 tablespoon chopped walnuts
¼ cup bottled Italian dressing
1 ripe avocado, peeled, seeded
  and chopped
lemon juice
lettuce leaves

Cook the pasta shells in boiling salted water until just tender. Drain and
cool.
   Mix the pasta shells with the celery, green pepper, mushrooms and
walnuts. Add the dressing and toss together. Sprinkle the avocado with
lemon juice to prevent discoloration, then add to the salad and mix well.
   Line a serving dish with lettuce leaves and pile the salad on top.
Serves 4 to 6

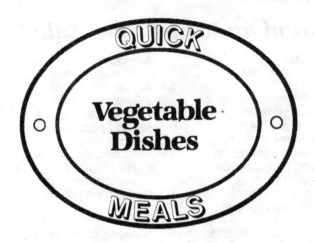

Stuffed Baked Aubergines (Eggplants)

Metric/Imperial
2 large aubergines, halved
 lengthways
salt and pepper
2 tablespoons oil
1 onion, chopped
1 garlic clove, crushed
1 × 400 g/14 oz can tomatoes,
 drained
2 tablespoons tomato purée
1 teaspoon dried mixed herbs
1 × 200 g/7 oz can tuna fish,
 drained and flaked
175 g/6 oz Cheddar cheese,
 grated

American
2 large eggplants, halved
 lengthwise
salt and pepper
2 tablespoons oil
1 onion, chopped
1 garlic clove, crushed
1 × 16 oz can tomatoes,
 drained
2 tablespoons tomato paste
1 teaspoon dried mixed herbs
1 × 7 oz can tuna fish, drained
 and flaked
1½ cups grated Cheddar cheese

Scoop out the flesh from the aubergine (eggplant) halves, leaving the
shells about 5 mm/¼ inch thick. Chop the flesh and sprinkle it with salt.
Leave to drain for 20 minutes, then rinse and pat dry with kitchen paper
towels.

Heat the oil in a saucepan. Add the onion and garlic and fry until
softened. Stir in the tomatoes, tomato purée (paste), herbs and chopped
aubergine (eggplant). Cover and simmer for 15 minutes. Stir in the tuna,
and salt and pepper to taste.

Divide the tuna mixture between the aubergine (eggplant) shells and
arrange them in a shallow ovenproof dish. Sprinkle the cheese on top.
Cover with foil and bake in a preheated moderately hot oven
(190°C/375°F, Gas Mark 5) for 30 to 35 minutes.
Serves 4

Tomato Walnut Casserole

Metric/Imperial
100 g/4 oz short-cut macaroni
salt and pepper
1 × 400 g/14 oz can tomatoes
1 tablespoon grated onion
2 bay leaves
100 g/4 oz Cheddar cheese,
    grated
100 g/4 oz walnuts, chopped

American
¼ lb elbow macaroni
salt and pepper
1 × 16 oz can tomatoes
1 tablespoon grated onion
2 bay leaves
1 cup grated Cheddar cheese
1 cup chopped walnuts

Cook the macaroni in boiling salted water until tender.

Meanwhile place the tomatoes with their juice, the onion, bay leaves and salt and pepper to taste in a saucepan. Bring to the boil, mashing the tomatoes with a spoon to break them up, and simmer until the mixture is thick.

Drain the macaroni thoroughly. Discard the bay leaves from the tomato sauce.

Make alternate layers of macaroni, tomato sauce, cheese and walnuts in a greased ovenproof dish, ending with tomato sauce and cheese. Cook in a preheated moderately hot oven (200°C/400°F, Gas Mark 6) for about 25 minutes or until bubbling and the top is golden brown. Serve hot.
Serves 4

Bacon and Cheese Rosti

Metric/Imperial
1 kg/2 lb potatoes, halved
500 g/1 lb streaky bacon
    rashers, derinded and chopped
1 onion, chopped
100 g/4 oz Cheddar cheese,
    grated
salt and pepper

American
2 lb potatoes, halved
1 lb bacon slices, chopped
1 onion, chopped
1 cup grated Cheddar cheese
salt and pepper

Parboil the potatoes in boiling water for 5 minutes. Drain and dry on kitchen paper towels.

Fry the bacon and onion in a frying pan (skillet) until golden. Grate the potatoes coarsely into the pan and add the cheese and salt and pepper to taste. Mix well, then spread out and smooth the surface. Cook until the underside is crisp and brown.

Place the pan under a preheated grill (broiler) and cook for a further 5 minutes or until the potatoes are tender and the top is golden brown. Serve hot.
Serves 4

Spicy Spinach

Metric/Imperial
25 g/1 oz butter or margarine
2 large onions, chopped
½-1 teaspoon chilli powder
1 kg/2 lb spinach, torn into
  pieces
salt

American
2 tablespoons butter or
  margarine
2 large onions, chopped
½-1 teaspoon chili powder
2 lb spinach, torn into pieces
salt

Melt the butter or margarine in a frying pan (skillet). Add the onions and fry until golden brown. Stir in the chilli powder and cook for 1 minute, then stir in the spinach. Cover the pan and cook gently for about 4 minutes or until the spinach is tender. Season with salt and serve hot.
Serves 4

Potato Pancakes

Metric/Imperial
500 g/1 lb potatoes, grated
225 g/8 oz onions, grated
2 eggs, beaten
salt and pepper
oil for frying

American
1 lb potatoes, grated
½ lb onions, grated
2 eggs, beaten
salt and pepper
oil for frying

Mix together the potatoes, onions, eggs and salt and pepper to taste.
  Heat a little oil in a frying pan (skillet). Drop large spoonfuls of the potato mixture into the pan, spacing them well apart, and flatten with a spatula. Fry for 4 minutes on each side, then remove from the pan and keep hot while you cook the remaining pancakes, in batches, in the same way. Serve hot.
Serves 4

Corn Parcels

Metric/Imperial
4 corn on the cob, husks and
  silk removed
65 g/2½ oz butter or margarine,
  melted
1 teaspoon dried thyme
salt and pepper

American
4 ears of corn, shucked
5 tablespoons butter or
  margarine, melted
1 teaspoon dried thyme
salt and pepper

Blanch the corn in boiling water for 3 minutes. Drain well. Place each ear on a sheet of foil large enough to enclose it.
  Mix together the butter or margarine, thyme and salt and pepper to taste. Drizzle over the corn, then fold up the foil to make neat parcels. Place on a baking sheet.
  Cook in a preheated moderate oven (160°C/325°F, Gas Mark 3) for 10 minutes or until the corn is tender. Serve hot.
Serves 4

Baked Stuffed Courgettes (Zucchini)

Metric/Imperial
8 large courgettes
1 × 326 g/11½ oz can sweetcorn
  kernels, drained
1 large onion, chopped
50 g/2 oz Cheddar cheese,
  grated
25 g/1 oz black olives,
  stoned and chopped
1 egg, beaten
salt and pepper

American
8 large zucchini
1 × 11½ oz can whole kernel corn,
  drained
1 large onion, chopped
½ cup grated Cheddar cheese
¼ cup chopped pitted ripe olives
1 egg, beaten
salt and pepper

Blanch the courgettes (zucchini) in boiling water for 3 minutes. Drain and cool slightly, then cut in half lengthwise and scoop out the seeds.

Mix together the remaining ingredients with salt and pepper to taste. Arrange the courgette (zucchini) halves, cut sides up, in one layer in a greased shallow ovenproof dish. Fill the hollows with the corn mixture.

Cook in a preheated moderate oven (180°C/350°F, Gas Mark 4) for 35 minutes or until the courgettes (zucchini) are tender and the stuffing is golden brown. Serve hot.
Serves 4 to 6

Crusty Mushroom Loaf

Metric/Imperial
1 loaf of French bread
25 g/1 oz butter or margarine
2 tablespoons plain flour
300 ml/½ pint milk
100 g/4 oz mushrooms, sliced
2 hard-boiled eggs, chopped
1 tablespoon chopped parsley
salt and pepper

American
1 loaf of French bread
2 tablespoons butter or
  margarine
2 tablespoons all-purpose flour
1¼ cups milk
1 cup sliced mushrooms
2 hard-cooked eggs, chopped
1 tablespoon chopped parsley
salt and pepper

Slice off the top from the loaf and scoop out the soft centre. Place the bread shell and top on a baking sheet and cook in a preheated moderate oven (180°C/350°F, Gas Mark 4) for 10 to 15 minutes or until crisp inside.

Meanwhile melt the butter or margarine in a saucepan. Stir in the flour and cook for 1 minute, then gradually stir in the milk. Bring to the boil, stirring, and simmer until thickened. Add the mushrooms, eggs, parsley and salt and pepper to taste.

Pour the mushroom mixture into the bread shell and replace the top. Return to the oven and cook for 10 minutes. Serve hot.
Serves 4

Bacon Corn Fritters

Metric/Imperial	American
100 g/4 oz plain flour	1 cup all-purpose flour
pinch of salt	pinch of salt
1 egg	1 egg
150 ml/¼ pint milk	¾ cup milk
1 teaspoon Worcestershire sauce	1 teaspoon Worcestershire sauce
1 × 200 g/7 oz can sweetcorn kernels, drained	1 × 7 oz can whole kernel corn, drained
4 bacon rashers, derinded, chopped and fried	4 bacon slices, fried and crumbled
25 g/1 oz butter	2 tablespoons butter
1 tablespoon oil	1 tablespoon oil

Sift the flour and salt into a bowl. Add the egg, milk and Worcestershire sauce and beat to a smooth batter. Stir in the corn and bacon.

Melt the butter with the oil in a large frying pan (skillet). Drop in tablespoons of the batter, keeping them well spaced apart as they will spread out, and fry until crisp and golden brown on both sides. Serve hot.
Serves 3 to 4

Barbecued Beans

Metric/Imperial	American
1 × 275 g/10 oz packet frozen butter beans	1 × 10 oz package frozen lima beans
2 tablespoons oil	2 tablespoons oil
1 onion, chopped	1 onion, chopped
1 garlic clove, crushed	1 garlic clove, crushed
2 tomatoes, skinned and chopped	2 tomatoes, peeled and chopped
1 tablespoon brown sugar	1 tablespoon brown sugar
pinch of dry mustard	pinch of dry mustard
pinch of chilli powder	pinch of chili powder
1 tablespoon tomato ketchup	1 tablespoon tomato ketchup
salt and pepper	salt and pepper

Cook the beans in boiling water according to the instructions on the packet.

Meanwhile heat the oil in a saucepan. Add the onion and garlic and fry until softened. Stir in the tomatoes, sugar, mustard, chilli powder, ketchup and salt and pepper to taste. Simmer for 10 minutes.

Drain the beans and fold into the sauce. Serve hot.
Serves 4

Corn Pilaf

Metric/Imperial	American
100 g/4 oz long-grain rice	½ cup rice
salt and pepper	salt and pepper
50 g/2 oz butter or margarine	4 tablespoons butter or
1 onion, chopped	margarine
100 g/4 oz mushrooms, sliced	1 onion, chopped
2 streaky bacon rashers, derinded	1 cup sliced mushrooms
and diced	2 bacon slices, diced
225 g/8 oz cooked meat, diced	1 cup diced cooked meat
1 × 300 g/11½ oz can sweetcorn	1 × 11 oz can whole kernel
kernels, drained	corn, drained
50 g/2 oz Parmesan cheese,	½ cup grated Parmesan
grated	cheese
2 tomatoes, sliced	2 tomatoes, sliced

Cook the rice in boiling salted water for about 20 minutes or until tender. Drain, if necessary, and keep hot.

Melt the butter or margarine in a frying pan (skillet). Add the onion and fry until softened. Stir in the mushrooms and bacon and continue frying until the bacon is crisp. Add the meat, corn and salt and pepper to taste and heat through. Stir in the rice and reheat if necessary.

Stir in the cheese and pile on a warmed serving dish. Garnish with the tomato slices and serve hot.
Serves 4

Corn Fritters

Metric/Imperial	American
3 large eggs, separated	3 large eggs, separated
50 g/2 oz plain flour, sifted	½ cup all-purpose flour, sifted
1 × 326 g/11½ oz can sweetcorn	1 × 11½ oz can whole kernel corn,
kernels, drained	drained
salt and pepper	salt and pepper
oil for frying	oil for frying

Beat the egg yolks and flour together until smooth. Stir in the corn and salt and pepper to taste. Beat the egg whites until stiff and fold into the mixture.

Heat a little oil in a frying pan (skillet). Drop tablespoonfuls of the corn mixture onto the pan, spacing them well apart as they spread, and cook for 2 minutes on each side. Remove from the pan and keep hot while you cook the remaining fritters, in batches, in the same way.

Serve hot.
Serves 4

Stir-Fried Bean Sprouts

Metric/Imperial	American
3 tablespoons oil	3 tablespoons oil
2 garlic cloves, crushed	2 garlic cloves, crushed
2 slices fresh root ginger, peeled and shredded	2 slices fresh ginger root, peeled and shredded
500 g/1 lb bean sprouts	1 lb bean sprouts
salt and pepper	salt and pepper
2 tablespoons soy sauce	2 tablespoons soy sauce
3 spring onions, cut into 5 cm/2 inch pieces	3 scallions, cut into 2 inch pieces
1½ teaspoons sesame seed oil (optional)	1½ teaspoons sesame seed oil (optional)

Heat the oil in a frying pan (skillet). Add the garlic and ginger and stir-fry for 10 seconds. Add the bean sprouts with salt and pepper to taste and stir to coat with the oil. Add the soy sauce and spring onions (scallions) and stir-fry for 2 minutes.

Sprinkle over the sesame seed oil, if using, and serve hot.
Serves 4

Mixed Vegetable Curry

Metric/Imperial	American
4 potatoes, diced	4 potatoes, diced
4 carrots, diced	4 carrots, diced
¼ turnip, diced	¼ turnip, diced
100 g/4 oz frozen peas	1 cup frozen peas
100 g/4 oz runner beans, chopped	1 cup chopped green beans
1 tablespoon oil	1 tablespoon oil
1 onion, chopped	1 onion, chopped
1 garlic clove, crushed	1 garlic clove, crushed
1 tablespoon curry powder	1 tablespoon curry powder
2 tablespoons tomato purée	2 tablespoons tomato paste
1 tablespoon desiccated coconut	1 tablespoon shredded coconut
2 teaspoons lemon juice	2 teaspoons lemon juice
salt	salt

Parboil the potatoes, carrots, turnip, peas and beans in boiling water for 5 minutes. Drain, reserving the water.

Heat the oil in a frying pan (skillet). Add the onion and garlic and fry until golden brown. Stir in the curry powder, tomato purée (paste) and enough of the reserved water to make a thick gravy. Cover and simmer gently for 10 minutes.

Add the parboiled vegetables, coconut, lemon juice and salt to taste and simmer, covered, until the vegetables are tender. Serve hot.
Serves 6

Spiced Mushrooms

Metric/Imperial
50 g/2 oz butter or margarine
2 onions, chopped
2 tablespoons tomato purée
½ teaspoon ground cinnamon
½ teaspoon ground cloves
500 g/1 lb mushrooms, sliced
2 tablespoons water
150 ml/¼ pint plain yogurt
300 ml/½ pint beef stock
salt and pepper

American
4 tablespoons butter or
    margarine
2 onions, chopped
2 tablespoons tomato paste
½ teaspoon ground cinnamon
½ teaspoon ground cloves
1 lb mushrooms, sliced
2 tablespoons water
⅔ cup plain yogurt
1¼ cups beef stock or broth
salt and pepper

Melt the butter or margarine in a frying pan (skillet). Add the onions and fry until softened. Stir in the tomato purée (paste), cinnamon and cloves and cook for 2 minutes. Add the mushrooms and water and mix well. Cook, stirring, until the mushrooms are lightly browned.

Add the yogurt, stock and salt and pepper to taste and simmer gently for 15 minutes. Serve hot.
Serves 6

Spiced Fruit and Vegetables

Metric/Imperial
1 tablespoon oil
1 onion, chopped
4 celery sticks, chopped
1 tablespoon plain flour
1 tablespoon curry powder
300 ml/½ pint chicken stock
1 teaspoon ground ginger
grated rind and juice of
    1 lemon
1 × 400 g/14 oz can apricot
    halves, drained
2 bananas, thickly sliced
500 g/1 lb cooking apples,
    peeled, cored and quartered
100 g/4 oz raisins
150 ml/¼ pint soured cream

American
1 tablespoon oil
1 onion, chopped
4 celery stalks, chopped
1 tablespoon all-purpose flour
1 tablespoon curry powder
1¼ cups chicken stock or broth
1 teaspoon ground ginger
grated rind and juice of
    1 lemon
1 × 16 oz can apricot halves,
    drained
2 bananas, thickly sliced
1 lb apples, peeled, cored and
    quartered
⅔ cup raisins
⅔ cup sour cream

Heat the oil in a saucepan. Add the onion and celery and fry until the onion is golden. Stir in the flour and curry powder and cook for 2 minutes, then gradually stir in the stock. Add the ginger and lemon rind and juice and bring to the boil.

Add the fruit and raisins and stir well, then cover and cook gently for about 15 minutes or until the apples are very tender. Stir in the sour cream and serve hot.
Serves 6

Chinese Cabbage (Bok Choy) with Tomatoes

Metric/Imperial
1 medium Chinese cabbage,
    quartered
salt and pepper
50 g/2 oz butter or margarine
150 ml/¼ pint chicken stock
1 onion, sliced
1 garlic clove, crushed
100 g/4 oz tomatoes, chopped
1 tablespoon chopped parsley

American
1 medium head Chinese cabbage
    (bok choy), quartered
salt and pepper
4 tablespoons butter or
    margarine
⅔ cup chicken stock or broth
1 onion, sliced
1 garlic clove, crushed
½ cup chopped tomatoes
1 tablespoon chopped parsley

Blanch the cabbage in boiling salted water for 5 minutes. Drain well.

Melt 25 g/1 oz (2 tablespoons) of the butter or margarine in a frying pan (skillet). Add the cabbage, stock and salt and pepper to taste. Cover and cook gently for 10 minutes.

Meanwhile melt the remaining butter or margarine in a saucepan. Add the onion and garlic and fry until softened. Stir in the tomatoes, parsley and salt and pepper to taste. Cook gently for 5 minutes.

Drain the cabbage, reserving the cooking liquid, and place in a warmed serving dish. Stir 4 to 6 tablespoons of the cooking liquid into the tomato mixture, then pour over the cabbage. Serve hot.
Serves 4

Saucy Vegetable Casserole

Metric/Imperial
2 medium potatoes
salt and pepper
225 g/8 oz leeks, sliced
3 tomatoes, skinned and
    quartered
1 × 275 g/10 oz can condensed
    cream of chicken soup
½ teaspoon dried mixed herbs
50 g/2 oz Gouda cheese, grated
25 g/1 oz fresh breadcrumbs

American
2 medium potatoes
salt and pepper
½ lb leeks, sliced
3 tomatoes, peeled and
    quartered
1 × 10 oz can condensed cream
    of chicken soup
½ teaspoon dried mixed herbs
½ cup grated Gouda cheese
½ cup soft bread crumbs

Parboil the potatoes in boiling salted water for 10 minutes. Meanwhile parboil the leeks in boiling salted water for 5 minutes. Drain both vegetables. Chop the potatoes.

Mix the leeks and potatoes with the tomatoes, undiluted soup and herbs. Season to taste with salt and pepper and put into an ovenproof dish. Mix together the cheese and breadcrumbs and sprinkle on top.

Cook in a preheated moderately hot oven (190°C/375°F, Gas Mark 5) for 25 to 30 minutes or until the vegetables are tender and the top is golden brown. Serve hot.
Serves 4

Orange Glazed Carrots

Metric/Imperial
500 g/1 lb carrots, sliced
salt and pepper
3 tablespoons orange juice
1½ tablespoons brown sugar
50 g/2 oz butter or margarine
pinch of ground cloves
chopped parsley to garnish

American
1 lb carrots, sliced
salt and pepper
3 tablespoons orange juice
1½ tablespoons brown sugar
4 tablespoons butter or
  margarine
pinch of ground cloves
chopped parsley for garnish

Cook the carrots in boiling salted water until just tender. Drain well. Place in a warmed serving dish and keep hot.

Put the orange juice, sugar, butter or margarine, cloves and salt and pepper to taste in the saucepan and bring to the boil, stirring to melt the fat. Pour this sauce over the carrots. Sprinkle with parsley and serve hot.
Serves 4

Herbed Courgettes (Zucchini)

Metric/Imperial
750 g/1½ lb courgettes,
  sliced
salt and pepper
25 g/1 oz butter or margarine
2 teaspoons chopped fresh
  tarragon

American
½ lb zucchini, sliced
salt and pepper
2 tablespoons butter or
  margarine
2 teaspoons chopped fresh
  tarragon

Cook the courgettes (zucchini) in boiling salted water for 5 minutes or until just tender. Drain well and return to the pan. Add the butter or margarine, tarragon and salt and pepper to taste and mix well. Serve hot.
Serves 4

Creamy Corn with Peppers

Metric/Imperial
1 onion, chopped
1 carrot, diced
1 celery stick, chopped
1 green pepper, cored, seeded
    and diced
1 red pepper, cored, seeded
    and diced
1 bay leaf
350 g/12 oz frozen sweetcorn
    kernels
25 g/1 oz butter or margarine
25 g/1 oz plain flour
150 ml/¼ pint milk
salt and pepper

American
1 onion, chopped
1 carrot, diced
1 celery stalk, chopped
1 green pepper, seeded
    and diced
1 red pepper, seeded
    and diced
1 bay leaf
¾ lb frozen whole kernel corn
2 tablespoons butter or
    margarine
¼ cup all-purpose flour
¾ cup milk
salt and pepper

Put the onion, carrot, celery, green and red peppers and bay leaf in a saucepan and cover with water. Bring to the boil and simmer for 5 minutes. Stir in the corn and simmer for a further 5 minutes or until all the vegetables are tender.

Discard the bay leaf. Drain the vegetables, reserving 150 ml/¼ pint (¾ cup) of the cooking liquid. Keep the vegetables hot.

Melt the butter or margarine in the saucepan. Stir in the flour and cook for 2 minutes, then gradually stir in the reserved cooking liquid and the milk. Bring to the boil, stirring and simmer until thickened. Season to taste with salt and pepper.

Stir the vegetables into the sauce and reheat if necessary. Serve hot.
Serves 4

Tomatoes with Yogurt

Metric/Imperial
50 g/2 oz butter or margarine
500 g/1 lb tomatoes, skinned
    and chopped
pinch of sugar
300 ml/½ pint plain yogurt
2 tablespoons chopped fresh
    basil
salt and pepper
25 g/1 oz pine nuts (optional)

American
4 tablespoons butter or
    margarine
1 lb tomatoes, peeled and
    chopped
pinch of sugar
1¼ cups plain yogurt
·2 tablespoons chopped fresh
    basil
salt and pepper
¼ cup pine nuts (pignoli)
    (optional)

Melt the butter or margarine in a saucepan. Add the tomatoes and cook gently until just softened. Remove from the heat and stir in the sugar, yogurt, basil and salt and pepper to taste.

Pour into a shallow serving dish and sprinkle over the pine nuts, if using. Serve warm.
Serves 4

Stir-Fried Mixed Vegetables

Metric/Imperial
1 tablespoon oil
1 large onion, chopped
1 garlic clove, crushed
50 g/2 oz streaky bacon rashers,
  derinded and chopped
1 tablespoon peeled and grated
  fresh root ginger
50 g/2 oz mushrooms, sliced
500 g/1 lb mange tout
225 g/8 oz Chinese cabbage
  or other cabbage, shredded
100 g/4 oz bean sprouts
25 g/1 oz unsalted peanuts
1 tablespoon soy sauce
5 tablespoons water
salt and pepper

American
1 tablespoon oil
1 large onion, chopped
1 garlic clove, crushed
3 bacon slices, chopped
1 tablespoon peeled and grated
  fresh ginger root
½ cup sliced mushrooms
1 lb mange tout (snow peas)
2 cups shredded Chinese cabbage
  (bok choy) or other cabbage
¼ lb bean sprouts
¼ cup unsalted peanuts
1 tablespoon soy sauce
5 tablespoons water
salt and pepper

Heat the oil in a wok or frying pan (skillet). Add the onion, garlic, bacon and ginger and stir-fry for 3 minutes.

Add the mushrooms, mange tout and cabbage and stir-fry for 2 minutes.

Add the remaining ingredients, with salt and pepper to taste, and stir-fry for a further 5 minutes or until the vegetables are tender but still crisp and most of the liquid has evaporated. Serve hot.
Serves 4 to 6

Greek Courgette (Zucchini) Pancakes

Metric/Imperial
3 medium courgettes, grated
225 g/8 oz feta cheese,
  grated
2 teaspoons chopped fresh mint
salt and pepper
3 tablespoons plain flour
3 eggs, beaten
butter or margarine for frying

American
3 medium-size zucchini, grated
½ lb feta cheese, grated
  (about 2 cups)
2 teaspoons chopped fresh mint
salt and pepper
3 tablespoons all-purpose flour
3 eggs, beaten
butter or margarine for frying

Squeeze the courgettes (zucchini) in a tea (dish) towel to remove excess moisture. Mix the courgettes (zucchini) with the cheese, mint and salt and pepper to taste. Add the flour and eggs and mix well.

Melt a little butter or margarine in a frying pan (skillet). Drop tablespoonfuls of the mixture into the pan, spacing them well apart, and cook until golden and crisp on both sides. Drain on kitchen paper towels and keep hot while you cook the remaining pancakes in the same way. Serve hot.
Serves 4

Baked Stuffed Tomatoes

Metric/Imperial	American
4 large tomatoes	4 large tomatoes
2 tablespoons oil	2 tablespoons oil
100 g/4 oz mushrooms, diced	1 cup diced mushrooms
2 shallots, finely chopped	2 shallots, finely chopped
2 tablespoons fresh breadcrumbs	2 tablespoons soft bread crumbs
25 g/1 oz ground hazelnuts	1/4 cup ground hazelnuts
1 teaspoon chopped parsley	1 teaspoon chopped parsley
1/4 teaspoon dried thyme	1/4 teaspoon dried thyme
2 tablespoons grated Parmesan cheese	2 tablespoons grated Parmesan cheese
salt and pepper	salt and pepper

Cut a lid off the rounded end of each tomato, then scoop out the seeds.
Heat the oil in a frying pan (skillet). Add the mushrooms and shallots and fry for 3 minutes. Remove from the heat and stir in the remaining ingredients with salt and pepper to taste. Fill the tomato shells with this mixture and replace the lids.
Arrange the tomatoes in an ovenproof dish. Cook in a preheated moderate oven (180°C/350°F, Gas Mark 4) for 15 to 20 minutes or until tender and heated through. Serve hot.
Serves 4

Curried Cauliflower

Metric/Imperial	American
25 g/1 oz butter or margarine	2 tablespoons butter or margarine
1 onion, chopped	1 onion, chopped
1/2 teaspoon dry mustard	1/2 teaspoon dry mustard
1 teaspoon ground turmeric	1 teaspoon ground turmeric
1/4 teaspoon garlic powder	1/4 teaspoon garlic powder
1/2 teaspoon ground ginger	1/2 teaspoon ground ginger
1/2 teaspoon chilli powder	1/2 teaspoon chili powder
salt	salt
4 tablespoons water	1/4 cup water
1 cauliflower, broken into florets	1 cauliflower, broken into florets
1 teaspoon garam masala	1 teaspoon garam masala

Melt the butter or margarine in a saucepan. Add the onion and fry until golden brown. Stir in the mustard, turmeric, garlic powder, ginger, chilli powder and salt to taste. Cook for 2 minutes, then stir in the water.
Add the cauliflower, cover and cook gently for 5 minutes. Sprinkle over the garam masala and continue cooking until the cauliflower is just tender. Serve hot.
Serves 4

Vegetable Brochettes

Metric/Imperial
225 g/8 oz courgettes, sliced
8 small tomatoes
1 large onion, cut into wedges
  with skin
8 button mushrooms
1 green pepper, cored, seeded
  and cut into squares
1 tablespoon oil
1 tablespoon lemon juice
1 tablespoon chopped fresh
  thyme
salt and pepper

American
½ lb zucchini, sliced
8 cherry tomatoes
1 large onion, cut into
  wedges with skin
8 button mushrooms
1 green pepper, seeded
  and cut into squares
1 tablespoon oil
1 tablespoon lemon juice
1 tablespoon chopped fresh
  thyme
salt and pepper

Blanch the courgettes (zucchini) in boiling water for 1 minute. Drain well.
   Thread the courgettes (zucchini) onto skewers alternating with the
other vegetables. Mix together the oil, lemon juice, thyme and salt and
pepper to taste. Brush the vegetables with the mixture.
   Place the brochettes under a preheated grill (broiler) and cook for 5 to
10 minutes, turning and basting with the oil mixture from time to time.
Serve hot.
Serves 4

Petits Pois à la Française

Metric/Imperial
25 g/1 oz butter or margarine
1 lettuce heart, shredded
12 spring onions (white part
  only)
1 teaspoon caster sugar
1 tablespoon chopped fresh mint
salt and pepper
500 g/1 lb frozen petits pois

American
2 tablespoons butter or
  margarine
1 lettuce heart, shredded
12 scallions (white part only)
1 teaspoon sugar
1 tablespoon chopped fresh mint
salt and pepper
1 lb frozen peas

Melt the butter or margarine in a saucepan. Add the lettuce, spring onions
(scallions), sugar, mint and salt and pepper to taste and simmer gently for
10 minutes.
   Stir in the peas, cover and simmer for a further 3 to 5 minutes or until
the peas are tender. Serve hot.
Serves 4 to 6

Spiced Beans

Metric/Imperial	American
3 tablespoons oil	3 tablespoons oil
3 shallots, thinly sliced	3 shallots, thinly sliced
1 teaspoon ground ginger	1 teaspoon ground ginger
pinch of grated nutmeg	pinch of grated nutmeg
pinch of chilli powder	pinch of chili powder
500 g/1 lb French beans, halved crossways	1 lb green beans, halved crosswise
salt and pepper	salt and pepper
1 chicken stock cube	1 chicken bouillon cube
6 tablespoons boiling water	6 tablespoons boiling water

Heat the oil in a frying pan (skillet). Add the shallots and fry for 1 minute. Stir in the spices, beans and salt and pepper to taste and cook for 2 minutes.

Dissolve the stock (bouillon) cube in the water and add to the pan. Stir well, then cover and simmer for 5 minutes.

Remove the lid and cook for a further 2 to 3 minutes, stirring, until the beans are tender. Serve hot.

Serves 4

Stir-Fried Carrots and Cauliflower

Metric/Imperial	American
6 carrots, sliced	6 carrots, sliced
1 cauliflower, broken into florets	1 cauliflower, broken into florets
2 tablespoons oil	2 tablespoons oil
1 garlic clove, crushed	1 garlic clove, crushed
2 spring onions, chopped	2 scallions, chopped
1 tablespoon soy sauce	1 tablespoon soy sauce
pinch of chilli powder	pinch of chili powder
pinch of ground ginger	pinch of ground ginger
salt	salt

Blanch the carrots and cauliflower in boiling water for 3 minutes. Drain well.

Heat the oil in a wok or frying pan (skillet). Add the garlic and fry for 30 seconds, then stir in the spring onions (scallions) and soy sauce. Add the carrots and cauliflower and sprinkle over the chilli powder, ginger and salt. Stir-fry for 2 to 3 minutes or until the vegetables are just tender but still crisp. Serve hot.

Serves 4

Tipsy Grapes

Metric/Imperial
225 g/8 oz green and black
   grapes, halved and pipped
1½ tablespoons white wine
3 egg whites
75 g/3 oz caster sugar

American
½ lb green and purple grapes,
   halved and pitted
1½ tablespoons white wine
3 egg whites
6 tablespoons sugar

Sprinkle the grapes with the wine and leave to marinate for about 1 hour, stirring occasionally.

Beat the egg whites until frothy, then gradually beat in the sugar. Continue beating until the mixture is stiff. Fold in the grapes. Divide the mixture between four stemmed dessert glasses and serve immediately.
Serves 4

Strawberries Cordon Bleu

Metric/Imperial
500 g/1 lb strawberries,
   hulled and sliced
100 g/4 oz ratafias or
   macaroons, crushed
grated rind and juice of
   1 orange
25 g/1 oz caster sugar
150 ml/¼ pint double cream

American
1 lb strawberries, hulled and
   sliced
1 cup crushed ratafias or
   macaroons
grated rind and juice of
   1 orange
2 tablespoons sugar
⅔ cup heavy cream

Fold together the strawberries, ratafia or macaroon crumbs and orange rind. Divide between four dessert glasses.

Dissolve the sugar in the orange juice. Add the cream and whip until thick. Spoon on top of the strawberry mixture and serve.
Serves 4

Apple Crunch

Metric/Imperial
4 medium cooking apples, peeled,
  cored and chopped
100 g/4 oz sugar
1 tablespoon plain flour
1 tablespoon lemon juice
1 teaspoon ground cinnamon
50 g/2 oz butter or margarine
2 tablespoons water
100 g/4 oz digestive biscuits,
  crushed
whipped cream to decorate

American
4 medium-size apples, peeled,
  cored and chopped
½ cup sugar
1 tablespoon all-purpose flour
1 tablespoon lemon juice
1 teaspoon ground cinnamon
4 tablespoons butter or
  margarine
2 tablespoons water
1 cup graham cracker crumbs
whipped cream to decorate

Put the apples in a saucepan and add the sugar, flour, lemon juice, cinnamon, butter or margarine and water. Cook gently, stirring occasionally, until the apples have pulped. Beat the mixture until it is smooth, then allow to cool.

Divide the biscuit (graham cracker) crumbs between dessert glasses and spoon the apple mixture on top. Decorate with whipped cream to serve.
Serves 4 to 6

Summer Orange Whip

Metric/Imperial
300 ml/½ pint plain yogurt
1 × 175 g/6 oz can frozen
  concentrated orange juice,
  thawed
7 g/¼ oz gelatine
4 tablespoons hot water
2 oranges
2 egg whites
mint sprigs to decorate

American
1 ¼ cups plain yogurt
1 × 6 oz can frozen concentrated
  orange juice, thawed
1 envelope unflavored gelatin
¼ cup hot water
2 oranges
2 egg whites
mint sprigs to decorate

Put the yogurt and orange juice into a blender or food processor and process until mixed.

Dissolve the gelatine in the water. Grate the rind from the oranges, then peel them, removing all the white pith. Chop the flesh, discarding any seeds. Add the orange rind and flesh and dissolved gelatine to the yogurt mixture and process until well combined. Pour into a bowl and chill until almost set.

Beat the egg whites until stiff and fold into the orange mixture. Spoon into individual glasses and chill until set. Serve decorated with mint sprigs.
Serves 4 to 6

Raspberry Cheese Mousse

Metric/Imperial
1 packet raspberry jelly
300 ml/½ pint hot water
100 g/4 oz raspberries
2 eggs, separated
50 g/2 oz caster sugar
1 × 75 g/3 oz packet cream
  cheese
whipped cream to decorate

American
1 package raspberry-flavored
  gelatin
1 cup hot water
¼ lb raspberries
2 eggs, separated
¼ cup sugar
1 × 3 oz package cream cheese
whipped cream to decorate

Dissolve the jelly (gelatin) in the water and leave until almost set. Meanwhile, purée the raspberries in a blender or food processor. Sieve (strain) to remove the seeds.

Beat the egg yolks and sugar together until pale and thick. (If not using an electric mixer, it will be necessary to do this in a heatproof bowl placed over a pan of simmering water.) Beat in the raspberry purée.

Beat the cream cheese with 1 tablespoon of the setting jelly (gelatin), then fold into the egg yolk mixture with the remaining jelly. Beat the egg whites until stiff and fold into the mixture. Spoon into individual glasses and chill until set. Serve topped with a whirl of whipped cream.
Serves 4 to 6

Maraschino Apples

Metric/Imperial
4 dessert apples, peeled,
  cored and thinly sliced
juice of 1 lemon
175 ml/6 fl oz double cream
1 small jar maraschino cherries
caster sugar to taste
2 macaroons, crushed
2 tablespoons flaked almonds,
  toasted

American
4 apples, peeled, cored and
  thinly sliced
juice of 1 lemon
¾ cup heavy cream
1 small jar maraschino cherries
sugar to taste
2 macaroons, crushed
2 tablespoons sliced almonds,
  toasted

Toss the apple slices in lemon juice to prevent discoloration.

Whip the cream until thick. Drain the cherries, reserving the syrup. Halve the cherries. Mix 3 to 4 teaspoons of the syrup into the cream, then fold in the cherries and apple slices. Sweeten to taste with sugar and divide between four stemmed glasses.

Sprinkle the tops with the crushed macaroons and almonds and serve lightly chilled.
Serves 4

Quick Raspberry Dessert

Metric/Imperial
150 g/5 oz golden syrup
1 × 425 g/15 oz can creamed
  rice pudding
225 g/8 oz raspberries

American
½ cup maple syrup
1 × 16 oz can creamed rice
  pudding
½ lb raspberries

Put 1 tablespoon of the syrup in each of four dessert glasses. Put the remaining syrup in a bowl and add the rice pudding and most of the raspberries. Beat well together. Divide between the dessert glasses and chill. Just before serving, decorate with the reserved raspberries.
Serves 4

Danish Apple Dessert

Metric/Imperial
750 g/1½ lb cooking apples,
  peeled, cored and chopped
75 g/3 oz butter or margarine
75 g/3 oz sugar
100 g/4 oz fresh breadcrumbs
150 ml/¼ pint double cream
redcurrant jelly

American
1½ lb apples, peeled, cored
  and chopped
6 tablespoons butter or
  margarine
6 tablespoons sugar
2 cups soft bread crumbs
⅔ cup heavy cream
red currant jelly

Put the apples in a saucepan with just enough water to cover the bottom of the pan. Cook gently until the apples are very soft. Add 25 g/1 oz (2 tablespoons) of the butter or margarine and sugar and beat well until smooth. Cool.
    Melt the remaining butter or margarine in a frying pan (skillet). Add the breadcrumbs and fry until golden. Stir in the remaining sugar and cool.
    Make alternate layers of the breadcrumbs and apple mixture in a glass dish, ending with crumbs. Whip the cream and spread over the top.
    Warm the jelly until it is melted, then drizzle over the top. Chill.
Serves 4 to 6

Swiss Fruit Delight

Metric/Imperial
2 tablespoons rolled oats
150 ml/¼ pint plain yogurt
2 bananas, sliced
2 oranges, peeled and chopped
grated rind of 1 lemon
100 g/4 oz seedless grapes
1 red dessert apple, cored
  and chopped
caster sugar to taste

American
2 tablespoons rolled oats
⅔ cup plain yogurt
2 bananas, sliced
2 oranges, peeled and chopped
grated rind of 1 lemon
¼ lb seedless grapes
1 red-skinned apple, cored
  and chopped
sugar to taste

Mix together the oats and yogurt. Fold in the fruit and sweeten to taste. Chill well before serving.
Serves 4

Cinnamon Pear Delight

Metric/Imperial	American
4 pears, peeled, halved and cored	4 pears, peeled, halved and cored
300 ml/½ pint cider	1¼ cups hard or apple cider
1 teaspoon ground cinnamon	1 teaspoon ground cinnamon
3 tablespoons demerara sugar	3 tablespoons raw brown sugar
150 ml/¼ pint double cream	⅔ cup heavy cream
grated rind of 1 lemon	grated rind of 1 lemon
chopped walnuts to decorate	chopped walnuts to decorate

Place the pears in a saucepan and add the cider, cinnamon and sugar. Cover and poach gently for 10 to 15 minutes or until the pears are tender. Leave to cool.

Whip the cream with the lemon rind until thick. Place two pears on each of four serving dishes and spoon over a little of the poaching liquid. Spoon or pipe the cream on top and sprinkle with chopped walnuts.
Serves 4

Strawberries Romanoff

Metric/Imperial	American
1 kg/2 lb strawberries	2 lb strawberries
6 tablespoons icing sugar	6 tablespoons confectioners sugar
3 tablespoons rum	3 tablespoons rum
3 tablespoons orange liqueur	3 tablespoons orange liqueur
300 ml/½ pint double cream	1¼ cups heavy cream
3 tablespoons brandy	3 tablespoons brandy

Mix the strawberries with 4 tablespoons of the sugar, the rum and orange liqueur. Cover and chill for 1 hour.

Whip the cream with the remaining sugar and the brandy until thick. Fold into the strawberries. Serve chilled.
Serves 6 to 8

Sherried Melon Cup

Metric/Imperial	American
2 medium ogen melons, halved and seeded	2 medium-sized cantaloup melons, halved and seeded
1 tablespoon grated orange rind	1 tablespoon grated orange rind
120 ml/4 fl oz medium sherry	½ cup medium sherry
4 maraschino cherries	4 maraschino cherries

Scoop the flesh out of the melon halves using a melon baller, or cut it into cubes. Keep the melon shells intact.

Mix the melon balls or cubes with the orange rind and sherry and return to the shells. Decorate with the cherries and chill lightly before serving.
Serves 4

Prunes in Red Wine

Metric/Imperial
300 ml/½ pint red wine
2 tablespoons clear honey
1 teaspoon lemon juice
500 g/1 lb prunes, soaked
   overnight and drained, or
   canned prunes

American
1¼ cups red wine
2 tablespoons honey
1 teaspoon lemon juice
1 lb prunes, soaked overnight
   and drained, or canned
   prunes

Put the wine, honey and lemon juice in a saucepan and bring to the boil.
Simmer for 10 minutes. Add the prunes and simmer for a further
10 minutes. Cool, then chill. Serve with whipped cream.
Serves 6

Strawberries with Liqueur Cream

Metric/Imperial
350 ml/12 fl oz double cream
2 tablespoons caster sugar
2 tablespoons liqueur such as
   Cointreau, Grand Marnier
   or Kirsch
350 g/12 oz strawberries, sliced

American
1½ cups heavy cream
2 tablespoons sugar
2 tablespoons liqueur such as
   Cointreau, Grand Marnier
   or Kirsch
¾ lb strawberries, sliced

Whip the cream with the sugar and liqueur until thick. Fold in the
strawberries. Chill lightly before serving.
Serves 4

Variation: Use other soft fruit, such as raspberries, blackberries or
loganberries instead of strawberries.

Fruit Salad Brûlée

Metric/Imperial
2 peaches, peeled, stoned
   and sliced
2 pears, peeled, cored and
   sliced
2 bananas, sliced
225 g/8 oz strawberries, sliced
lemon juice
300 ml/½ pint double cream
75 g/3 oz dark brown sugar

American
2 peaches, peeled, pitted
   and sliced
2 pears, peeled, cored and
   sliced
2 bananas, sliced
½ lb strawberries, sliced
lemon juice
1¼ cups heavy cream
½ cup firmly packed dark
   brown sugar

Place the peaches, pears, bananas and strawberries in a flameproof
serving dish. Sprinkle over a little lemon juice and toss together.
   Whip the cream until thick and spread over the fruit. Sprinkle the brown
sugar on top to cover the cream completely.
   Place under a preheated grill (broiler) and cook until the brown sugar
melts and caramelizes. Cool, then chill before serving.
Serves 4 to 6

Alpine Oranges

Metric/Imperial	American
4 oranges, peeled and segmented	4 oranges, peeled and segmented
25 g/1 oz caster sugar	2 tablespoons sugar
4 tablespoons sherry	¼ cup sherry
150 ml/¼ pint double cream	⅔ cup heavy cream
¼ teaspoon vanilla essence	¼ teaspoon vanilla
4 bought or homemade meringue shells, crushed	4 bought or homemade meringue shells, crushed

Divide the orange segments between four dessert glasses. Stir in the sugar and sherry. Chill.

Whip the cream with the vanilla until thick and fold in the meringue. Spoon on top of the oranges and serve immediately.

Serves 4

Sunshine Fruit Salad

Metric/Imperial	American
juice of 2 large oranges	juice of 2 large oranges
juice of 1 lemon	juice of 1 lemon
2 tablespoons orange liqueur	2 tablespoons orange liqueur
225 g/8 oz strawberries, halved	½ lb strawberries, halved
2 large peaches, peeled, stoned and sliced	2 large peaches, peeled, pitted and sliced
2 large bananas, sliced	2 large bananas, sliced
2 passion fruit or pomegranates, halved	2 passion fruit or pomegranates, halved

Place the orange and lemon juices and liqueur in a serving bowl. Add the strawberries, peaches and bananas and fold together gently. Scoop the flesh and seeds out of the passion fruit or pomegranate halves and add to the bowl. Mix gently. Chill before serving.

Serves 4

Lemon Syllabub

Metric/Imperial	American
grated rind and juice of 1 lemon	grated rind and juice of 1 lemon
100 g/4 oz caster sugar	½ cup sugar
150 ml/¼ pint sweet white wine or sherry	⅔ cup sweet white wine or sherry
300 ml/½ pint double cream	1¼ cups heavy cream
sponge fingers to serve	lady fingers to serve

Mix together the lemon rind and juice, sugar and wine or sherry and leave to stand for at least 1 hour.

Strain the lemon mixture into another bowl and add the cream. Whip until the mixture thickens. Spoon into tall glasses and chill. Serve with sponge (lady) fingers.

Serves 4

Cranberry Orange Dessert

Metric/Imperial	American
450 ml/¾ pint orange juice	2 cups orange juice
7 g/¼ oz powdered gelatine	1 envelope unflavored gelatin
25 g/1 oz caster sugar	2 tablespoons sugar
2 egg whites	2 egg whites
4 tablespoons cranberry sauce	¼ cup cranberry sauce
whipped cream to decorate	whipped cream to decorate

Pour a little of the orange juice into a cup. Add the gelatine and leave to soak. Stir the sugar into the remaining orange juice until dissolved.

Place the cup in a pan of simmering water and stir until the gelatine has dissolved. Add to the sweetened orange juice. Chill until the mixture is the consistency of unbeaten egg white.

Beat the egg whites until stiff and fold into the orange mixture. Put a tablespoon of cranberry sauce in the bottom of four stemmed glasses and top with the orange mixture. Chill until set.

Top with a whirl of whipped cream before serving.
Serves 4

Tipsy Syllabub

Metric/Imperial	American
25 g/1 oz medium oatmeal	¼ cup oatmeal
300 ml/½ pint double cream	1¼ cups heavy cream
100 g/4 oz clear honey	⅓ cup honey
5 tablespoons whiskey	5 tablespoons whiskey
1 teaspoon lemon juice	1 teaspoon lemon juice

Toast the oatmeal under the grill (broiler) until golden brown. Cool.

Whip the cream with the honey, whiskey and lemon juice until thick. Fold in the oatmeal. Divide between dessert glasses and chill lightly before serving.
Serves 4 to 6

Yogurt Fluff

Metric/Imperial	American
2 egg whites	2 egg whites
50 g/2 oz caster sugar	¼ cup sugar
150 ml/¼ pint fruit yogurt	⅔ cup fruit yogurt
1 tablespoon toasted coconut	1 tablespoon toasted coconut

Beat the egg whites until frothy, then gradually beat in the sugar. Continue beating until the mixture is stiff. Fold in the yogurt.

Divide the mixture between four dessert glasses and sprinkle the coconut on top. Serve immediately.
Serves 4

Marmalade Creams

Metric/Imperial	American
250 ml/8 fl oz double cream	1 cup heavy cream
4 tablespoons marmalade	¼ cup marmalade
1 tablespoon lemon juice	1 tablespoon lemon juice
75 g/3 oz digestive biscuits, crushed	1 cup crushed graham crackers
½ teaspoon ground cinnamon	½ teaspoon ground cinnamon

Whip the cream until thick. Fold in the marmalade and lemon juice. Mix together the biscuit (graham cracker) crumbs and cinnamon.

Make alternate layers of the cream mixture and crumbs in four tall glasses, ending with the cream mixture. Chill lightly before serving.
Serves 4

Peppermint Chocolate Pears

Metric/Imperial	American
10-12 mint chocolate creams	10-12 mint chocolate creams
150 ml/¼ pint single cream	⅔ cup light cream
4 ripe comice pears, peeled	4 ripe bartlett pears, peeled
25 g/1 oz walnuts, chopped	¼ cup chopped walnuts

Place the chocolate creams and cream in a heatproof bowl over a pan of hot water and melt gently, stirring occasionally.

Meanwhile core the pears from the bottom and cut a slice from the bottom of each to make a flat surface. Stand the pears in four dessert glasses.

Pour the sauce over the pears and sprinkle the walnuts on top. Serve immediately.
Serves 4

Gingered Mandarin Oranges

Metric/Imperial	American
1 × 300 g/11 oz can mandarin oranges, drained	1 × 11 oz can mandarin oranges, drained
300 ml/½ pint sweetened apple purée	1¼ cups sweetened apple sauce
25 g/1 oz stem ginger, chopped	¼ cup chopped preserved stem ginger
2 tablespoons ginger syrup	2 tablespoons ginger syrup
½ teaspoon grated nutmeg	½ teaspoon grated nutmeg
1 tablespoon clear honey	1 tablespoon honey
2 teaspoons lemon juice	2 teaspoons lemon juice

Mix together all the ingredients. Chill lightly before serving with whipped cream.
Serves 4

Chocolate Pots

Metric/Imperial	American
1 large egg, separated	1 large egg, separated
2 tablespoons cornflour	2 tablespoons cornstarch
50 g/2 oz caster sugar	¼ cup sugar
150 ml/¼ pint milk	⅔ cup milk
50 g/2 oz plain chocolate, broken into pieces	2 × 1 oz squares semi-sweet chocolate, broken into pieces
1 tablespoon rum	1 tablespoon rum
whipped cream to decorate	whipped cream to decorate

Beat the egg yolk with the cornflour (cornstarch), sugar and a little of the milk. Put the remaining milk in a saucepan and heat to just below boiling point. Pour the hot milk onto the egg yolk mixture, stirring well, then pour the mixture back into the pan. Cook gently, stirring, until the custard thickens. Stir in the chocolate until melted. Stir in the rum. Remove from the heat and cool.

Beat the egg white until stiff and fold into the chocolate mixture. Spoon into four small pots and chill until set. Serve topped with a whirl of whipped cream.

Serves 4

Chocolate Mousse

Metric/Imperial	American
100 g/4 oz plain chocolate	4 × 1 oz squares semi-sweet chocolate
4 teaspoons liqueur or water	4 teaspoons liqueur or water
4 eggs, separated	4 eggs, separated
whipped cream to decorate	whipped cream to decorate

Melt the chocolate gently with the liqueur or water. Remove from the heat and cool slightly, then beat in the egg yolks.

Beat the egg whites until stiff and fold into the chocolate mixture. Divide between four dessert glasses and chill well. Just before serving, decorate with whipped cream.

Serves 4

Marmalade Sundae

Metric/Imperial	American
100 g/4 oz marmalade	½ cup marmalade
120 ml/4 fl oz water	½ cup water
2 tablespoons brandy	2 tablespoons brandy
vanilla ice cream	vanilla ice cream

Put the marmalade, water and brandy in a saucepan and heat gently, stirring, until the ingredients are well blended. Strain and pour over vanilla ice cream. The sauce may also be served cold, if preferred.

Serves 4

Banana and Pasta Caramel

Metric/Imperial	American
150 g/5 oz small pasta shapes	5 oz (1¼ cups) small pasta shapes
salt	salt
4 egg yolks	4 egg yolks
3 tablespoons caster sugar	3 tablespoons sugar
2 tablespoons cornflour	2 tablespoons cornstarch
300 ml/½ pint milk	1¼ cups milk
300 ml/½ pint single cream	1¼ cups light cream
3-4 bananas, sliced	3-4 bananas, sliced
100 g/4 oz demerara sugar	⅔ cup raw brown sugar

Cook the pasta shapes in boiling salted water until just tender. Drain and cool.

Beat the egg yolks, sugar, cornflour (cornstarch) and 3 tablespoons of the milk together until creamy. Place the remaining milk in a saucepan with the cream and heat until bubbles form around the edges. Gradually stir into the egg yolk mixture, then pour back into the pan. Cook very gently, stirring, until the custard thickens enough to coat the back of a wooden spoon. Stir in the pasta shapes. Pour into a shallow flameproof serving dish and cool.

Arrange the banana slices on the custard. Sprinkle the demerara (brown) sugar over the top to cover completely. Place the dish under a preheated grill (broiler) and cook for 3 to 4 minutes or until the sugar melts and caramelizes. Cool and chill before serving.
Serves 6 to 8

Orange Macaroni Dessert

Metric/Imperial	American
225 g/8 oz short cut macaroni	½ lb elbow macaroni
salt	salt
2 oranges	2 oranges
150 ml/¼ pint single cream	⅔ cup light cream
1 × 225 g/8 oz packet cream cheese	1 × 8 oz package cream cheese
½ teaspoon ground cinnamon	½ teaspoon ground cinnamon
2 tablespoons toasted flaked almonds	2 tablespoons toasted sliced almonds

Cook the macaroni in boiling salted water until just tender. Drain and cool.

Grate the rind from one of the oranges and set aside. Peel both oranges, removing all the white pith, and divide them into segments.

Beat the cream and cream cheese together until smooth. Beat in the orange rind and cinnamon, then fold in the macaroni and orange segments. Divide between individual dessert glasses and sprinkle the almonds on top. Serve chilled.
Serves 6 to 8

Raspberry Chantilly

Metric/Imperial
500 g/1 lb raspberries
2 tablespoons orange liqueur
1 egg white
150 ml/¼ pint plain yogurt
grated rind of ½ lemon
1 tablespoon caster sugar
toasted flaked almonds to
   decorate

American
1 lb raspberries
2 tablespoons orange liqueur
1 egg white
⅔ cup plain yogurt
grated rind of ½ lemon
1 tablespoon sugar
toasted sliced almonds to
   decorate

Divide the raspberries between four dessert glasses and spoon over the liqueur.
    Beat the egg white until stiff. Fold in the yogurt, lemon rind and sugar. Spoon on top of the raspberries and sprinkle almonds over the top. Serve immediately.
Serves 4

Yogurt Ice

Metric/Imperial
2 egg whites
2 tablespoons icing sugar
600 ml/1 pint peach melba or
   other fruit yogurt

American
2 egg whites
2 tablespoons confectioners
   sugar
2½ cups peach or other fruit-
   flavored yogurt

Beat the egg whites until foamy. Gradually beat in the sugar until the mixture holds stiff peaks. Lightly beat in the yogurt.
    Pour into a freezer container and freeze until firm, beating the mixture once or twice during freezing.
Serves 4 to 6

Butterscotch Meringue Glacé

Metric/Imperial
4 homemade or bought meringue
   shells
4 scoops of vanilla ice cream
Sauce:
4 tablespoons brown sugar
1 tablespoon golden syrup
2 tablespoons milk
25 g/1 oz butter or margarine
⅛ teaspoon vanilla essence

American
4 homemade or bought meringue
   shells
4 scoops of vanilla ice cream
Sauce:
¼ cup brown sugar
1 tablespoon corn syrup
2 tablespoons milk
2 tablespoons butter or
   margarine
⅛ teaspoon vanilla

Put all the sauce ingredients in a saucepan and bring to the boil, stirring to dissolve the sugar. Boil for 4 minutes.
    Place a meringue shell in each of four individual dishes and top with a scoop of ice cream. Pour over the sauce and serve.
Serves 4

Quick Chocolate Whip

Metric/Imperial	American
4 tablespoons semolina	¼ cup cream of wheat
4 tablespoons cocoa powder	¼ cup unsweetened cocoa
50 g/2 oz caster sugar	¼ cup sugar
900 ml/1½ pints milk	3½ cups milk
3 eggs, separated	3 eggs, separated
chopped mixed nuts to decorate	chopped mixed nuts to decorate

Put the semolina (cream of wheat), cocoa and sugar in a bowl and stir in enough milk to make a thin paste. Place the remaining milk in a saucepan and bring to the boil. Stir into the cocoa mixture, then pour back into the saucepan and heat, stirring, until thickened. Simmer for 5 minutes. Remove from the heat and cool.

Beat the egg yolks into the chocolate mixture. Beat the egg whites until stiff and fold into the mixture. Divide between four to six serving glasses and sprinkle nuts on top.
Serves 4 to 6

Pasta Melba

Metric/Imperial	American
1.2 litres/2 pints milk	5 cups milk
100 g/4 oz small pasta shapes	1 cup small pasta shapes
25 g/1 oz cornflour	¼ cup cornstarch
sugar to taste	sugar to taste
150 ml/¼ pint double cream	⅔ cup heavy cream
2 tablespoons brandy	2 tablespoons brandy
6 canned peach halves	6 canned peach halves
6 scoops of vanilla ice cream	6 scoops of vanilla ice cream
6 tablespoons raspberry jam, warmed	6 tablespoons raspberry jam, warmed

Place all but 6 tablespoons of the milk in a saucepan and bring to the boil. Add the pasta shapes and simmer gently for 15 minutes, stirring occasionally. Dissolve the cornflour (cornstarch) in the reserved milk. Add to the pan and cook, stirring, until thickened. Stir in sugar to taste and leave to cool.

Whip the cream until thick and fold into the pasta mixture with the brandy. Divide between six dessert glasses. Top each serving with a peach half and a scoop of ice cream. Drizzle the jam over the top and serve.
Serves 6

Lemon Flummery

Metric/Imperial	American
300 ml/½ pint water	1½ cups water
25 g/1 oz butter or margarine	2 tablespoons butter or margarine
grated rind and juice of 1 lemon	grated rind and juice of 1 lemon
25 g/1 oz plain flour	¼ cup all-purpose flour
100 g/4 oz caster sugar	½ cup sugar
1 egg, separated	1 egg, separated

Place the water, butter or margarine and lemon rind in a saucepan and bring to the boil, stirring to melt the fat. Mix the flour and sugar in a bowl. Gradually stir in the hot liquid. Add a little of this mixture to the egg yolk and mix well, then stir into the remaining mixture. Return to the saucepan and cook gently for 5 minutes, stirring frequently.

Pour the mixture into a bowl and stir in the lemon juice. Beat the egg white until stiff and fold into the mixture. Serve hot or cold with fruit.
Serves 4

Melon Sherbet

Metric/Imperial	American
175 g/6 oz sugar	¾ cup sugar
300 ml/½ pint water	1¼ cups water
1 melon (about 750 g/1½ lb), halved and seeded	1 melon (about 1½ lb), halved and seeded
juice of 1 orange	juice of 1 orange
juice of 1 lemon	juice of 1 lemon

Put the sugar and water in a saucepan and bring to the boil, stirring to dissolve the sugar. Boil for 5 minutes, then cool.

Scoop the melon flesh out of the skins and purée in a blender or food processor. Mix the melon purée with the sugar syrup and fruit juices. Pour into a freezer container and freeze until firm, beating the mixture once or twice during freezing.
Serves 4 to 6

Ginger Syllabub

Metric/Imperial	American
2 pieces of stem ginger, finely chopped	2 pieces of preserved stem ginger, finely chopped
2 tablespoons ginger syrup	2 tablespoons ginger syrup
2 tablespoons sherry	2 tablespoons sherry
25 g/1 oz caster sugar	2 tablespoons sugar
150 ml/¼ pint double cream	⅔ cup heavy cream

Mix together the ginger, ginger syrup, sherry and sugar. Whip the cream until thick and fold in the ginger mixture. Chill well.

Whip the mixture just before serving.
Serves 4

Easy Vanilla Ice Cream

Metric/Imperial
175 ml/6 fl oz sweetened
  condensed milk
450 ml/¾ pint double cream
1 teaspoon vanilla essence

American
¾ cup sweetened condensed
  milk
2 cups heavy cream
1 teaspoon vanilla

Put all the ingredients in a bowl and chill for 30 minutes.
  Beat the mixture until it forms stiff peaks, then pour into a freezer container. Freeze until firm.
Serves 4 to 6

Variations:

Chocolate Ice Cream: Heat the condensed milk with 100 g/4 oz plain chocolate (4 × 1 oz squares semi-sweet chocolate) until the chocolate has melted. Cool, then follow the directions above.

Benedictine Ice Cream: Substitute 5 tablespoons Benedictine or other liqueur for the vanilla.

Banana Marshmallow Pie

Metric/Imperial
175 g/6 oz digestive biscuits,
  crushed
75 g/3 oz butter or margarine,
  melted
Filling:
1 packet banana-flavoured
  dessert mix
milk
100 g/4 oz marshmallows
1 large banana, sliced
lemon juice

American
1½ cups crushed graham crackers
6 tablespoons butter or
  margarine, melted
Filling:
1 package banana-flavored instant
  dessert mix
milk
¼ lb marshmallows
1 large banana, sliced
lemon juice

Mix together the biscuit (graham cracker) crumbs and butter or margarine and press over the bottom and sides of a greased 20 cm/8 inch pie plate (pan). Chill until set.
  To make the filling, make up the dessert mix with milk according to the instructions on the packet. Cut the marshmallows into pieces using wet scissors and fold into the dessert. Pour into the crumb crust and chill until set.
  Dip the slices of banana in lemon juice to prevent discoloration and use to decorate the top of the pie.
Serves 4 to 6

Iced Honey and Brandy Mousse

Metric/Imperial	American
3 eggs, separated	3 eggs, separated
2 tablespoons clear honey	2 tablespoons honey
2 tablespoons lemon juice	2 tablespoons lemon juice
2 tablespoons brandy	2 tablespoons brandy
2 tablespoons water	2 tablespoons water
150 ml/¼ pint double cream	⅔ cup heavy cream

Beat the egg yolks, honey, lemon juice, brandy and water together until the mixture is thick and light and has doubled or tripled in volume. (If not using an electric beater, it will be necessary to do this in a heatproof bowl over a pan of hot water.)

Whip the cream until thick and fold into the mixture. Beat the egg whites until stiff and fold in. Pour into a 600 ml/1 pint (2½ cup) freezerproof serving dish. Cover and freeze until firm.
Serves 4

Banana Rum Ice Cream

Metric/Imperial	American
175 ml/6 fl oz sweetened condensed milk	¾ cup sweetened condensed milk
250 ml/8 fl oz double cream	1 cup heavy cream
5 ripe bananas	5 ripe bananas
juice of 1 lemon	juice of 1 lemon
2 tablespoons caster sugar	2 tablespoons sugar
2 tablespoons dark rum	2 tablespoons dark rum

Put the milk and cream in a bowl and chill for 30 minutes.

Meanwhile, purée the bananas in a blender or food processor. Add the lemon juice, sugar and rum and mix well.

Beat the cream mixture until it forms stiff peaks. Add the banana mixture and whip them together lightly. Pour into a freezer container and freeze until firm.
Serves 4 to 6

Lemon Cheese Soufflé

Metric/Imperial	American
2 × 75 g/3 oz packets cream cheese	2 × 3 oz packages cream cheese
50 g/2 oz caster sugar	¼ cup sugar
grated rind and juice of ½ lemon	grated rind and juice of ½ lemon
2 eggs, separated	2 eggs, separated
150 ml/¼ pint double cream	⅔ cup heavy cream

Cream the cream cheese with the sugar, lemon rind and juice and egg yolks. Whip the cream until thick and fold into the lemon mixture. Beat the egg whites until stiff and fold in. Spoon into a serving dish and chill.
Serves 6

Strawberry Cheese Dreams

Metric/Imperial
1 × 225 g/8 oz packet cream
  cheese
50 g/2 oz caster sugar
2 tablespoons single cream
1 egg yolk
⅛ teaspoon vanilla essence
1 teaspoon lemon juice
4 tablespoons strawberry jam
strawberries to decorate

American
1 × 8 oz package cream cheese
¼ cup sugar
2 tablespoons light cream
1 egg yolk
⅛ teaspoon vanilla
1 teaspoon lemon juice
¼ cup strawberry jam
strawberries to decorate

Cream the cream cheese, sugar, cream, egg yolk, vanilla and lemon juice together until light and fluffy.
Put 1 tablespoon of jam in each of four dessert glasses and spoon the cream cheese mixture on top. Decorate with whole or sliced strawberries.
Serves 4

Marrons Mont Blanc

Metric/Imperial
50 g/2 oz unsalted butter
25 g/1 oz caster sugar
1 × 225 g/8 oz can sweetened
  chestnut purée
2 tablespoons sherry
lemon juice
150 ml/¼ pint double cream

American
4 tablespoons unsalted butter
2 tablespoons sugar
1 × 8 oz can sweetened
  chestnut purée
2 tablespoons sherry
lemon juice
⅔ cup heavy cream

Cream the butter with the sugar until light and fluffy. Beat in the chestnut purée. Add the sherry and lemon juice to taste.
Pile the chestnut mixture in four dessert dishes. Whip the cream until thick and swirl it on top of the chestnut mixture to resemble snow on the mountain. Serve lightly chilled.
Serves 4

Dutch Banana Cream

Metric/Imperial
½ × 225 g/8 oz packet cream
  cheese
grated rind and juice of
  1 lemon
50 g/2 oz caster sugar
3 bananas, mashed
1 tablespoon kirsch
1 tablespoon gelatine
2 tablespoons hot water
toasted flaked almonds to
  decorate

American
½ × 8 oz package cream
  cheese
grated rind and juice of
  1 lemon
¼ cup sugar
3 bananas, mashed
1 tablespoon kirsch
1 envelope (1 tablespoon)
  unflavored gelatin
2 tablespoons hot water
toasted sliced almonds to
  decorate

Beat the cream cheese with the lemon rind and juice, sugar, bananas and kirsch until smooth.

Dissolve the gelatine in the water. Add to the banana mixture and stir well. Divide between four glasses and chill until set. Decorate with almonds before serving.
Serves 4

Crunchy Lemon Tart

Metric/Imperial
200 g/7 oz digestive biscuits,
  crushed
75 g/3 oz butter or margarine,
  melted
Filling:
1 small can sweetened condensed
  milk
150 ml/¼ pint double cream
grated rind of 1 lemon
6 tablespoons lemon juice

American
1¾ cups graham cracker
  crumbs
6 tablespoons butter or
  margarine, melted
Filling:
1 small can sweetened condensed
  milk
⅔ cup heavy cream
grated rind of 1 lemon
6 tablespoons lemon juice

Mix 175 g/6 oz (1½ cups) of the biscuit (graham cracker) crumbs with the melted butter or margarine. Press over the bottom and sides of a 20 cm/8 inch flan or quiche pan. Chill for 10 minutes.

Meanwhile place the filling ingredients in a bowl and beat until thick. Pour into the crumb crust and chill until set.

Sprinkle the remaining biscuit (graham cracker) crumbs over the top before serving.
Serves 6

Frosted Almond Creams

Metric/Imperial
2 eggs, separated
50 g/2 oz brown sugar
50 g/2 oz blanched almonds,
  chopped and toasted
300 ml/½ pint plain yogurt
2 tablespoons orange liqueur
toasted flaked almonds to
  decorate

American
2 eggs, separated
⅓ cup firmly packed brown
  sugar
½ cup chopped toasted almonds
1¼ cups plain yogurt
2 tablespoons orange liqueur
toasted sliced almonds to
  decorate

Beat the egg yolks and sugar together until thick and creamy. Stir in the chopped nuts, yogurt and liqueur. Beat the egg whites until stiff and fold into the mixture.

Divide between six freezerproof dessert dishes. Cover and freeze until firm.

Leave to soften at room temperature for 15 minutes before serving, decorated with the almonds.
Serves 6

Chocolate Fudge Sundae

Metric/Imperial
vanilla ice cream
chocolate ice cream
whipped cream
toasted chopped nuts
Sauce:
50 g/2 oz plain chocolate
120 ml/4 fl oz sweetened
  condensed milk
4 tablespoons water
25 g/1 oz butter or margarine

American
vanilla ice cream
chocolate ice cream
whipped cream
toasted chopped nuts
Sauce:
2 × 1 oz squares semi-sweet
  chocolate
½ cup sweetened condensed
  milk
¼ cup water
2 tablespoons butter or
  margarine

To make the sauce, put the chocolate and condensed milk in a heatproof bowl placed over a pan of simmering water. Heat until the chocolate has melted, stirring occasionally. Stir in the water and butter or margarine.

Put a scoop of vanilla and chocolate ice cream in each of four sundae glasses. Spoon over the chocolate fudge sauce and top with a whirl of whipped cream. Sprinkle with nuts and serve.
Serves 4

Minted Apple Snow

Metric/Imperial	American
1 kg/2 lb cooking apples, peeled, cored and sliced	2 lb apples, peeled, cored and sliced
grated rind and juice of 1 orange	grated rind and juice of 1 orange
3 tablespoons clear honey	3 tablespoons honey
4 large mint sprigs	4 large mint sprigs
2 egg whites	2 egg whites

Place the apples, orange rind and juice and honey in a saucepan. Add the mint sprigs, reserving the top leaves for decoration. Cover and cook gently for about 15 minutes or until the apples are very soft.

Discard the mint, then beat the apple mixture until smooth. Cool.

Beat the egg whites until stiff and fold into the apple mixture. Spoon into dessert glasses and decorate with the reserved mint leaves. Chill before serving.

Serves 4

Chocolate Pear Sundae

Metric/Imperial	American
4 scoops of vanilla ice cream	4 scoops of vanilla ice cream
8 canned pear halves	8 canned pear halves
4 ratafia biscuits, crushed	4 amaretti cookies, crushed
Sauce:	Sauce:
100 g/4 oz plain chocolate	4 × 1 oz squares semi-sweet chocolate
3 tablespoons golden syrup	3 tablespoons light corn syrup
6 tablespoons single cream	6 tablespoons light cream

First make the sauce. Place the chocolate in a heatproof bowl over a pan of hot water and melt, stirring occasionally. Stir in the syrup and cream and heat through gently.

Put a large scoop of vanilla ice cream in each of four dessert dishes and press two pear halves onto each scoop. Pour over the sauce and sprinkle the biscuits (cookies) on top. Serve immediately.

Serves 4

Quick Chocolate Custard

Metric/Imperial	American
225 g/8 oz plain chocolate	8 × 1 oz squares semi-sweet
350 ml/12 fl oz milk	chocolate
2 teaspoons instant coffee	1½ cups milk
powder	2 teaspoons instant coffee
2 teaspoons gelatine	powder
2 eggs, beaten	2 teaspoons unflavored gelatin
1 teaspoon vanilla essence	2 eggs, beaten
	1 teaspoon vanilla

Place the chocolate and milk in a saucepan and heat, stirring to melt the chocolate. Remove from the heat and stir in the instant coffee and gelatine until dissolved. Beat in the eggs and vanilla.

Pour into a serving dish and chill until set. Serve decorated with whipped cream.

Serves 4

Chestnut Whip

Metric/Imperial	American
1 × 500 g/1 lb can unsweetened	1 × 16 oz can unsweetened
chestnut purée	chestnut purée
¼ teaspoon vanilla essence	¼ teaspoon vanilla
grated rind and juice of	grated rind and juice of
1 small orange	1 small orange
2 tablespoons rum	2 tablespoons rum
100 g/4 oz brown sugar	⅔ cup firmly packed brown
2 egg whites	sugar
orange slices to decorate	2 egg whites
	orange slices to decorate

Mix together the chestnut purée, vanilla, orange rind and juice, rum and sugar. Beat the egg whites until stiff and fold into the mixture. Divide between six dessert glasses.

Chill for at least 1 hour. Decorate with twisted orange slices before serving.

Serves 6

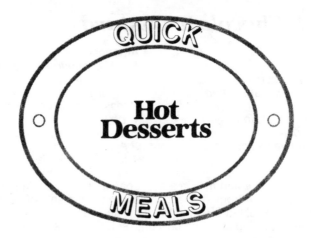

QUICK
Hot
Desserts
MEALS

Burgundy Velvet

Metric/Imperial
6 egg yolks
75 g/3 oz caster sugar
4 tablespoons burgundy-type
*   wine*
grated rind of 1 lemon
2 tablespoons lemon juice
1 tablespoon brandy

American
6 egg yolks
6 tablespoons sugar
¼ cup burgundy-type
*   wine*
grated rind of 1 lemon
2 tablespoons lemon juice
1 tablespoon brandy

Beat all the ingredients together in a large heatproof bowl. Place over a pan of hot water and continue beating until the mixture is very thick and will hold a peak.

Spoon into six stemmed glasses and serve immediately.
Serves 6

Zabaglione

Metric/Imperial
4 egg yolks
4 tablespoons caster sugar
4 tablespoons Marsala
1 teaspoon grated lemon rind
*   (optional)*

American
4 egg yolks
¼ cup sugar
¼ cup Marsala
1 teaspoon grated lemon rind
*   (optional)*

Put the egg yolks and sugar in a heatproof bowl and place over a pan of simmering water. Beat until pale and thick. Add the Marsala and lemon rind, if using, and continue beating until the mixture is very thick. Serve immediately.
Serves 4 to 6

Rhubarb Brûlée

Metric/Imperial	American
500 g/1 lb rhubarb, chopped	1 lb rhubarb, chopped
2 teaspoons water	2 teaspoons water
½ teaspoon ground cinnamon	½ teaspoon ground cinnamon
50 g/2 oz granulated sugar	¼ cup granulated sugar
150 ml/¼ pint soured cream	⅔ cup sour cream
75 g/3 oz light brown sugar	½ cup firmly packed light brown sugar

Place the rhubarb in a saucepan with the water, cinnamon and granulated sugar. Cook until soft.
Divide the rhubarb between four flameproof dessert dishes. Top with the sour cream. Sprinkle the brown sugar on top to make a 5 mm/¼ inch layer.
Place under a preheated grill (broiler) and cook until the sugar melts and caramelizes. Serve hot.
Serves 4

Variation:
Other fruits may be used instead of rhubarb, and the spice changed according to taste.

Baked Blackberry Alaska

Metric/Imperial	American
1 × 23 cm/9 inch bought or homemade sponge cake	1 × 9 inch bought or homemade sponge cake
600 ml/1 pint vanilla ice cream, softened	1 pint vanilla ice cream, softened
3 egg whites	3 egg whites
175 g/6 oz caster sugar	¾ cup sugar
1 × 400 g/14 oz can blackberries, drained	1 × 16 oz can blackberries, drained

Place the cake on an ovenproof serving plate. Top with the ice cream, spreading it to within 1 cm/½ inch of the edge of the cake. Level the top. Cover and freeze until the ice cream is firm again.
Meanwhile beat the egg whites until frothy. Gradually beat in the sugar and continue beating until the meringue is stiff and glossy.
Spoon the blackberries over the ice cream, then top with the meringue, spreading it all over to cover the berries and ice cream completely. Seal it to the edge of the cake.
Bake in a preheated hot oven (220°C/425°F, Gas Mark 7) for 5 minutes or until the meringue is lightly tinged brown. Serve immediately.
Serves 6 to 8

Jamaican Bananas

Metric/Imperial
40 g/1½ oz butter or margarine
4 large bananas, halved
  lengthways
juice of ½ lemon
2 tablespoons rum
brown sugar

American
3 tablespoons butter or
  margarine
4 large bananas, halved
  lengthwise
juice of ½ lemon
2 tablespoons rum
brown sugar

Melt the butter or margarine in a flameproof serving dish or chafing dish. Add the bananas, cut sides down, and fry until golden. Turn the bananas over, sprinkle with the lemon juice and fry until the other sides are beginning to brown.

Warm the rum in a ladle, pour it over the bananas and set alight. Serve flaming, with brown sugar and cream.
Serves 4

Hot Apricots in Brandy

Metric/Imperial
120 ml/4 fl oz sweet white wine
250 ml/8 fl oz water
2 tablespoons honey
1 × 2.5 cm/1 inch cinnamon stick
1 teaspoon lemon juice
350 g/12 oz dried apricots,
  soaked overnight and drained
1 tablespoon brandy
50 g/2 oz flaked almonds, toasted

American
½ cup sweet white wine
1 cup water
2 tablespoons honey
1 × 1 inch cinnamon stick
1 teaspoon lemon juice
2 cups dried apricots,
  soaked overnight and drained
1 tablespoon brandy
½ cup sliced almonds, toasted

Put the wine, water, honey, cinnamon stick and lemon juice in a saucepan and bring to the boil. Add the apricots and simmer for 15 minutes. Stir in the brandy. Pour the apricot mixture into a serving dish and sprinkle the almonds on top. Serve hot with cream.
Serves 4

Rhubarb Compôte

Metric/Imperial
1 × 500 g/1 lb 3 oz can
  rhubarb
75 g/3 oz sultanas
50 g/2 oz demerara sugar
1 banana, sliced
¼ teaspoon ground cinnamon

American
1 × 1 lb 3 oz can rhubarb
½ cup golden raisins
⅓ cup raw brown sugar
1 banana, sliced
¼ teaspoon ground cinnamon

Put all the ingredients in a saucepan and heat gently, stirring to dissolve the sugar. Serve hot, with cream.
Serves 4

Apple Flipovers

Metric/Imperial	American
100 g/4 oz plain flour	1 cup all-purpose flour
pinch of salt	pinch of salt
2 teaspoons baking powder	2 teaspoons baking powder
2 teaspoons caster sugar	2 teaspoons sugar
2 eggs, separated	2 eggs, separated
150 ml/¼ pint milk	¾ cup milk
2 cooking apples, peeled, cored and grated	2 apples, peeled, cored and grated
oil for frying	oil for frying

Sift the flour, salt, baking powder and sugar into a bowl. Add the egg yolks and milk and beat until smooth. Fold in the apples. Beat the egg whites until stiff and fold into the batter.

Lightly oil a frying pan (skillet) and heat. Drop tablespoonfuls of the batter onto the pan and cook until the flipovers have puffed up and are lightly browned on the underside. Turn over and cook the other sides.

Serve hot with whipped cream or ice cream.
Serves 4

Banana Fritters

Metric/Imperial	American
100 g/4 oz plain flour	1 cup all-purpose flour
½ teaspoon salt	½ teaspoon salt
1 egg	1 egg
150 ml/¼ pint evaporated milk	¾ cup evaporated milk
4 firm bananas, halved lengthways and then crossways	4 firm bananas, halved lengthwise and then crosswise
juice of 1 lemon	juice of 1 lemon
oil for deep frying	oil for deep frying
2 tablespoons brown sugar	2 tablespoons brown sugar
½ teaspoon ground cinnamon	½ teaspoon ground cinnamon

Sift the flour and salt into a bowl. Add the egg and milk and beat to a smooth batter. Leave for 30 minutes.

Toss the banana pieces in lemon juice to prevent discoloration. Dip the banana pieces in the batter, then deep fry in oil heated to 190°C/375°F for about 4 minutes or until golden brown. Drain on kitchen paper towels.

Mix together the sugar and cinnamon. Sprinkle over the banana fritters and serve hot.
Serves 4

Chocolate Cream Crêpes

Metric/Imperial
100 g/4 oz plain flour
1 egg
1 egg yolk
300 ml/½ pint milk
1 teaspoon lemon juice
1 tablespoon oil
oil for frying
Filling:
300 ml/½ pint double cream
50 g/2 oz plain chocolate,
  melted and cooled
25 g/1 oz walnuts, chopped

American
1 cup all-purpose flour
1 egg
1 egg yolk
1½ cups milk
1 teaspoon lemon juice
1 tablespoon oil
oil for frying
Filling:
1¼ cups heavy cream
2 × 1 oz squares sweet dark
  chocolate, melted and cooled
¼ cup chopped walnuts

Sift the flour into a bowl. Add the egg, egg yolk, half the milk, the lemon juice and oil and beat until smooth. Gradually beat in the remaining milk to make a smooth thin batter.

Lightly oil an 18 cm/7 inch omelette or frying pan (skillet). Pour in just enough batter to cover the bottom of the pan, tilting the pan to spread out the batter evenly. Cook until the underside is golden, then toss or turn the crêpe and cook the other side for 1 to 2 minutes. Slide onto a plate and keep hot while you cook the remaining crêpes. This batter should make eight crêpes.

Whip the cream until thick. Add the chocolate and whip until well combined. Fold in the nuts. Divide the filling between the crêpes and roll them up. Serve immediately.
Serves 4 to 6

Variations:
Banana Crêpes: Replace the chocolate with 6 sliced bananas. Decorate the rolled stuffed crêpes with chocolate sauce, and more sliced bananas.
Apple Crêpes: Mix 300 ml/½ pint (1¼ cups) sweetened apple purée or sauce with 50 g/2 oz sultanas (⅓ cup golden raisins) and a pinch of ground cinnamon. Use to fill the crêpes, then roll up.

Plum Cream Crêpes

Metric/Imperial
300 ml/½ pint double cream
1 tablespoon kirsch
1 × 400 g/14 oz can dessert
  plums, drained, stoned and
  chopped
8 hot crêpes (see recipe above)
sifted icing sugar

American
1¼ cups heavy cream
1 tablespoon kirsch
1 × 16 oz can plums, drained,
  pitted and chopped
8 hot crêpes (see recipe above)
sifted confectioners sugar

Whip the cream with the kirsch until thick. Fold in the plums.

Divide the mixture between the crêpes and fold them into quarters. Sprinkle with icing (confectioners) sugar and serve hot.
Serves 4

Orange and Cream Cheese Crêpes

Metric/Imperial
2 × 75 g/3 oz packets cream
  cheese
2 tablespoons single cream
2 tablespoons clear honey
50 g/2 oz sultanas
grated rind of 1 orange
8 hot crêpes (see recipe left)
Sauce:
juice of 2 oranges
grated rind of 1 orange
1 tablespoon arrowroot
25 g/1 oz soft brown sugar
1 tablespoon clear honey

American
2 × 3 oz packages cream cheese
2 tablespoons light cream
2 tablespoons honey
⅓ cup golden raisins
grated rind of 1 orange
8 hot crêpes (see recipe left)
Sauce:
juice of 2 oranges
grated rind of 1 orange
1 tablespoon arrowroot
3 tablespoons brown sugar
1 tablespoon honey

Beat the cream cheese, cream and honey together until smooth. Add the sultanas (raisins) and orange rind and mix well.

To make the sauce, make up the orange juice to 300 ml/½ pint (1½ cups) with water. Pour into a saucepan and add the orange rind, arrowroot, sugar and honey. Heat, stirring, until the sauce thickens.

Divide the cream cheese mixture between the crêpes and roll them up. Arrange on a warmed serving dish. Pour over a little of the sauce and serve the rest separately. Serve hot.
Serves 4

Nutty Apple Crêpes

Metric/Imperial
1 × 425 g/15 oz can apricot
  pie filling
50 g/2 oz hazelnuts, chopped
5 tablespoons demerara sugar
8 hot crêpes (see recipe left)

American
1 × 16 oz can apricot pie filling
½ cup chopped hazelnuts
5 tablespoons raw brown sugar
8 hot crêpes (see recipe left)

Put the pie filling in a saucepan and stir in the nuts and 1 tablespoon of the sugar. Heat through gently, then divide between the crêpes and fold into quarters.

Arrange in a flameproof serving dish. Sprinkle over the remaining sugar and place under a preheated grill (broiler). Cook until the sugar melts, then serve hot.
Serves 4

Wholewheat Honey Crêpes

Metric/Imperial
100 g/4 oz wholewheat flour
1 teaspoon baking powder
pinch of salt
1 egg, beaten
300 ml/½ pint milk
4 tablespoons clear honey
50 g/2 oz raisins
pinch of grated nutmeg
oil for frying

American
1 cup wholewheat flour
1 teaspoon baking powder
pinch of salt
1 egg, beaten
1½ cups milk
¼ cup honey
⅓ cup raisins
pinch of grated nutmeg
oil for frying

Put the flour, baking powder and salt into a bowl. Add the egg and milk and beat until smooth. In another bowl, mix the honey with the raisins and nutmeg.

Lightly oil an 18 cm/7 inch omelette or frying pan (skillet). Pour in just enough batter to cover the bottom of the pan, tilting the pan to spread out the batter evenly. Cook until the underside is golden, then toss or turn the crêpe and cook the other side for 1 to 2 minutes. Slide onto a plate and keep hot while you cook the remaining crêpes. This batter should make eight crêpes.

Spread each crêpe with a little of the honey mixture and fold into quarters. Serve hot.
Serves 4

Chestnut Crêpes

Metric/Imperial
1 × 200 g/7 oz can sweetened
   chestnut purée
2 tablespoons medium sherry
150 ml/¼ pint double cream
8 hot crêpes (see recipe on page
   230)
sifted icing sugar

American
1 × 7 oz can sweetened chestnut
   purée
2 tablespoons medium sherry
⅔ cup heavy cream
8 hot crêpes (see recipe on page
   230)
sifted confectioners sugar

Place the chestnut purée and sherry in a saucepan and heat through gently, stirring frequently. Whip the cream until thick and fold into the chestnut mixture. Divide between the crêpes and fold into quarters. Sprinkle with the sugar and serve hot.
Serves 4

Apple Griddle Cakes

Metric/Imperial
100 g/4 oz plain flour
2 teaspoons baking powder
2 tablespoons caster sugar
2 eggs, separated
150 ml/¼ pint milk
15 g/½ oz butter or margarine,
   melted
2 apples, peeled, cored and
   grated
oil for frying

American
1 cup all-purpose flour
2 teaspoons baking powder
2 tablespoons sugar
2 eggs, separated
¾ cup milk
1 tablespoon butter or
   margarine, melted
2 apples, peeled, cored and
   grated
oil for frying

Sift the flour, baking powder and half the sugar into a bowl. Add the egg yolks, milk and butter or margarine and beat until smooth. Beat the egg whites until stiff and fold in with the apples.

Lightly oil a griddle or heavy-based frying pan (skillet). Drop tablespoonfuls of the batter into the pan, spacing them well apart as they spread, and cook for 1 to 2 minutes or until the undersides are golden brown and bubbles appear on the surface. Turn over the cakes and cook the other sides until lightly browned. Remove from the pan and keep hot while you cook the remaining cakes in the same way.

Sprinkle over the remaining sugar and serve hot.
Serves 4

Variation:
Use 2 chopped bananas instead of apples.

Pineapple Igloos

Metric/Imperial
3 egg whites
175 g/6 oz caster sugar
4 canned pineapple rings
600 ml/1 pint sorbet or
   ice cream of choice
4 glacé cherries

American
3 egg whites
¾ cup sugar
4 canned pineapple rings
1 pint sherbet or ice cream
   of choice
4 glacé cherries

Beat the egg whites until stiff. Add 4 tablespoons of the sugar and continue beating for 1 minute or until the mixture is very stiff and glossy. Fold in the remaining sugar.

Place the pineapple rings on a baking sheet. Pile the sorbet (sherbet) or ice cream on top, making sure it does not hang over the edge of the pineapple. Cover completely with the meringue, sealing it to the pineapple. Top with the cherries.

Cook in a preheated hot oven (230°C/450°F, Gas Mark 8) for 4 to 5 minutes or until the meringue is just tinged with brown. Serve immediately.
Serves 4

Pain Perdu

Metric/Imperial
1 egg
1 tablespoon milk
few drops of vanilla essence
2 tablespoons caster sugar
4 slices of white bread,
    crusts removed
40 g/1½ oz butter or margarine
sifted icing sugar

American
1 egg
1 tablespoon milk
few drops of vanilla
2 tablespoons sugar
4 slices of white bread,
    crusts removed
3 tablespoons butter or
    margarine
sifted confectioners sugar

Lightly beat the egg with the milk in a shallow dish. Add the vanilla and sugar. Dip the bread in the mixture to coat both sides.

Melt the butter or margarine in a frying pan (skillet) and fry the bread until golden brown on both sides. Sprinkle with icing (confectioners) sugar and serve hot.
Serves 2 to 4

Hot Berry Snow

Metric/Imperial
500 g/1 lb mixed red berries
    (strawberries, raspberries,
    redcurrants, etc.)
1 tablespoon clear honey
150 ml/¼ pint plain yogurt
2 eggs, separated
1 tablespoon plain flour
25 g/1 oz ground almonds
2 tablespoons brown sugar

American
1 lb mixed red berries
    (strawberries, raspberries,
    etc.)
1 tablespoon honey
⅔ cup plain yogurt
2 eggs, separated
1 tablespoon all-purpose flour
¼ cup ground almonds
2 tablespoons brown sugar

Place the fruit in an ovenproof dish and spoon over the honey.

Beat together the yogurt, egg yolks, flour and almonds. Beat the egg whites until stiff and fold into the yogurt mixture. Pour over the fruit and sprinkle the sugar on top.

Cook in a preheated moderately hot oven (200°C/400°F, Gas Mark 6) for 15 to 20 minutes or until the topping is risen and golden brown. Serve immediately.
Serves 4

Pineapple Meringue Pudding

Metric/Imperial
3 trifle sponge cakes, halved
   lengthways
3 tablespoons sherry
1 tablespoon lemon juice
1 × 425 g/15 oz can pineapple
   rings
2 egg whites
100 g/4 oz caster sugar
Sauce:
1 teaspoon arrowroot
1 teaspoon sugar
1 teaspoon lemon juice

American
4 slices of pound cake
3 tablespoons sherry
1 tablespoon lemon juice
1 × 15 oz can pineapple rings
2 egg whites
½ cup sugar
Sauce:
1 teaspoon arrowroot
1 teaspoon sugar
1 teaspoon lemon juice

Arrange the cake slices on the bottom of a shallow ovenproof dish.
Sprinkle with the sherry and lemon juice. Drain the pineapple rings,
reserving the syrup for the sauce. Place the pineapple rings on the cake.

Beat the egg whites until stiff. Add 2 tablespoons of the sugar and
continue beating for 1 minute. Fold in the remaining sugar. Spoon or pipe
the meringue over the pineapple rings. Cook in a preheated moderately
hot oven (190°C/375°F, Gas Mark 5) for 8 to 10 minutes or until the
meringue is lightly browned.

Meanwhile make the sauce. Dissolve the arrowroot in the reserved
pineapple syrup in a saucepan. Add the sugar and lemon juice and bring
to the boil, stirring. Simmer until thickened. Serve this sauce with the hot
pudding.
Serves 4 to 6

French Plum Pudding

Metric/Imperial
750 g/1½ lb ripe plums, stoned
100 g/4 oz caster sugar
75 g/3 oz plain flour
3 eggs, beaten
450 ml/¾ pint milk
½ teaspoon almond essence
15 g/½ oz butter or margarine
sifted icing sugar

American
1½ lb ripe plums, pitted
½ cup sugar
¾ cup all-purpose flour
3 eggs, beaten
2 cups milk
½ teaspoon almond extract
1 tablespoon butter or
   margarine
sifted confectioners sugar

Arrange the plums in a buttered ovenproof dish. Sprinkle over
2 tablespoons of the sugar.

Sift the flour and remaining sugar into a bowl. Add the eggs, milk and
almond essence (extract) and beat until smooth. Pour over the plums and
dot the top with the butter or margarine.

Cook in a preheated hot oven (220°C/425°F, Gas Mark 7) for 25
minutes or until set and golden brown. Cool slightly, then dredge with
icing (confectioners) sugar. Serve warm.
Serves 4

Christmas Alaska

Metric/Imperial	American
4-6 slices of Christmas pudding or cake	4-6 slices of plum pudding or rich fruit cake
2 tablespoons brandy or sherry	2 tablespoons brandy or sherry
4-6 scoops of vanilla ice cream	4-6 scoops of vanilla ice cream
150 ml/¼ pint double cream	⅔ cup heavy cream
3 egg whites	3 egg whites
175 g/6 oz caster sugar	¾ cup sugar

Arrange the pudding or cake slices on an ovenproof plate. Sprinkle over the brandy or sherry. Pile the ice cream on top. Whip the cream until thick and spread over the ice cream. Place in the refrigerator or freezer while you make the meringue.

Beat the egg whites until stiff. Add 3 tablespoons of the sugar and continue beating for 1 minute. Fold in the remaining sugar.

Completely cover the cream, ice cream and pudding or cake with the meringue. Cook in a preheated moderately hot oven (200°C/400°F, Gas Mark 6) for about 3 minutes or until the meringue is just tinged golden brown. Serve immediately.

Serves 4 to 6

Orange Bread and Butter Pudding

Metric/Imperial	American
½ large loaf of white bread, sliced and crusts removed	½ large loaf of white bread, sliced and crusts removed
butter or margarine	butter or margarine
50 g/2 oz sultanas	⅓ cup golden raisins
300 ml/½ pint milk	1¼ cups milk
2 eggs	2 eggs
½ × 190 g/6½ oz can frozen concentrated orange juice, thawed	½ × 6½ oz can frozen concentrated orange juice, thawed
50 g/2 oz caster sugar	¼ cup sugar

Spread the bread slices with butter or margarine, then arrange them, buttered sides up, in a large ovenproof dish. Scatter over the sultanas (raisins).

Beat together the milk, eggs, orange juice and sugar and pour over the bread. Cook in a preheated moderately hot oven (190°C/375°F, Gas Mark 5) for 30 to 40 minutes or until set and golden. Serve hot.

Serves 4 to 6

Cherry Soufflé Omelette

Metric/Imperial
1 × 425 g/15 oz can black
  cherries, drained and
  stoned
8 eggs, separated
50 g/2 oz caster sugar
few drops of vanilla extract
50 g/2 oz butter or margarine
sifted icing sugar

American
1 × 16 oz can bing cherries,
  drained and pitted
8 eggs, separated
¼ cup sugar
few drops of vanilla
4 tablespoons butter or
  margarine
sifted confectioners sugar

Place the cherries in a saucepan and leave to heat through gently while you make the omelettes.

Beat the egg yolks with the sugar and vanilla until thick and pale. Beat the egg whites until stiff and fold into the yolk mixture.

Melt 15 g/½ oz (1 tablespoon) of the butter or margarine in a frying pan (skillet). Add one-quarter of the egg mixture and cook gently until the omelette is set and golden underneath. Place the pan under a preheated grill (broiler) and cook until the omelette is risen and golden on top.

Using a slotted spoon, place one-quarter of the cherries on the omelette. Fold over and slide onto a warmed serving plate. Keep hot while you cook the remaining three omelettes in the same way.

Dredge the omelettes with icing (confectioners) sugar and serve hot.
Serves 4

Rhubarb and Raisin Charlotte

Metric/Imperial
175 g/6 oz fresh breadcrumbs
100 g/4 oz soft brown sugar
25 g/1 oz butter or margarine
1 × 425 g/15 oz can rhubarb,
  drained
100 g/4 oz raisins

American
3 cups soft bread crumbs
⅔ cup firmly packed brown sugar
2 tablespoons butter or
  margarine
1 × 16 oz can rhubarb, drained
⅔ cup raisins

Cover the bottom of a greased 1.2 litre/2 pint (5 cup) ovenproof dish with one-third of the breadcrumbs. Sprinkle over one-third of the sugar and dot with one-third of the butter or margarine. Add half the rhubarb and raisins. Repeat the layers, then finish with breadcrumbs, sugar and butter or margarine.

Cook in a preheated moderately hot oven (190°C/375°F, Gas Mark 5) for 40 minutes or until the top is golden and crisp. Serve hot.
Serves 6

Peach Charlotte

Metric/Imperial
1 × 425 g/15 oz can peach
  slices
50 g/2 oz caster sugar
¼ teaspoon mixed spice
50 g/2 oz fresh brown
  breadcrumbs
50 g/2 oz butter or margarine

American
1 × 16 oz can peach slices
¼ cup sugar
¼ teaspoon apple pie spice
1 cup soft brown bread crumbs
4 tablespoons butter or
  margarine

Drain the peaches, reserving the syrup. Mix together the sugar and spice.
Make alternate layers of the peaches, spiced sugar and breadcrumbs in a
deep ovenproof dish, reserving about 1 tablespoon of the breadcrumbs
for the topping. Pour over the reserved peach syrup, dot with the butter or
margarine and sprinkle the reserved breadcrumbs on top.

Cook in a preheated moderately hot oven (190°C/375°F, Gas Mark 5)
for about 35 minutes or until golden and crisp on top. Serve with whipped
cream.

Serves 4

Beignets

Metric/Imperial
40 g/1½ oz butter or margarine
150 ml/¼ pint water
65 g/2½ oz plain flour,
  sifted
pinch of salt
2 eggs, beaten
oil for deep frying
50 g/2 oz caster sugar
½ teaspoon ground cinnamon

American
3 tablespoons butter or
  margarine
¾ cup water
½ cup plus 2 tablespoons
  all-purpose flour, sifted
pinch of salt
2 eggs, beaten
oil for deep frying
¼ cup sugar
½ teaspoon ground cinnamon

Put the butter or margarine and water in a saucepan and bring to the boil,
stirring to melt the fat. Remove from the heat and add the flour and salt.
Beat until the mixture pulls away from the sides of the pan. Gradually beat
in the eggs to make a smooth, shiny batter.

Place the batter in a piping (pastry) bag fitted with a plain 1 cm/½ inch
nozzle. Pipe small rounds into oil heated to 185°C/360°F and deep fry
until puffed up and golden brown. Alternatively, the batter may be
dropped into the oil from a teaspoon. Drain the puffs on kitchen paper
towels and keep hot until they are all fried.

Mix the sugar with the cinnamon and sprinkle over the puffs. Serve hot.

Serves 6

Hot Chocolate Soufflé

Metric/Imperial
25 g/1 oz butter or margarine
2 tablespoons plain flour
2 tablespoons cornflour
300 ml/½ pint milk
50 g/2 oz caster sugar
100 g/4 oz plain chocolate
3 egg yolks
4 egg whites

American
2 tablespoons butter or
  margarine
2 tablespoons all-purpose flour
2 tablespoons cornstarch
1½ cups milk
¼ cup sugar
4 × 1 oz squares semi-sweet
  chocolate
3 egg yolks
4 egg whites

Melt the butter or margarine in a saucepan. Stir in the flour and cornflour (cornstarch) and cook for 1 minute, then gradually stir in the milk. Bring to the boil, stirring, and simmer until thickened. Stir in the sugar. Add the chocolate and stir until melted.

Remove from the heat and cool slightly, then beat in the egg yolks. Beat the egg whites until stiff and fold into the mixture. Spoon into a greased 1.2 litre/2 pint (5 cup) soufflé dish and cook in a preheated moderately hot oven (190°C/375°F, Gas Mark 5) for 35 minutes or until well risen and firm. Serve immediately.
Serves 4 to 6

Honey Sesame Noodles

Metric/Imperial
225 g/8 oz egg noodles
salt
50 g/2 oz butter or margarine
2 teaspoons sesame seeds
2 tablespoons sultanas
3 tablespoons clear honey
pinch of ground cinnamon
150 ml/¼ pint soured cream

American
½ lb egg noodles
salt
4 tablespoons butter or
  margarine
2 teaspoons sesame seeds
2 tablespoons golden raisins
3 tablespoons honey
pinch of ground cinnamon
⅔ cup sour cream

Cook the noodles in boiling salted water until just tender. Drain and keep warm.

Melt the butter or margarine in a frying pan (skillet). Add the sesame seeds and fry until golden. Stir in the sultanas (raisins), honey, cinnamon and noodles and heat through. Serve hot, topped with the sour cream.
Serves 4

Noodles Jubilee

Metric/Imperial
225 g/8 oz egg noodles
salt
2 tablespoons clear honey
1 × 425 g/15 oz can black
  cherries
2 teaspoons arrowroot
2 tablespoons brandy
  (optional)
50 g/2 oz flaked almonds

American
½ lb egg noodles
salt
2 tablespoons honey
1 × 16 oz can bing cherries
2 teaspoons arrowroot
2 tablespoons brandy
  (optional)
½ cup sliced almonds

Cook the noodles in boiling salted water until just tender. Drain and stir in the honey. Keep warm.
    Drain the cherries, reserving the syrup. Dissolve the arrowroot in a little of the syrup, then place in a saucepan with the rest of the syrup. Bring to the boil, stirring, and simmer until thickened. Stir in the cherries and brandy, if using, and heat through. Add the noodles and fold together. Spoon into a warmed serving dish and sprinkle the almonds on top. Serve hot, with cream.
Serves 4

Noodle Mallow Pudding

Metric/Imperial
225 g/8 oz egg noodles
salt
100 g/4 oz butter or margarine
3 tablespoons brown sugar
100 g/4 oz marshmallows
2 tablespoons single cream
½ teaspoon vanilla essence
50 g/2 oz walnuts, chopped

American
½ lb egg noodles
salt
½ cup butter or margarine
3 tablespoons brown sugar
¼ lb marshmallows
2 tablespoons light cream
½ teaspoon vanilla
½ cup chopped walnuts

Cook the noodles in boiling salted water until just tender. Drain and keep warm.
    Melt the butter or margarine in a clean saucepan. Add the sugar, marshmallows and cream and heat gently, stirring, until the marshmallows have melted. Stir in the vanilla and noodles and reheat if necessary.
    Spoon into a warmed serving dish, sprinkle the walnuts on top and serve hot.
Serves 4

QUICK

Breads, Cakes and Biscuits (Cookies)

MEALS

Drop Scones

Metric/Imperial
225 g/8 oz self-raising flour
2 teaspoons baking powder
25 g/1 oz caster sugar
pinch of salt
1 tablespoon golden syrup
1 egg, beaten
200 ml/⅓ pint milk
oil for frying

American
2 cups self-rising flour
2 teaspoons baking powder
2 tablespoons sugar
pinch of salt
1 tablespoon light corn syrup
1 egg, beaten
1¼ cups milk
oil for frying

Sift the flour, baking powder, sugar and salt into a bowl. Add the syrup, egg and milk and beat to make a smooth thick batter.

Lightly oil a griddle or frying pan (skillet) and heat. Drop tablespoonfuls of the batter onto the pan, well spaced apart as they spread, and cook until the undersides are golden and bubbles appear on the surface. Turn the scones over and cook the other sides until golden. Remove from the pan and keep hot while you cook the remaining scones, in batches, in the same way. Serve hot or cold.
Makes about 30

Hazel Nutties

Metric/Imperial
100 g/4 oz ground toasted
* hazelnuts*
100 g/4 oz demerara sugar
about ½ egg, beaten

American
1 cup ground toasted hazelnuts
⅔ cup firmly packed raw brown
* sugar*
about ½ egg, beaten

Mix together the ingredients to make a pliable dough. Place on an oiled surface and roll out very thinly using an oiled rolling pin. Cut into 4 cm/1½ inch rounds and place on baking sheets lined with non-stick parchment paper.

Cook in a preheated moderate oven (180°C/350°F, Gas Mark 4) for 10 to 12 minutes or until golden brown. Cool on a wire rack.
Makes about 24

Cheese Ring Rolls

Metric/Imperial
225 g/8 oz plain flour
4½ teaspoons baking powder
1 teaspoon salt
1 teaspoon paprika
225 g/8 oz Cheddar cheese,
  grated
4 tablespoons chopped piccalilli
  or other pickle
1 large egg
150 ml/¼ pint milk

American
2 cups all-purpose flour
4½ teaspoons baking powder
1 teaspoon salt
1 teaspoon paprika
2 cups grated Cheddar cheese
¼ cup chopped piccalilli or
  similar pickle relish
1 large egg
¾ cup milk

Sift the flour, baking powder, salt and paprika into a bowl. Rub in 200 g/7 oz (1¾ cups) of the cheese. Add the piccalilli. Lightly beat the egg with the milk and add to the mixture. Mix to a soft dough.

Divide the dough into six portions and shape each into a ball. Place on a greased baking sheet in a ring and press down slightly. Brush with the egg and milk mixture remaining on the sides of the bowl, then sprinkle over the remaining cheese.

Cook in a preheated hot oven (220°C/425°F, Gas Mark 7) for 25 minutes or until golden brown. Cool on a wire rack. Serve warm or cold.
Makes 6

Scottish Treacle (Molasses) Scones

Metric/Imperial
500 g/1 lb plain flour
1 teaspoon bicarbonate of soda
½ teaspoon cream of tartar
1 teaspoon ground cinnamon
1 teaspoon mixed spice
½ teaspoon salt
50 g/2 oz butter or margarine
2 teaspoons sugar
2 tablespoons black treacle
300 ml/½ pint milk
milk to glaze

American
4 cups all-purpose flour
1 teaspoon baking soda
½ teaspoon cream of tartar
1 teaspoon ground cinnamon
1 teaspoon apple pie spice
½ teaspoon salt
4 tablespoons butter or
  margarine
2 teaspoons sugar
2 tablespoons molasses
1¾ cups milk
milk to glaze

Sift the flour, soda, cream of tartar, spices and salt into a bowl. Rub in the butter or margarine, then stir in the sugar. Add the treacle (molasses) and milk and mix to a soft dough.

Roll out the dough on a floured surface to 1 cm/½ inch thick. Cut into 7.5 cm/3 inch triangles and place on a baking sheet. Brush the tops of the triangles with milk.

Cook in a preheated hot oven (220°C/425°F, Gas Mark 7) for about 15 minutes or until risen and golden brown. Serve warm.
Makes 10

Welsh Cakes

Metric/Imperial
225 g/8 oz self-raising flour
¼ teaspoon salt
½ teaspoon mixed spice
75 g/3 oz butter or margarine
50 g/2 oz caster sugar
50 g/2 oz currants
1 egg, beaten
1 tablespoon milk
oil for frying

American
2 cups self-rising flour
¼ teaspoon salt
½ teaspoon apple pie spice
6 tablespoons butter or
  margarine
¼ cup sugar
⅓ cup currants
1 egg, beaten
3 tablespoons milk
oil for frying

Sift the flour, salt and spice into a bowl. Rub in the butter or margarine
until the mixture resembles breadcrumbs. Stir in the sugar and currants,
then mix to a firm dough with the egg and milk.

Roll out the dough on a floured surface to about 5 mm/¼ inch thick.
Cut into 6 cm/2½ inch rounds.

Lightly oil a griddle or frying pan (skillet) and heat. Add the cakes, a few
at a time, and cook for 2 to 3 minutes on each side or until golden brown.
Serve hot.
Makes about 12

Chocolate Brandy Slice

Metric/Imperial
100 g/4 oz butter or margarine
100 g/4 oz caster sugar
100 g/4 oz plain chocolate,
  melted
6 tablespoons strong black
  coffee
2 tablespoons brandy
40 petit beurre or other
  oblong biscuits
50 g/2 oz flaked almonds
glacé cherry halves to decorate

American
½ cup butter or margarine
½ cup sugar
4 × 1 oz squares semi-sweet
  chocolate, melted
6 tablespoons strong black
  coffee
2 tablespoons brandy
40 oblong plain sweet cookies
½ cup sliced almonds
glacé cherry halves to decorate

Cream the butter or margarine with the sugar until light and fluffy. Beat in
the chocolate.

Mix together the coffee and brandy. Moisten 10 biscuits (cookies) with
the brandy mixture, then arrange them close together in two rows on an
oblong plate. Spread with about one-fifth of the chocolate mixture.
Continue making layers in this way, ending with biscuits (cookies).
Spread the remaining chocolate mixture over the top and sides of the
cake. Press the flaked (sliced) almonds onto the sides of the cake and
decorate the top with the cherries. Chill before serving.
Serves 10 to 12

Belgian Fudge Cake

Metric/Imperial
100 g/4 oz butter or margarine
2 tablespoons golden syrup
225 g/8 oz digestive
  biscuits, crushed
2 tablespoons raisins
50 g/2 oz glacé cherries,
  chopped
150 g/5 oz plain chocolate,
  chopped
Icing:
50 g/2 oz plain chocolate
25 g/1 oz butter or margarine
2 tablespoons water
175 g/6 oz icing sugar,
  sifted

American
½ cup butter or
  margarine
2 tablespoons light corn syrup
2 cups graham cracker crumbs
2 tablespoons raisins
⅓ cup chopped glacé cherries
5 × 1 oz squares semi-sweet
  chocolate, chopped
Frosting:
2 × 1 oz squares semi-sweet
  chocolate
2 tablespoons butter or
  margarine
2 tablespoons water
1½ cups confectioners sugar,
  sifted

Place the butter or margarine and syrup in a saucepan and heat, stirring, until the fat has melted. Remove from the heat and stir in the biscuit (graham cracker) crumbs, raisins, cherries and chocolate. Press the mixture firmly into a greased and lined 500 g/1 lb loaf tin (4 × 3 inch loaf pan). Chill until set.

To make the icing (frosting), place the chocolate, butter or margarine and water in a saucepan and heat until the chocolate and fat have melted. Remove from the heat and gradually beat in the sugar.

Remove the cake from the pan, peel off the paper and cut the cake into three layers. Use two-thirds of the icing (frosting) to sandwich the layers together and spread the remainder over the top of the cake. Chill before serving.
Serves 6 to 8

Wholewheat Soda Bread

Metric/Imperial
350 g/12 oz wholewheat flour
100 g/4 oz plain flour
1 teaspoon salt
1 teaspoon bicarbonate of soda
25 g/1 oz lard
300 ml/½ pint buttermilk

American
3 cups wholewheat flour
1 cup all-purpose flour
1 teaspoon salt
1 teaspoon baking soda
2 tablespoons shortening
1¾ cups buttermilk

Place the flours, salt and soda in a bowl. Rub in the lard (shortening), then mix in the buttermilk to make a soft dough. Shape the dough into an 18 cm/7 inch round on a floured surface.

Place the round on a greased baking sheet and score it into quarters with a sharp knife. Cook in a preheated moderately hot oven (200°C/400°F, Gas Mark 6) for about 35 minutes or until risen and golden brown. Cool on a wire rack.
Makes one 18 cm/7 inch round loaf

Quick Chocolate Cake

Metric/Imperial	American
2 eggs, beaten	2 eggs, beaten
2 tablespoons caster sugar	2 tablespoons sugar
225 g/8 oz butter or margarine, melted	1 cup butter or margarine, melted
225 g/8 oz plain chocolate, melted	8 × 1 oz squares semi-sweet chocolate, melted
225 g/8 oz digestive biscuits, broken into small pieces	½ lb plain sweet cookies, broken into small pieces

Lightly beat the eggs with the sugar. Gradually beat in the melted butter or margarine, then mix in the chocolate. Fold in the biscuits (cookies).

Spoon into a greased 15 cm/6 inch loose-bottomed (springform) cake pan and spread out evenly. Chill overnight.

The next day, remove from the pan and serve with whipped cream.

Serves 6

Yogurt Wholewheat Scones

Metric/Imperial	American
225 g/8 oz wholewheat flour	2 cups wholewheat flour
½ teaspoon salt	½ teaspoon salt
1½ teaspoons baking powder	1½ teaspoons baking powder
50 g/2 oz butter	4 tablespoons butter
150 ml/¼ pint plain yogurt	1 cup plain yogurt

Place the flour, salt and baking powder in a bowl. Rub in the butter until the mixture resembles breadcrumbs, then mix in the yogurt to make a soft dough.

Roll out the dough on a floured surface to about 2 cm/¾ inch thick and cut out 5 cm/2 inch rounds. Place on greased baking sheets.

Cook in a preheated moderately hot oven (200°C/400°F, Gas Mark 6) for 12 minutes or until risen and lightly browned. Cool on a wire rack.

Makes 10

Spicy Flapjacks

Metric/Imperial	American
225 g/8 oz oatmeal	2¼ cups oatmeal
100 g/4 oz dark brown sugar	⅔ cup firmly packed dark brown sugar
1 teaspoon ground ginger	1 teaspoon ground ginger
75 g/3 oz butter or margarine, melted	6 tablespoons butter or margarine, melted
¼ teaspoon salt	¼ teaspoon salt

Mix together all the ingredients. Press into a greased 18 cm/7 inch square cake pan. Cook in a preheated moderate oven (180°C/350°F, Gas Mark 4) for 45 minutes or until brown and firm. Mark into squares, then leave to cool in the pan.

Makes about 20

Chocolate Log

Metric/Imperial
100 g/4 oz mixed glacé fruit
  (cherries, pineapple, etc.),
  chopped
1 tablespoon brandy
225 g/8 oz stale cake crumbs
225 g/8 oz cottage cheese,
  sieved
1 × 75 g/3 oz packet cream
  cheese
50 g/2 oz plain chocolate,
  grated
25 g/1 oz caster sugar
Icing:
150 ml/¼ pint double cream
50 g/2 oz plain chocolate,
  melted
Christmas decorations
sifted icing sugar

American
½ cup chopped mixed glacé or
  candied fruit (cherries,
  pineapple, etc.)
1 tablespoon brandy
4 cups stale cake crumbs
1 cup cottage cheese,
  strained
1 × 3 oz package cream cheese
2 × 1 oz squares semi-sweet
  chocolate, grated
2 tablespoons sugar
Frosting:
⅔ cup heavy cream
2 × 1 oz squares semi-sweet
  chocolate, melted
Christmas decorations
sifted confectioners sugar

Sprinkle the fruit with the brandy and leave to soak for 10 minutes. Add the remaining cake ingredients and mix well together. Spread out on a 28 × 18 cm/11 × 7 inch sheet of greaseproof (waxed) paper or foil and roll up like a Swiss (jelly) roll, using the paper or foil to help lift the chocolate mixture. Chill until set.

To make the icing (frosting), whip the cream until thick and fold in the chocolate. Place the cake on a serving plate and cover with the icing (frosting). Add Christmas decorations, if liked, and icing (confectioners) sugar to resemble snow. Chill before serving.
Serves 6 to 8

Cottage Cheese Griddle Cakes

Metric/Imperial
25 g/1 oz butter or margarine,
  melted
100 g/4 oz cottage cheese
2 eggs, beaten
50 g/2 oz plain flour, sifted
1 teaspoon baking powder
1 tablespoon milk
oil for frying

American
2 tablespoons butter or
  margarine, melted
½ cup cottage cheese
2 eggs, beaten
½ cup all-purpose flour, sifted
1 teaspoon baking powder
3 tablespoons milk
oil for frying

Mix together the butter or margarine and cottage cheese, then beat in the remaining ingredients to make a thick batter.

Lightly oil a griddle or frying pan (skillet). Drop tablespoonfuls of the batter onto the pan, spacing them well apart as they spread, and cook for 1 minute on each side or until golden brown. Remove from the pan and keep hot while you cook the remaining griddle cakes, in batches, in the same way. Serve hot.
Serves 4

Chocolate Chews

Metric/Imperial	American
50 g/2 oz caster sugar	1/4 cup sugar
2 tablespoons golden syrup	2 tablespoons light corn syrup
75 g/3 oz butter	6 tablespoons butter
225 g/8 oz quick-cook oats	2 2/3 cups quick-cook oats
3 tablespoons cocoa powder	3 tablespoons unsweetened cocoa
1 teaspoon vanilla essence	1 teaspoon vanilla
25 g/1 oz walnuts, chopped	1/4 cup chopped walnuts
50 g/2 oz raisins, chopped	1/3 cup chopped raisins

Place the sugar, syrup and butter in a saucepan and heat, stirring to dissolve the sugar and melt the fat. Bring to the boil, then remove from the heat and stir in the remaining ingredients.

Pour into a greased 20 cm/8 inch square cake pan and spread out evenly. Chill until firm. Cut into 5 cm/2 inch squares to serve.
Makes 16

Cream Scones (Biscuits)

Metric/Imperial	American
150 g/5 oz plain flour	1 1/4 cups all-purpose flour
1/2 teaspoon salt	1/2 teaspoon salt
2 teaspoons baking powder	2 teaspoons baking powder
150 ml/1/4 pint single cream	1 cup light cream

Sift the flour, salt and baking powder into a bowl and add the cream. Mix to a soft dough.

Roll out the dough on a floured surface to 1 cm/1/2 inch thick. Cut into 5 cm/2 inch rounds and place on a floured baking sheet. Cook in a preheated hot oven (220°C/425°F, Gas Mark 7) for 12 to 15 minutes or until well risen and golden brown. Cool on a wire rack.
Makes 9

Tapioca Coconut Balls

Metric/Imperial	American
225 g/8 oz tapioca	1 1/3 cups tapioca
225 g/8 oz soft dark brown sugar	1 1/3 cups firmly packed dark brown sugar
1/2 teaspoon salt	1/2 teaspoon salt
900 ml/1 1/2 pints water	3 3/4 cups water
100 g/4 oz desiccated coconut	1 cup shredded coconut
2 teaspoons caster sugar	2 teaspoons sugar

Place the tapioca, brown sugar, salt and water in a saucepan and bring to the boil, stirring. Simmer for about 10 minutes or until the mixture becomes thick and the tapioca softens. Stir frequently.

Pour the mixture into a greased shallow dish and leave to cool.

Scoop out tablespoonfuls of the mixture and shape into balls. Mix together the coconut and sugar and use to coat the balls.
Serves 6 to 8

Date and Hazelnut Fingers

Metric/Imperial
2 eggs
175 g/6 oz dark brown sugar
75 g/3 oz self-raising flour,
  sifted
pinch of salt
50 g/2 oz bran cereal
50 g/2 oz hazelnuts, chopped
100 g/4 oz dates, stoned and
  chopped

American
2 eggs
1 cup firmly packed dark
  brown sugar
¾ cup self-rising flour, sifted
pinch of salt
1 cup bran cereal
½ cup chopped hazelnuts
1 cup chopped pitted dates

Beat the eggs and sugar together until light and creamy. Stir in the remaining ingredients until well mixed. Pour into a greased and lined 28 × 18 cm/11 × 7 inch baking pan and spread out evenly.
   Cook in a preheated moderate oven (180°C/350°F, Gas Mark 4) for 30 minutes. Cool in the pan. Cut into fingers to serve.
Makes 12

Chocolate Crispies

Metric/Imperial
100 g/4 oz milk chocolate
2 tablespoons milk
2 tablespoons golden syrup
100 g/4 oz cornflakes, crushed
50 g/2 oz desiccated coconut

American
4 oz milk chocolate
2 tablespoons milk
2 tablespoons light corn syrup
3 cups crushed cornflakes
½ cup shredded coconut

Place the chocolate, milk and syrup in a heavy-based saucepan and heat gently until the chocolate has melted. Remove from the heat and fold in the cornflakes and coconut. Divide the mixture between 12 to 14 paper cake cases and chill until set.
Makes 12 to 14

Chocolate Fruit Bars

Metric/Imperial
90 g/3½ oz butter or margarine
1 tablespoon golden syrup
225 g/8 oz muesli
25 g/1 oz raisins, chopped
50 g/2 oz glacé cherries,
  chopped
100 g/4 oz plain or milk chocolate,
  melted

American
7 tablespoons butter or
  margarine
1 tablespoon light corn syrup
2⅔ cups granola
3 tablespoons chopped raisins
⅓ cup chopped glacé cherries
4 × 1 oz squares semi-sweet
  or milk chocolate, melted

Place the butter or margarine and syrup in a saucepan and heat until the fat has melted. Remove from the heat and stir in the muesli (granola), raisins and cherries. Press into a greased 18 cm/7 inch square cake pan.
   Spread the melted chocolate over the mixture in the pan. Chill until set. Cut into bars to serve.
Makes 12

Coffee Coconut Cookies

Metric/Imperial	American
50 g/2 oz butter or margarine	4 tablespoons butter or
75 g/3 oz caster sugar	margarine
75 g/3 oz mashed potatoes	6 tablespoons sugar
1 egg, beaten	½ cup mashed potatoes
100 g/4 oz self-raising flour,	1 egg, beaten
sifted	1 cup self-rising flour, sifted
50 g/2 oz desiccated coconut	⅔ cup shredded coconut
1 tablespoon strong black	¼ cup strong black coffee
coffee	

Cream the butter or margarine with the sugar until light and fluffy. Beat in the remaining ingredients.

Place small spoonfuls of the mixture on greased baking sheets. Cook in a preheated moderately hot oven (200°C/400°F, Gas Mark 6) for 10 to 15 minutes or until golden brown. Cool on a wire rack.

Makes 12

Chestnut Loaf Cake

Metric/Imperial	American
100 g/4 oz butter or margarine	½ cup butter or margarine
100 g/4 oz caster sugar	½ cup sugar
1 × 450 g/16 oz can unsweetened	1 × 16 oz can unsweetened
chestnut purée	chestnut purée
225 g/8 oz plain chocolate,	8 × 1 oz squares semi-sweet
melted	chocolate, melted
¼ teaspoon vanilla essence	¼ teaspoon vanilla
whipped cream to decorate	whipped cream to decorate

Cream the butter or margarine with the sugar until light and fluffy. Beat in the chestnut purée, chocolate and vanilla until smooth. Spoon into a greased and lined 500 g/1 lb loaf tin (4 × 3 inch loaf pan) and smooth the top. Chill overnight.

Invert the cake onto a serving plate and peel off the paper. Decorate with whipped cream before serving.

Serves 8

Oaty Crunchies

Metric/Imperial
75 g/3 oz plain flour
75 g/3 oz caster sugar
75 g/3 oz rolled oats
75 g/3 oz butter or margarine
1 tablespoon golden syrup
1 tablespoon milk
½ teaspoon bicarbonate of soda

American
¾ cup all-purpose flour
6 tablespoons sugar
1 cup rolled oats
6 tablespoons butter or
  margarine
1 tablespoon light corn syrup
1 tablespoon milk
½ teaspoon baking soda

Sift the flour into a bowl and stir in the sugar and oats.

Put the butter or margarine, syrup and milk in a saucepan and heat gently, stirring to melt the fat. Stir in the soda, then add the liquid to the dry ingredients. Mix well together.

Shape the mixture into 20 balls and place well apart on greased baking sheets. Cook in a preheated cool oven (150°C/300°F, Gas Mark 2) for 20 minutes. Cool slightly on the baking sheets, then transfer to a wire rack to cool completely.
Makes 20

Chocolate Crunch

Metric/Imperial
50 g/2 oz golden syrup
75 g/3 oz butter or margarine
25 g/1 oz caster sugar
2 tablespoons cocoa powder
225 g/8 oz digestive biscuits,
  crushed
1 tablespoon brandy or rum
50 g/2 oz plain chocolate,
  melted

American
3 tablespoons light corn syrup
6 tablespoons butter or
  margarine
2 tablespoons sugar
2 tablespoons unsweetened cocoa
2 cups graham cracker crumbs
1 tablespoon brandy or rum
2 × 1 oz squares semi-sweet
  chocolate, melted

Place the syrup and butter or margarine in a saucepan and heat until the fat has melted. Remove from the heat and stir in the sugar, cocoa, biscuit (graham cracker) crumbs and brandy or rum. Press into a greased 18 cm/6 inch loose-bottomed (springform) cake pan. Chill until set.

Spread the chocolate over the top of the cake and chill until set. Remove from the pan and cut into wedges to serve.
Serves 4 to 6

Apple Muffins

Metric/Imperial
225 g/8 oz plain flour
1 tablespoon baking powder
1 teaspoon salt
50 g/2 oz caster sugar
1 teaspoon ground cinnamon
2 eggs, beaten
150 ml/¼ pint milk
50 g/2 oz butter or margarine,
  melted
2 dessert apples, peeled,
  cored and grated

American
2 cups all-purpose flour
1 tablespoon baking powder
1 teaspoon salt
¼ cup sugar
1 teaspoon ground cinnamon
2 eggs, beaten
¾ cup milk
4 tablespoons butter or
  margarine, melted
2 apples, peeled, cored and
  grated

Sift the flour, baking powder, salt, sugar and cinnamon into a bowl. Add the remaining ingredients and mix together quickly. Divide between 24 greased bun (muffin) tins.

Cook in a preheated hot oven (220°C/425°F, Gas Mark 7) for 15 to 20 minutes or until risen and golden brown. Serve warm.
Makes 24

Vanilla Biscuits (Cookies)

Metric/Imperial
225 g/8 oz butter or margarine
175 g/6 oz caster sugar
350 g/12 oz plain flour
1 teaspoon baking powder
pinch of salt
2 teaspoons vanilla essence
sifted icing sugar

American
1 cup butter or margarine
¾ cup sugar
3 cups all-purpose flour
1 teaspoon baking powder
pinch of salt
2 teaspoons vanilla
sifted confectioners sugar

Cream the butter or margarine with the sugar until light and fluffy. Sift the flour with the baking powder and salt, then add to the creamed mixture with the vanilla. Work together to make a smooth dough.

Form the dough into two rolls about 5 cm/2 inches in diameter and wrap in plastic wrap. Chill for 1 hour, or until required. (The dough may be kept in the refrigerator for up to 4 days, and sliced and baked as wanted.)

Cut the rolls into 5 mm/¼ inch thick slices and arrange on greased baking sheets. Cook in a preheated moderately hot oven (190°C/375°F, Gas Mark 5) for about 15 minutes or until lightly browned. Cool on a wire rack, then dredge with icing (confectioners) sugar.
Makes about 40

Coffee Biscuit (Cookie) Cake

Metric/Imperial
100 g/4 oz butter or margarine
175 g/6 oz icing sugar, sifted
1 egg, separated
120 ml/4 fl oz strong black
   coffee
1 tablespoon cocoa powder
40 petit beurre or other
   oblong biscuits
6 blanched almonds, halved

American
½ cup butter or margarine
1½ cups confectioners sugar,
   sifted
1 egg, separated
½ cup strong black coffee
1 tablespoon unsweetened cocoa
40 oblong plain sweet cookies
6 blanched almonds, halved

Cream the butter or margarine until soft, then gradually beat in the sugar. Beat in the egg yolk, 2 tablespoons of the coffee and the cocoa. Beat the egg white until stiff and fold into the mixture.

Moisten 10 biscuits (cookies) in the remaining coffee, then arrange them close together in two rows on an oblong plate. Spread with about one-fifth of the mocha mixture. Continue making layers in this way, ending with biscuits (cookies). Spread the remaining mocha mixture over the top and sides of the cake. Decorate with the almonds and chill before serving.
Serves 10 to 12

Sky Rockets

Metric/Imperial
75 g/3 oz digestive biscuits,
   crushed
75 g/3 oz dates, stoned and
   chopped
50 g/2 oz currants
40 g/1½ oz glacé cherries,
   chopped
3 tablespoons apricot jam
225 g/8 oz marzipan
food colourings
small sweets

American
¾ cup graham cracker crumbs
½ cup chopped pitted dates
⅓ cup currants
3 tablespoons chopped glacé
   cherries
3 tablespoons apricot jam
½ lb marzipan
food colorings
small candies

Mix together the biscuit (graham cracker) crumbs, dates, currants, glacé cherries and jam. Divide into eight portions and shape into barrels with pointed ends.

Colour three-quarters of the marzipan orange (or another colour) and the remainder green (or another colour). Roll out the orange marzipan on a sugared surface and cut into eight pieces. Wrap around the barrels. Roll out the green marzipan and use to cover the pointed ends. Decorate with small sweets (candies).
Makes 8

Chestnut Layer Gâteau

Metric/Imperial
1 x 400 g/14 oz packet frozen
  puff pastry, thawed
1 x 225 g/8 oz can unsweetened
  chestnut purée
300 ml/½ pint double cream
100 g/4 oz plain chocolate,
  melted
50 g/2 oz icing sugar, sifted

American
1 x 17¾ oz package frozen puff
  pastry, thawed
1 x 8 oz can unsweetened
  chestnut purée
1¼ cups heavy cream
4 x 1 oz squares semi-sweet
  chocolate, melted
½ cup confectioners sugar, sifted

Roll out the pastry dough thinly and cut into three 18 cm/7 inch rounds.
Place the rounds on greased baking sheets and prick all over with a fork.
Cook in a preheated hot oven (220°C/425°F, Gas Mark 7) for 12 to 15
minutes or until golden brown and puffed up. Cool.
   Place the chestnut purée, cream, half the chocolate and the sugar in a
bowl and beat until thick. Use to sandwich together the pastry rounds.
Spread the remaining chocolate over the top. If liked, decorate with
whipped cream. Serve as soon as possible after assembling.
Serves 8

Honey Nut Squares

Metric/Imperial
100 g/4 oz plain flour
1 teaspoon ground cinnamon
1 teaspoon ground ginger
½ teaspoon bicarbonate of soda
¼ teaspoon salt
3 tablespoons oil
3 tablespoons clear honey
3 tablespoons black treacle
50 g/2 oz demerara sugar
1 egg, beaten
2 tablespoons milk
50 g/2 oz sultanas (optional)
25 g/1 oz walnuts, chopped

American
1 cup all-purpose flour
1 teaspoon ground cinnamon
1 teaspoon ground ginger
½ teaspoon baking soda
¼ teaspoon salt
3 tablespoons oil
3 tablespoons honey
3 tablespoons molasses
⅓ cup firmly packed raw brown
  sugar
1 egg, beaten
5 tablespoons milk
⅓ cup golden raisins (optional)
¼ cup chopped walnuts

Sift the flour, spices, soda and salt into a bowl. Add the oil, honey, treacle
(molasses), sugar, egg and milk and beat until smooth. Stir in the sultanas
(raisins), if using.
   Pour into a greased 18 cm/7 inch square cake pan and spread out
evenly. Scatter over the walnuts.
   Cook in a preheated moderate oven (180°C/350°F, Gas Mark 4) for
30 minutes or until firm. Cool in the pan, then cut into squares.
Makes 9

Index

256